STORYTELLING GAMES

Creative Activities for Language, Communication, and Composition across the Curriculum

by
Doug Lipman

Oryx Press
1995

The rare Arabian Oryx is believed to have inspired the myth of the unicorn. This desert antelope became virtually extinct in the early 1960s. At that time several groups of international conservationists arranged to have 9 animals sent to the Phoenix Zoo to be the nucleus of a captive breeding herd. Today the Oryx population is over 800, and nearly 400 have been returned to reserves in the Middle East.

© 1995 by The Oryx Press
4041 North Central at Indian School Road
Phoenix, Arizona 85012-3397

Cover photo of Doug Lipman, Chelli Keshavan, Edwin Lok, Megan Van der Kloot, and Kate Van der Kloot by Susan Wilson

Published simultaneously in Canada

Printed and Bound in the United States of America

♾ The paper used in this publication meets the minimum requirements of American National Standard for Information Science—Permanence of Paper for Printed Library Materials, ANSI Z39.48, 1984.

Library of Congress Cataloging-in-Publication Data
Lipman, Doug.
  Storytelling games : creative activities for language, communication, and composition across the curriculum / by Doug Lipman.
  Includes bibliographical references and indexes.
  ISBN 0-89774-848-4 (alk. paper)
  1. Storytelling—Handbooks, manuals, etc. 2. Education, Elementary—Activity programs—Handbooks, manuals, etc. 3. English language—Composition and exercises—Study and teaching (Elementary)—Handbooks, manuals, etc. 4. Interdisciplinary approach in education—Handbooks, manuals, etc. I. Title.
  LB1042.L53 1995
  372.6'23—dc20   94-38939
                                                                              CIP

Dedication

To the memory of Mischa Borodkin
and to Ethel Borodkin,
who loved me as their son.

TABLE OF CONTENTS

■ ■ ■

PREFACE
Imagination, Language, and Joy

■ ■ ■

This book gives you everything you need to lead story games in a wide variety of situations. It helps you find a game, learn it, present it, adapt it, and use it to teach a variety of subjects.

Story games help players to have fun with oral language in a structured way. You can use story games to encourage flexible thinking, imagination, and freedom of expression—as well as to reinforce learning in almost any subject.

In a group setting, you can use these games to promote cooperation, acceptance of diversity, and self-confidence.

STORY GAMES

What's a Story Game?

A story game is a game in which players tell stories. Each player may tell a complete story, a section of a story, a sentence, or a single word—or a player may just create a movement or sound that can be used in storytelling.

Story games are played by both individuals and teams. Some games include movements, pencil and paper, or props—but most require nothing but a few minutes of time. Some involve guessing and problem-solving, hints and deceptions, puns and proverbs, or slyness and sharing. In some games, players tell stories of personal experiences; in others, they rework traditional stories; in still others, they draw on their imaginations for original stories.

Where Do Story Games Come From?

Although this book is the first collection of story games ever published, many of the games have been around for decades, if not centuries.

I am both a folk musician and a storyteller. Once, while browsing through a collection of Texas folk songs, I noticed the singing game "Old Bloody Bones" (p. 28),which required storytelling. I was surprised to see that a game could involve storytelling. I thought, "What an oddity!"

As it happened, the next book I browsed through—a collection of Irish children's lore—contained the game "Towns and Counties" (p. 73), which also involved telling a story. Seeing these two games in the same week, I began to think of them as a category. I played them with children, and with adults, and began an active search for more such games.

Over the years, I collected many story games—some traditional, some new. Approximately a third of the 46 games in this collection are adapted from traditional games, including nineteenth-century parlor games. Another third are adapted from games that were originally devised for educational purposes or theatrical training. Only 18 of these games originally involved storytelling; to the rest, I added the storytelling element. The final third are original games, published here for the first time in any form.

EASY AND FLEXIBLE

The story games in this collection are easy to teach, easy to find, easy to fit to your needs, and can be used by almost anyone in a large variety of settings.

Who Can Use This Book?

Anyone who wants to lead creative games with children or adults can use this book.

The games are written especially to meet the needs of those who live, work, or play with children: parents, teachers, librarians childcare workers, community workers, and recreation and scout leaders. Because the games use spoken language so extensively, they are of special interest to English teachers, speech pathologists, and teachers of English as a second language.

These games do more for the classroom than give enjoyable use of language. They can actually help teach specific concepts in oral communication, language, and literature.

Teachers of other subjects will find story games that are specific to their curricula as well, whether in geography, history, mathematics, multiculturalism, science, social studies, or thinking skills.

By adapting the activities somewhat, teachers of other languages will also find many useful games that can survive translation.

Parents, librarians, and after-school activity leaders can also use these games for enjoyable exploration and review of school subjects.

Many of the games presented here were played originally by adults. More than half of the games remain suitable for adult entertainment. Don't be deterred by the frequent mention of curriculum and of the needs of young players. If you are a teacher of adults, an adult-recreation leader, or the host of an adult party, these games are for you, too.

Easy to Teach

You won't need any prior knowledge of games or of storytelling—nor will your group. Each game is self-contained, and its description is complete.

Each game is described twice: first, succinctly, and then in detail. If you're an old hand at teaching games, you'll be able to get the idea quickly; if you need more help, you can follow the step-by-step recipe. Sample stories are provided, along with lists of words or phrases that may help you when playing particular games.

The games are accompanied by "Hints"—how to handle unexpected responses, how to accommodate a range of abilities, or how to explain a game in more detail if necessary. Most games also list "Variations," which help you adapt a game for different groups and different purposes.

These games are starting points for the players' creativity—and for your creativity as a leader. Both you and the players are given specific, manageable tasks—as well as ways to extend and adapt them in the spirit of play and openness.

Easy to Find

To help you find a game that fits your objectives, the games are grouped into four chapters by subject matter—starting with the skills of oral language itself, then moving through language concepts, other subjects from the humanities, and finally on to math, science, and thinking skills.

Each chapter of games is divided into smaller sections, by specific subject. Each section describes how its games relate to that subject.

The Game Finder Index (p. 156) makes it easy to find a game for a particular group. For each age level, it tells you which games are appropriate, which games are especially suited for introducing story games to that age group, and the games' complexity and game type. It even shows how large or small a group each game works for and includes any special requirements for space or materials.

For a cross-referenced index of games on a particular subject, you can use the Subject Index (p. 164).

Once you turn to the description of a particular game, you'll find convenient summaries of all these characteristics: grade level, space or materials needed, complexity, and game type.

If you want to know the exact demands that a game makes on players—in communicating, storytelling, thinking, or curricular areas—turn to the listing of "Skills Reinforced" at the end of each game. The Subject Index can also guide you to other games that reinforce the same skills.

Flexible

The games in this book work for a wide range of ages, settings, and purposes.

The primary age range for these games is kindergarten through junior high—although at least one fifth of the games are suitable for preschoolers, and many others work well with highschoolers and adults. Each game is marked with a range of grade levels, and the Game Finder Index makes it easy to find just those games suitable for your group.

Whatever the age of your players, at least half the games in this book will work with them.

Whatever the size of your group—whether just one player and you, a handful of neighbors, a class full of students, or a hall full of scouts—you will find games in this collection that can get your group participating.

Whatever length of time you have available—whether three minutes of waiting, a fifteen-minute activity slot, a one-hour class, or a three-day car trip—you'll find games that will make the time memorable.

Whatever your purpose—whether to entertain, to build group skills, or to teach values, communication, or a particular subject—you'll find games easily adaptable to your needs.

SPEAKING AND LISTENING— PLAYFULLY

The games in this book use oral language playfully. They allow players to practice essential skills used in spoken communication. As a result, players may improve their self-confidence and even gain a sense of mastery of the spoken word. Along the way, players can develop important social skills as well.

Oral Language

In recent years, educators have increasingly emphasized the importance of oral language as a basis for written language. Too often, however, this empha-sis has been more evident in theory than in practice. Students still spend too little time speaking.

The present collection aims to make it easy for students to speak—with discipline, meaning, creativity, enjoyment, and cooperation. It includes activities that work in class settings, that interest children, that supplement various areas of the curriculum, and that encourage the full scope of oral language expression.

Before anyone ever had an educational theory, however, human beings craved—and created—playful opportunities for oral language expression. Just as we need to exercise our muscles and our imaginations, we need to express ourselves to each other. Story games help meet this need.

The Confidence to Speak Out

As natural as it is to speak creatively to others, many people feel insecure speaking in front of groups. In fact, public speaking is chronically listed as the most feared activity by adults in the United States.

The simple games in this collection give people of any age an opportunity to gain confidence in speaking out. They give pleasant, nonthreatening, recurrent opportunities to think of a story idea and then put it into words.

Different games emphasize different aspects of creating and telling a story. Taken as a whole, the games in this collection provide an extensive course in storytelling—the most basic, versatile, and compelling form of spoken communication.

In a world of cellular telephones and teleconferenced meetings, it is increasingly vital to be able to speak out confidently and fluidly. To educate citizens in our society, we need to help them claim a practical—as well as political—freedom of speech.

The Magic of Listening

Listening is at the heart of many interactions at school, at home, and at work. Story games give meaningful practice in directed listening.

The games in this collection make it easy for players to take turns speaking and listening. They provide motivation for listening to the player speaking at the moment, as well as clear boundaries for the start and finish of a player's turn to speak.

One of the most powerful experiences a person can have is to be listened to. The full, nonjudgmental attention of our friends, family, or classmates has a great power to affirm. Story games allow this power to be unleashed.

Creating the Spirit of Joy

A book like this can give you ideas. It can introduce you to activities that will give your group new opportunities to learn, imagine, communicate, and cooperate. But the spirit in which the games are played must come from you.

The games create an environment in which players will want to practice language and other skills, saving you from needing to cajole them. If you take advantage of this opportunity to focus on spontaneity and the players' own motivations, you will give the games a spirit of freedom.

The games make every player valuable. If you take advantage of this opportunity to welcome each player's contribution, you will give the games a spirit of respect.

The games divert attention from "getting the right answer" to solving problems creatively. If you use this opportunity to encourage divergent responses—to delight in the humorous and the unexpected—you will give the games a spirit of discovery.

The games let you share your love of language as well as your expertise and experience. If you savor the games yourself—and if you cherish the players—you will give the games a spirit of joy.

ACKNOWLEDGMENTS

I thank the children and adults who have played these games with me over the years, starting with my first storytelling classes for adults at Mount Ida Junior College. I remember especially the many children and elders from Arts In Progress (Jamaica Plain, MA), the adults who came to my private storytelling classes in the late '70s and early '80s, and the adults who attended my five-day workshop in story games at the National Storytelling Institute. The children from the Bridgewater (MA) Public Schools, Etz Hayim Synagogue, and the Matthew Thornton School (both of Derry, NH) graciously gave their enthusiasm and criticism to experimental forms of many of these games.

I thank the ring of friends, coaches, and writing buddies who have given me their attention and support during the creation of this book, including my mainstays, Jay O'Callahan and Marsha Saxton, as well as Terry Marotta and Gail Zarren. Karen Golden, Lyn Hoopes, Elena Marqueta, Gail Newhall, Liz Shapiro, Christine Shumock, and Wanna Zinsmaster took time— often many hours—to discuss individual games and the project as a whole. Working space, decaf tea, and good humor were provided by Michael and Michael and the rest of the crew at the Brookline Deli.

I thank those who read versions of this book and gave their comments, including Julie Della Toree, Sherry DesEnfants, Catherine Ann Dillon, Rosemary Glenn, Lyn Hoopes, Liana Laughlin, Mary Joe TenEyck, Carrie van der Laan, Marjorie Vanderberg, Debra Gordon Zaslow, and Wanna Zinsmaster.

I thank Debbie Moulton, who recruited the following kind folks to help so generously with Susan Wilson's cover photo: Paulette Van der Kloot and her daughters Kate, Megan, and Elizabeth; Cathy McLaughlin and her niece Chelli Keshavan; and Ming Lok and his son Edwin. I thank the *National Storytelling Journal*, which first published my two part article on story games.

I thank the jewel in this crown of players, helpers, friends, and readers, Linda Palmström—my wife and my heart's dream come true.

HOW TO USE THIS BOOK

■ ■ ■

Story games have the potential to benefit your group in many ways. To gain those benefits, you need to locate an appropriate game, take it off the page, and introduce it to your players in a way that brings out their best.

This chapter takes you from finding the right game to learning, teaching, and adapting it. It helps you use the games to develop your group's creativity, social skills, and leadership.

FINDING A GAME

The first step in teaching a game successfully is to select a game that is appropriate both for your group's needs and for your goals.

This book is organized by the subjects that the games relate to; it is cross-indexed by each game's background and applicability. Whether you start with your group's needs or with your curricular goals, this book will lead you to what you want.

Once you choose a game to examine, you'll find that it includes all the information you need to evaluate and teach it.

Finding a Game for a Particular Group

Let's suppose you want a game for a class of 30 fifth-grade students. You plan just 15 minutes for this activity. The class has no experience with storytelling of any kind.

Turn to the Game Finder Index (p. 156). Look under the subheading labeled "Upper Elementary." You'll see that four games are labeled not only as especially appropriate for this grade level, but as appropriate for a first introduction to story games. All four are of low or medium complexity, so they should be easy to play within your 15-minute time period. Turn to the game descriptions, and choose the one that appeals to you most.

For another example, let's suppose that your group loves guessing games. Turn again to the "Upper Elementary" subheading of the Game Finder Index. There you'll find four games for guessing a sound or movement, eight games for guessing a word or phrase, one game for guessing a fact, and two games for guessing whether a story was true or false. Choose the form of guessing that sounds most appealing, and then turn to the individual game descriptions.

You can use the other table headings to check the grade level, complexity, and space or prop requirements of the games that interest you, if you wish, before turning to the descriptions—but this information also accompanies each game.

Finding a Game by Subject

Let's suppose you want a game to reinforce the connections between sound and meaning in words.

Look first at the Contents, where you'll see that the subjects have been divided into four groups:

CHAPTER 1: Mastering Oral Communication

CHAPTER 2: Learning about Language
CHAPTER 3: Exploring Places, Periods, and
Peoples
CHAPTER 4:. Practicing Math, Science, and
Thinking Skills

Each of these chapters is divided into sections. Thus, Learning about Language consists of six sections:

Letter Sounds

Words

Rhyming

Homonyms

Expressions and Proverbs

Grammar

Each of these sections begins with an explanation of the subject matter, and how story games relate to it. Thus, Homonyms starts with a brief explanation of homonyms—words with different meanings but the same sound—and their uses. Next come two subheadings:

Games in This Section

Games in Other Sections

"Games in This Section" introduces the two Homonym games and describes exactly how they connect to the subject of homonyms. "Games in Other Sections" describes how four games from other sections also support the subject. Thus, even though only two games are presented in this section, the whole collection contains six games that help with homonyms.

In your search for relating word meaning to word sound, you've already uncovered six possible games. Of course, the sections on Letter Sounds and Rhyming will lead you to still others.

You can also find specific terms like "homonyms" in the Subject Index.

What Appears with Each Game

Each game description gives you all the information you need to teach the game. After the game's title, you'll find the grade levels, complexity, and game type, as well as a brief summary of the game itself.

The grade levels given are necessarily approximate. Groups of a given grade level vary in their interests, verbal skills, and social skills. Further, at any one moment your group may be tired enough to need a simpler game than they usually prefer, or they may be primed and eager for a greater challenge than usual.

The complexity ratings are meant to give you a rough idea of how big a "project" each game represents. Games with low complexity are easy to explain quickly, require little set-up or equipment, and can be played successfully in very short time periods. Games with high complexity are the most involved to explain and play, for one or more of the following reasons: they require equipment, they involve several steps, or they require at least 15 minutes to play. Of course, all the games can be repeated in less time than it takes to teach them initially.

Most of the games use one of a handful of basic game types. As a result, if your group seems to love games that are labeled as "Combining elements" games, you can easily find other similar ones. Or, if you have already taught them several games that use "Audience response to story cues," you can try out a different type.

Here's the first part of one of the games from Homonyms, showing how the information is presented:

❆ ❆

TEAKETTLE STORIES

Grade levels: Grade 4 and up.

Complexity: Medium.

Game type: Guessing a word used in a story.

Quick summary: A player chooses a pair of secret words that sound the same (homonyms). The player tells a clue story that uses both words, substituting "teakettle" for the words. The group tries to guess the secret words.

After the "Quick summary," you'll find the detailed directions for introducing the game under the subheading "Directions." This part describes everything you need to say when teaching the game. It includes instructions to give, questions to ask, and hypothetical contributions from players along with ways you might respond to each contribution. For games which are best taught by telling a story, the directions also include at least one sample story.

After the description, you will find hints about teaching the game. Hints may help you with a wide variety of techniques, such as:

◆ How to describe a potentially confusing instruction in more detail;

◆ how to deal with a variety of player responses;

◆ how to avoid common pitfalls in teaching the game;

◆ extra questions to ask if your group gets stuck.

After "Hints" comes "Variations," which shows alternative ways to play the game. "Variations" gives ways to make the game easier or harder, to adapt it for different subject areas, or to change the team structure to include more or fewer groups of players.

At the end of each description comes a list of skills reinforced, divided into four areas. Where different, the skills of leader and group member are listed separately. Here are the skills you will reinforce for the game "Teakettle Stories":

Skills Reinforced

Communication:
Group: Attempting to understand a story in which some words are omitted.

Leader: Pronouncing story clue clearly to the entire group.

Storytelling:
Leader: Creating a story that contains both words of a homonym pair.

Thinking:
Group: Allowing the marker word "teakettle" to be understood with two meanings.

Leader: Using the marker word "teakettle" in place of the word to be guessed; keep track of the marker's dual meanings.

Curricular: Reviewing homonyms; exemplifying their dual meanings.

Communication skills involve any aspect of oral or written language, from word identification and pronunciation to turn-taking or gesturing. *Storytelling* skills pertain to the creating, shaping and telling of a story. *Thinking* skills are the specific cognitive tasks involved in playing the game. *Curricular* skills relate to school subjects, whether described in the same section of the book or elsewhere. All these skills are referenced in the Subject Index.

PREPARING FOR A GAME

It's possible to teach one of these games with no preparation at all by simply reading the instructions out loud to your group. This method will probably be less effective than imagining the game and describing it in your own words, but it will be better than not teaching the game at all.

You'll have an even better chance of creating excitement, learning, and joy if you spend some time learning a game before you teach it.

To learn a game, try to imagine it from the description. Speak aloud the directions and sample story; if you can think of one easily, tell your own sample story instead. Imagine how you think your group might respond and how you might react. Respond as a player to the challenge of the game, thinking of how you might respond if someone else were teaching the game.

If the directions seem hard to remember, try taking brief notes about the sequence of teaching the game. Jot down the main steps and any essential details.

After you have imagined teaching a game, try teaching it to one or two other people. If you are a parent who wants to play the game with your children, for example, try it out first with another adult, or with the child most likely to understand and enjoy the game.

If you are a teacher, try the game out first with a colleague, with your own family, or with a small group of students. When I taught nursery school, I would approach an individual child or a small group during recess, asking, "Do you want to try a secret new game?" If the children didn't like the game, they would just return to normal recess activities. By the end of recess, I had often tried the game with everyone in the class. When I introduced the game to the group later that day, I had experience in teaching the game, and everyone in the class had experience in playing it.

If any part of the game seemed confusing or difficult when you tried it out, refer to the "Hints" and "Variations" for ideas about clarifying or simplifying the game. Create your own modifications if necessary.

Please note that a quarter of the games in this book include chanted lines, some traditional and some original. Ten of these chants may also be sung, either to familiar tunes (as indicated with each game) or to the melodies that begin on page 147. The singing is optional. At this point, however, you will want to try out the chants. If you want to sing them to the indicated familiar tune, practice fitting the words to the melody. Whether spoken or sung, these lines are the one part of the game that will be more effective when memorized.

Now you are ready to prepare the group!

Preparing the Group

To play a story game, four conditions must be present: to understand what the game is, to feel safe enough to play, to have enough time and space to play, and to consent to play.

To understand a game, each group will need different preparation. If you usually play games with them, your players may need to understand what kind of a game you are about to teach. If necessary, let them know briefly how the game differs from their usual games—in activeness, in competitiveness, in the time allotted to play it, or in the use of the imagination. You might say something like, "This is a game where we make stories together." On the other hand, if you do not usually play games with this group, your players may need to understand that what follows will not be a test or a drill. Often, it's enough to say, "This is a game. We'll play it just for fun."

To feel safe enough to play, your group may need some ground rules. You may prefer to state these in advance, or you may want to wait until they come up in the course of playing. At a minimum, players need to know that they will be safe from judgment and humiliation: there will be no put-downs allowed and no grades or other evaluations given. It may also help them to know that the point of these games is to give everyone a fun chance to speak, not to find the right answer to anything.

Give your group enough time and space to play. Games are perfect for squeezing into leftover moments, especially when a group already knows and loves them. When you first introduce a game, however, you will need to choose a time and place where the group can concentrate adequately on this new activity. Later, once a game is familiar, you can try it in more difficult circumstances: a tired or upset group, an overcrowded or distracting location, or a short or uncertain time period.

To gain a group's consent to play, you need to make it clear that each individual has a choice. Depending on your situation, players may be free to leave the area to choose another activity or else to sit quietly without participating. In any case, a player who does not want to take a turn should not be forced to take one. You may be able to make this clear without mentioning it explicitly. Or you might say, "This is a story game. If you want a turn, you can have one." If a player appears reluctant to take a turn, you can say, "Would you like a turn?" or "If you don't want a turn now, you can pass," or "Should we come back to you?" Play is not play if it is coerced.

TEACHING A GAME

Before you introduce a game, prepare yourself and your group as described in the preceding section. Make sure you have imagined the game yourself and given the players the information, time, space, and any props they need. Do what you can to create the emotional safety necessary for true play.

As you introduce a game, elicit contributions from players. Part of your job is to help players feel safe to volunteer. You may choose to introduce brainstorming, a technique that can help suspend evaluation of ideas long enough to let creativity function.

After you have introduced a game, the greatest benefits come from repeating the game on other occasions, adapting it to fit the evolving needs and interests of your group.

Introducing a Game

Set aside some time with a minimum of distractions, if possible. Most games in this collection can be taught in 10 or 15 minutes. Some of the low complexity games can be taught in 5 minutes; the highest complexity games may require 20 minutes. In these time periods, you'll be able to demonstrate the game and offer turns to two or three players or groups. Once your players know a game, they will be able to repeat it in less time.

Most groups respond well to a new game if you ask for their opinion about it. I often preface an experimental game by saying, "This is a game I'm just trying out. I want to know if you enjoy it." Such a statement acknowledges my inexperience and vulnerability in addition to soliciting the group's advice. I have found that groups respond better to my honest ignorance than to my attempts to pretend I know what I'm doing. After the game, I take a moment to ask, "Did you enjoy that? Would it be a good one to try again?"

Whenever possible, keep your words of introduction to a minimum. Simply begin the game. Don't list the rules, just demonstrate how to play. Rules can usually be explained more clearly after they have been demonstrated.

When you call on a player for a contribution, call first on a player who you think understands what you want. The others will learn best from that player's successful example. Later, you can be sure that all get turns. In addition, when you repeat the game another day, you can give different players a chance to have the first turn.

Some of the games require sample stories. Tell them with enjoyment. Don't try to memorize them. Just imagine what happens in them, then tell them from your imagination. Even better, substitute your own sample story. It's more appealing to approximate a story and tell it with ease and enjoyment than to recite it grimly in exact detail.

Some games don't use sample stories but depend on contributions from your group. Don't try to memorize the directions for these games. Instead, try to understand them and apply them to your group's contributions. If at any time you're not sure how to proceed, consider asking the group for help: "I'm not sure how to go on from here. Can you help me figure out how this could work?"

Getting Players to Contribute

After you have modeled a game for a group, you need volunteers to tell stories or to contribute suggestions. If your group is comfortable with you, with each other, and with speaking out, you won't have trouble getting volunteers to contribute.

But what happens if no one volunteers? If players don't understand the game, you may need to explain more or to offer more sample stories. If they don't feel safe from your evaluation of them, you may need to remind them that you aren't grading their responses, that there is no right answer, and that it's just a game. If they don't feel safe from humiliation by each other, you may need to remind them that you won't let anyone be put down. Or you may need to persuade an acknowledged leader in the group to give the game a try, thus making it permissible for the rest.

If your players just haven't come up with an idea, you may need to stimulate their imaginations. Give another sample story or two. Or give them a list of possibilities. For example, when teaching "Apple Tree," I sometimes recite a list of possible subjects for personal stories while I wait for a volunteer. (See p. 124.) Such a litany of possibilities serves two functions: it may trigger memories, and it gives people time to get up their nerve to volunteer. With enough examples, coaxing, and occasional statements about how it is okay to be embarrassed, a volunteer can usually be enticed from even the most reluctant group.

When you call on a series of players for contributions, be aware of the group's dynamics. If the group has identifiable sub-groups, call on members of each of them. For example, if you call on three boys in a row, the girls in some groups will cease to volunteer.

Consider giving players a chance to tell their suggestions or stories to a partner before they share them with the entire group. Have players break into groups of two or three and brainstorm suggestions for a minute or two. Then ask groups to contribute ideas they liked.

Brainstorming

What if your group seems short of ideas? Try brainstorming—the rapid listing of ideas without stopping to evaluate them. Brainstorming involves suspending all evaluation in order to generate ideas as quickly as possible. After all, your group can't come up with a *good* idea unless it can come up with *some* idea.

To help your players brainstorm, explain to them that their job for the moment is to think of many ideas, whether good or bad. You might say something like, "This is brainstorming. We think of lots of ideas, but don't comment on them." State the question to be answered or the problem to be solved. Then respond enthusiastically to every contribution by repeating it or writing it down where all can see. Restate the question or problem frequently. Interrupt any evaluation of ideas by the group, saying, "This is brainstorming. For now, we just want lots of ideas." Resist especially any personal temptation you may feel to explain why something won't work; evaluation can come after brainstorming is over.

Once you have a list of ideas, have your group point out those with potential to work well. It's usually best not to dwell on why a particular idea won't work; just pass it over and speak of those that will. Your group will probably be more forthcoming in its next brainstorming session if no one's ideas are criticized in this session.

If your group latches onto an idea that you think will not work, you can say, "Let's look at the idea. Does it solve our problem?" If the players think it will, it most often makes sense to let them try it. After all, if it fails, you can always return to fix it or to try a different idea. In the rare case where a poor choice might jeopardize the introduction of the game, say, "The idea you like is worth exploring. Just to teach you the game, however, I'm going to choose this other idea. Later, you can come back and try the one you like."

Try brainstorming whenever your group needs help coming up with an idea. Does your group need to think of a two-syllable place name for "Towns and Counties"? Brainstorm place names of any number of syllables, then go back and choose the appropriate ones. Do you need to name an enjoyable activity for "You're Shaking Me Up"? Brainstorm things that your group does; later, players can decide which ones are actually enjoyable. Do you need six or seven good words beginning with the letter "B" for "Letter Echoes"? Brainstorm all the B-words you can think of, then choose the good ones. If you write down all the words suggested, by the way, it will become clear—without your having to mention it—which ones don't actually begin with "B."

Brainstorming can even help you relate games to curriculum. In "Hide the Words" (p. 43), for example, you can ask players to brainstorm words from a given area of curriculum. Spend a few minutes brainstorming words that have a connection to American colonial history, for example, then proceed with the game.

Playing Again

If your players enjoyed a game at all, play it with them again. Play it later the same day or week, or the next month, or the next time you travel on a bus together.

On subsequent playings, more players will be likely to participate. The stories created will probably become more complex, original, and ingenious. Only through repetition can all a game's potential be fully realized.

If group members love a game, they will be eager to play it, even in small installments. Only three minutes to play while driving to the store? Play just one turn of a game they have played before, such as "Towns and Counties" or "Letter Relay." Is your class lined up waiting for the bell to ring? Start a quick round of "Because." Did more groups create "Proverb Guessing" stories than had time to tell them? Save them to tell, one a day, at odd moments.

If the game still seems a little too hard, try to simplify it. Sometimes the "Hints" or "Variations" may help; if not, create your own simpler variation. Pay attention to your group's spontaneous variations, which may give you the approach you need.

If a game starts to seem easy or boring, check out the "Variations." Or be alert to variations created spontaneously by your players.

When you find a game that your group loves, look for other games like it. Refer to the Game Finder Index, p. 156.

MANAGING TURNS AND TEAMS

Story games require certain social skills, including the ability to take turns and, in some cases, the ability to form teams. With a little care, you can help your players implement the required social skills in a way that enhances the game experience.

Managing Turns

All of the games require taking turns. In most situations, you'll be able to use the group's existing social skills to determine smoothly who speaks next. In some situations, however, friction over turn-taking may threaten to destroy the atmosphere of safety and cooperation necessary to the game. In these cases, you may need special techniques to ensure fairness and smoothness.

If a few players dominate a game, you can always ask volunteers to raise their hands; then you call on players who have had the fewest turns. Or you can establish a rule or two, such as these:

◆ No one speaks twice until everyone has spoken once.
◆ No one speaks four times until everyone has spoken twice.
◆ Each player gets one turn (or two turns); then the game is over.

You can make such rules more concrete by giving a physical sign that a player has had a turn. For example, in a round-robin game you can have players stand; after taking a turn, a player sits down. Or you can give each player one or two bingo markers or slips of cardboard; to speak, a player puts a marker in a pile in the center of the room. To ensure that no player speaks twice until every player has spoken once, let each player get one red and one yellow marker; the yellow marker can be used for a first turn and the red one for a second turn.

Choosing Teams

Some of the games require teams. You can make the process of choosing teams as cooperative as the game playing itself.

At first thought, it would seem to empower players to allow them to choose teams in any way they like. To be sure, some groups can happily form teams by consent or through the sensible choices of team captains. In many cases, however, the choosing of teams becomes a drama of exclusion that leaves players with unpleasant feelings.

To avoid unnecessary feelings of rejection, try to choose teams through methods that rely on chance. For example, you can simply group players together who are already seated together. Or you can use the familiar (if impersonal) method of counting off, which adapts well to any size teams. Or have all the players toss coins simultaneously, and let all the "heads" go to one team and the "tails" to the other; if you need smaller teams, repeat the process within each half of your group. Similarly, you can have all the players jump in the air and land with feet either together or spread apart, or with either their left or their right foot in front.

Other random methods for choosing teams are based on facts about the players. These methods are most refreshing if you use a single method only once or twice. Please note that some of the following methods may not be appropriate for certain groups; for example, some of your players may not have telephone numbers, or some might not even know their parents' names.

Divide players by the day of their birthdays. For example, say,

Think of the day of the month of your birthday. I was born on December 23rd, so my day is 23. If your day is between one and fifteen, you're part of the first group. Otherwise, you're part of the second group.

Of course, you can group the days of the month into quarters (1–7, 8–14, etc.), or into odd and even numbers, or into numbers that give remainders of zero, one, or two when divided by three. Adjust the grouping of numbers, if necessary, to secure teams of more equal sizes.

Divide players into four groups by the season of their birth. Or group spring and fall birthdays against winter and summer. Another day, group spring with winter.

Have all those born in months beginning with "J," "M" or "N" form one team. Or make three teams: those born in months ending with "R," those born in months ending with "Y," and all others. Or number the months from one to twelve, grouping together those in even-numbered months.

Divide players by height, or by who is wearing a particular color or colors.

Divide players by the first letter of their first (or last) names, or by the last letters of their names. Or use the first or last letters of their mother's or father's names or of the locality of their birth. Or use the second letter of names or birthplaces.

Divide players by the first (or last) digit of their street addresses or phone numbers. If your players live near each other, of course, the first three digits of their phone numbers may be the same. In this case, use the fourth, fifth, sixth, or seventh digit.

Adapting the Team Structure

The use of teams in these games has both advantages and disadvantages. Keep in mind that you can alter the team structure to promote your own objectives.

On the positive side, team members tend to cooperate with each other. To tell a story together, they need to communicate among themselves. They also learn from each other, sharing ideas and helping each other over obstacles. Where an individual might be unable to create a certain kind of story, a team might succeed. In addition, the discussion among team members that precedes a team story has another value, since it may transfer to a pre-writing context, in which students discuss their writing ideas before committing them to paper.

Further, by dividing your group into many small teams to prepare stories, you increase the number of players who get turns to speak in a given time period. If you have small teams tell their stories to other teams, you increase this number even more. Players who are shy or fearful of speaking to your whole group may find speaking to small teams more comfortable.

On the negative side, teams tend to compete against other teams, taking the focus away from creating and communicating, and leaving players with feelings of failure if their team "loses." Also, while several smaller teams are preparing or sharing stories simultaneously, you cannot assist each one individually. The player who tells a story to a

small group usually receives attention that is less focused than the attention received by a player who tells it to a larger group. Further, dividing into teams can reduce the sense that everyone has shared a single experience.

To decide whether to change the team structure described with a particular game, you will have to take into account several factors.

First, evaluate your players' social skills. Can they easily wait while many players take turns to tell stories? Can they form themselves into teams without disruption? Can they work in small groups without your attention? Are they all eager to talk at once? Are they eager just to be together?

Second, if they have used the game's existing team structure previously, evaluate their reaction to it. Were they impatient or excited while one player spoke to the entire group? Did they break into teams that supported stereotyped groupings (all the girls together; all the Khmer-speakers together)? If so, did these groupings create a helpful sense of security and shared experience, or a hurtful sense of exclusion and comparison?

Third, think of your goals for the activity and their consequences for the team structure and use of small groups. Do you most want your players to have a relaxed chance to speak? This might cause you to lean toward using small groups. Do you most want the group members to gain a positive experience of the diversity of their verbal styles? This might cause you to lean toward keeping your players together.

Once you have evaluated these factors, try a likely structure and notice what happens. You can try a pure whole-group structure or a pure small-group structure. Alternatively, you can try a hybrid structure—such as having teams prepare stories in small groups then sharing the results with the whole group, or having small teams tell stories to other teams then letting a few of the teams retell their stories to the whole group. Depending on the result, re-use the structure next time or try an altered one.

Here are some possible team structures for story games that involve guessing:

- ◆ An individual tells a story clue; the others guess.
- ◆ A small group tells a story clue; the others guess.

- A small group tells a story clue; another small group guesses.
- An individual tells a story clue (in response to a secret provided by another team); the individual's teammates guess.

In some guessing games, a series of words are hidden within a story. If a small group tells such a story—with each group member including one of the words in the group member's segment of the story—the guessing players know they are searching for one word from each of the story segments. If an individual tells such a story, however, the story is not divided into segments; this makes guessing more difficult. The size of the small group or team in such a game is limited by the number of words to be hidden in the story.

RESPONDING TO PLAYERS

Once players volunteer a suggestion or a story, you have an opportunity to respond.

If you respond with criticism (or with a tone that signifies hearing the "right answer"), you will convince your group that you did not mean what you said about not evaluating contributions. The level of safety will plummet; you may get no contributions, or you may get contributions given only to please you from those group members who habitually contribute for a leader's benefit.

Try to respond with respect and pleasure. I often restate the contribution with a tone of approval, trying to repeat the player's exact words. This can help the group understand what the player said, and lets the player know that I heard the contribution. Here are some other simple responses you can make to any player's contribution:

Thank you!

Yes!

Good!

Great!

Marvelous!

If a player's contribution shows creativity, solves a problem, or follows up on another player's contribution, your response can show your appre-ciation of the player's achievement. If desired, you can repeat the player's contribution before or after any of these appreciative responses:

Good idea!

Great idea!

Good thinking!

Great thought!

That's a way to solve that!

That's a (new) way to . . . !

That's another way to think about that!

Wow!

That's fascinating!

You found a different way to solve the problem [of . . .]!

That takes ____'s idea and goes further with it!

Dealing with Inappropriate Responses

If a player's response does not seem appropriate, you can still treat it with respect. For example, even if you simply go on to restate the problem and listen to another player's contribution, you can first say a phrase similar to one of these:

So you thought of . . . !

I never thought of that!

Interesting!

That's certainly a way to do it!

Many times, however, your response can help elicit a clearer or more appropriate contribution. Try one of these:

Are you saying that . . . ?

Keep going!

[Restate the player's response, with exclamatory tone] "What else?" or "Then what?" or "Yes?"

I imagined you would say a way to . . . , but it sounds like you thought of a way to . . . . Is that right?

If a player simply restates your sample story (or a story told by another player), say, "You told the same story! Good job! Can anyone tell a different story about . . . ?"

If the contribution seems to contradict a turn of plot that a group story has already taken, you can clarify with one of the following responses. (Many times, I have asked for confirmation of my understanding of what a player said, only to discover that an apparently inappropriate contribution was in fact appropriate and creative.) Try saying:

Up to now, I think we've been imagining that . . . [e.g., the hero was a dog]; now you're imagining that . . . [e.g., the hero is a person under a magic spell to look like a dog]. Is that right?

Do we agree that . . . ? Can you say how what you said relates to that?

Wow! You're saying that . . . . I imagined you would think of . . . , but you thought . . . . Which way should we play this?

Often enough, the inappropriate contribution actually points up a misunderstanding or a decision about the story that the group has not all agreed to. You can use the apparently inappropriate contribution to help the group make an explicit decision:

I think we have a decision to make here . . . .

That brings up an important point. Is it true that . . . ?

You found a different way to solve the problem [of . . .]! Which way do we want to solve it?

Are you thinking that . . . [e.g., our hero is still stuck in dog form]? I thought that _____'s idea was to . . . [e.g., have her eat a magic wafer and turn back into a person]. Did we have a misunderstanding? Are you willing to let . . . [e.g., her turn back into a person]? How do you think the story should go?

You can think of your job as finding the laudable impulse in each player's contribution and then showing your appreciation of it. Many times, you will also be able to help the player shape that impulse to further the group project. Sometimes, however, you will have to settle for acknowledging the impulse and then going on to another player's contribution:

So you thought of a way to . . . ? Thank you! Who has a way to . . . [restate the original problem]?

It sounds like you're trying to get us to laugh at you. Is that right? Well, in this story I want us to put the funny things in the story. [Or: Well, can you help us solve the problem of . . . ?]

That's a different way the story could go. If you want, you can make your own story later.

In any case, you can focus on the group project—the story being created together—rather than on your personal authority. If a player refuses to assist the group project, you can see that player's refusal as a choice about working together, not as a personal affront to you.

Value and appreciate each contribution from your group with a response that is appropriate to the player and to the contribution. Remember that the unexpected player contribution has the potential to teach you—and your players—more than any other contribution.

HELPING PLAYERS BECOME LEADERS

When you teach a game, you will usually begin in the role of leader. In most games, this means that you will tell (or at least begin) a story for your group. Players will listen, guess, or respond with movements or words. As leader, you will also be the one who calls on group members for contributions to a group story, or to make a guess about the story you told.

In some situations, it will make sense for you to remain in the leader's role. Perhaps your group members need more examples before they understand the leader's role well enough to try it themselves. Perhaps your goals for the game are best met with your group in the role of listeners. Perhaps you just enjoy the leader's role in a particular game, but your group members don't.

Most often, however, the full potential of the game will be realized only when the players become leaders themselves, or even play without any intervention from you at all. Many of the skills reinforced by the games are used only by the leader. Further, there is no substitute for the satisfaction a group gets from having fun without outside intervention.

Your leading and teaching are valuable, but only as ways to produce enjoyment and learning. When enjoyment and learning can happen without you, it's time to stand back and let your group members exercise their full powers. This means letting them tell stories, of course, but also letting them call on other group members to make guesses or add contributions.

In a school setting, there is an additional advantage to allowing students to lead the games. Very often, the most successful storytellers are students who do not excel in conventional studies. By letting them have a turn to lead a story game, you may be providing them with a rare opportunity to savor success.

Helping Leaders Succeed

Of course, not all players will succeed immediately in the role of leader. You have an opportunity, then, to help them learn to succeed.

A common difficulty for new leaders is speaking too softly. Try standing at the opposite end of the room from a leader who can't be heard easily. In case the leader is directing the story at you, the leader will now automatically increase volume until you seem able to hear. If not, you can say, "What?" or "I can't hear you." This response gives the player a good reason to speak louder: to communicate to you.

Often, however, the leader is speaking softly out of fear of being noticed or judged. You may need to make it clear that no judgment or ridicule is intended or allowed. (See the sections earlier in this chapter on "Preparing the Group" and "Introducing a Game.") It may take several sessions to establish the required safety.

You may also need to make it feel safe enough to speak out loudly by giving the leader a series of successful experiences. Paradoxically, the leader's quietness itself can cause failure, if the group members become disinterested because they can't hear. To keep the group interested, try repeating loudly and energetically what the leader says: "You saw a large butterfly? It was flying right toward you? You jumped up on its back!"

Another difficulty for a leader may lie in telling too long a story. Especially in preschool and the primary grades, many children can talk for more minutes than they can hold the group's attention. Fortunately, the games give you opportunities to intervene that might not be present in other activities.

In the case of "Old Bloody Bones" (p. 28), for example—where the storyteller uses the cue words "old bloody bones" to signal the end of a story— you can gently interrupt a player who is telling a long story by saying, "It's time to say 'old bloody bones' soon." If the player continues, say, "It's time to say 'old bloody bones' now!" If necessary, go on to say, "I'm going to say 'old bloody bones' for you, now. Old bloody bones!" Then go into the movements that follow each leader's story.

In other games, you have similar built-in ways to end a player's turn by going on to the next phase of the game. In each case, the game carries its own momentum, replacing the leader's story with some sort of group activity.

Placing Limits on Leaders

Occasionally, you will need to limit the content of what a leader contributes, because it draws attention away from the game, is socially unacceptable, or leads the game to a dead end.

In the case of a player "hamming it up" in a way that distracts attention from the actual game, you can use the approach recommended in "Responding to Players," above (p. xix): find the laudable impulse in what the player does, respond to it, and attempt to enlist it in the service of the group goal. For example, if a player gets carried away making a lion sound, you can focus on the meaning of the story, saying something like this:

What a wonderful lion sound! Do you remember why you had a lion in the story? To scare the man? Tell us how the man reacted to such a scary lion!

Or you might focus on the dramatic impulse itself:

Did you notice how that great sound you made woke us up? That really got our attention. Now, the problem of a good actor or storyteller is what to do with our attention, once you have it. Where do you want the story to go from here?

In the case of content that is socially unacceptable because it is scatological, sexual, or oppressive of a particular group, you may have to prohibit it decisively. Without making the player seem bad, let the player know what is unacceptable, and why. For example, you might say, "That's okay to say privately, but I'm not comfortable with you saying it here around the campfire." Or you might have to say, "I know that you've probably heard other people tell jokes like that, but when I hear blond women described as stupid, it seems hurtful. No one should ever be judged by how she looks. I need us to change that part of the story. How can we do that?"

In the case of content that leads the story to a dead end, you have a larger range of viable choices. To be sure, the group purpose is undermined by the player who uses a turn in the round-robin story to kill off all the characters in a terrorist explosion, or who introduces gore and bloodshed at every chance.

In some situations, it will make sense to limit such derailment by making a "no violence" rule—or to prohibit content from video games, movies, or TV, saying, "I want something from your imagination."

In other situations, however, the players will learn more if you do not step in and save them from themselves, but allow them to see the consequences of their own actions. You might say, "Everyone is dead. Where do we go from here?" If no one can think of a way out, you can say, "Well, I guess that ends our story. How does that feel to you? Why?" In time, the group may choose to create its own form of a "no cheating us out of our story" rule.

In general, the rule of thumb is this: if the players seem engaged or "present" and the stories seem to be evolving at all, it is probably most efficient to let the players discover the limitations of violent plots on their own—with perhaps some guidance at opportune moments. On the other hand, if the players seem "absent" or "fevered" and their stories are strictly repetitious, it's probably a bigger favor to them to make a strict prohibition.

This book is designed to help you match a game not only with your group's needs and desires but also with your goals—whether for social skills, curriculum, creativity, or enjoyment.

The games themselves offer you the opportunity to treat your players with respect, to reveal the joy in learning, and to create opportunities for your players to communicate their astounding creativity. Dig in!

CHAPTER I
Mastering Oral Communication

■ ■ ■

Spoken language is our first language. Almost everyone has years of practice in oral communication before learning to communicate in writing.

To nurture—and capitalize on—our oral communication skills, we need to recognize the nature of oral language, to direct our attention to communicating orally with zest and caring, to develop sensory imagery, and to provide meaningful opportunities for practicing the component skills of oral language.

The Nature of Oral Language

Oral language uses much more than words. Oral language also communicates through movement, gesture, posture, facial expression, vocal inflection, tempo, rhythm, pitch, eye contact, and sometimes even touch and smell.

Oral language is multi-dimensional. At the same time that we speak words, we also turn toward or away from our listeners, gesture, roll our eyes, shrug our shoulders, move our head to one side, and change our tone of voice. Each dimension of oral language simultaneously modifies the meaning of the others. Our shrug can amplify our resigned tone of voice, while the fire in our eyes reveals our hidden determination to change the situation.

Oral language is too complex to teach in a linear fashion. It would take most of us years of intensive training to gain conscious control of the simultaneous processes that a four-year old might employ perfectly while uttering a single sentence. The child's words, for example, may ask politely for a parent's permission to be allowed to stay up beyond bedtime; the perfectly timed eye movements may suggest that the true audience is the visiting grandparent; the artistically exaggerated gestures may suggest subservience to the parent's decision; at the same time, the subtle modulation in the tone of voice may indicate that the parent would be foolish to refuse and thus appear hard-hearted.

Where detailed analysis might fail in helping this child go beyond such complex existing skills, whole-language activities like games and storytelling can sometimes succeed in exercising, exploring, and expanding these communicative abilities through creative play.

The sections in this chapter on movements and eye contact attempt to give players specific help in mastering the communicative power of these nonverbal elements. Most of the other games in this book give practice in the integrated use of oral communication.

The Importance of Imagery and Intention

Oral communication is enhanced when the speaker pays attention to imagery and intention.

To tell the story of your hard day at work, you call up images of what happened to you and what those events meant to you. Then you translate these images and intentions into a complex example of multidimensional oral communication.

If you can remember exactly how large the tray was that you were asked to carry, you will use your unconscious oral language skills to communicate its size through your eye movements, words, and gestures. If you can remember how ridiculous the request seemed to you, you will communicate how you felt through tone of voice, facial expression, and posture simultaneously.

If you take your attention away from these images and intentions, however, your communication will almost certainly suffer. Suddenly, you may be reduced to a more single-dimensional focus on consciously shaping your gestures or on maintaining subject-verb agreement. This type of focus is why the person who is a captivating natural storyteller may deliver such a flat, memorized report in school or on the job: the person's attention is on the words, not on the images and meanings.

As a result, it's usually most effective to work on oral communication in the context of responding to imagery, or of communicating an intention. Three sections in this chapter focus directly on developing sensory imagery. The remainder of the games in this book allow opportunities for unselfconsciously accomplishing a playful purpose through oral communication.

Developing Sensory Imagery

Most of us have a preferred mode of perception. For example, some people tend to notice first the visual aspects of our world, especially when storing or remembering information or incidents. Other people focus first on sounds, others on muscle feelings, still others on words and concepts.

For oral communication, the three most important kinds of sensory imagery are visual, sound, and kinesthetic (motion or muscular). These are the three most commonly used sensory modes for storing memories and ideas. In addition, they are the modes in which our listeners perceive us. Obviously, we are seen and heard by our listeners. In addition, our muscular tension affects both our appearance and our voice. As a result, our kinesthetic experiences are revealed both by how we look and by how we sound.

The most effective oral communicators are able to experience the world in all three of these modes, and to use sight, sound, and muscular configuration to communicate what they experience.

The sections on sound imagery, kinesthetic imagery, and visual imagery provide opportunities for players to pay attention to experiencing and expressing through each of these sensory modes.

Special Demands of Oral Presentation

In writing, time is not a major element of the communicative process. There is no correlation between the writer's speed of composition, for example, and the reader's speed of comprehending what was written. No matter how long it took me to write this paragraph, you can read it in a few moments. Further, I could rearrange it endlessly until I perfected the sequence of ideas—at no cost to you.

In oral communication, on the other hand, time is an essential part of the process. If I pause to gather my thoughts while speaking to you, you have to wait before you can hear more. If I confuse the order of ideas or events and have to backtrack, you share my confusion. As a result, oral communication makes extra demands on the speaker to keep things flowing in order.

The sections in this chapter on speaking out without a script and on remembering sequences both deal with these issues of time and order.

In addition, oral communicators may use one or more "expression clusters" that recur in a presentation. When you are tell-ing about your hard day at work, for example, you may imitate your boss's tempo of speech, way of standing, and size of gesture. If you say something later with those qualities of expression, your listeners will understand implicitly that your boss is speaking.

In a more abstract example, a speaker on psychology (or a comedian!) may be explaining different internal tendencies in response to a given event. When representing "denial of feelings" as a tendency, the speaker may always face to one side, tense the facial muscles, and use a lifeless tone of voice. These qualities of communication can become a cluster that will come to communicate to the listener that "what you now hear is the expression of the denial of feelings"—even when the speaker does not continue to identify explicitly that tendency.

The section on characterization deals with creating clusters of expressive qualities.

Finally, oral communication is fluid. It need not be predetermined, and it need never be the same twice. Before you can mail a letter to your uncle, you must decide how to end it. But you can begin to give oral comments without having decided exactly what you will end up saying. Indeed, the process of speaking aloud often brings unexpected thoughts. Furthermore, if you write a letter to your uncle, it uses the same words every time he reads it. But if you speak to him on the same subject, you can expand on the example that seems to be working while skipping over the one that leaves him looking puzzled.

The section on improvising plot is designed to help players become comfortable with the fluid nature of oral communication.

Speaking Out without a Script

The attention of a group of listeners is a double-edged sword. On the one hand, even two-year olds respond positively to the power of a group's attention. If they have an opportunity to speak or move while many people are watching, most toddlers will be drawn toward it.

On the other hand, the power of a group's attention is awesome. By the time most two-year olds have grown into adults, they associate this power with humiliation and paralysis, and many people list their biggest fear as "public speaking."

Games in This Section

The two games in this section ("Wolf, Are You Ready?" and "Janey Jo") are both adaptations of traditional chasing games. They give young players a way to speak to an entire group with a minimum of self-consciousness. Each game creates a dialogue between the group and a single player who improvises simple statements within a clear framework. In both cases, the main focus of the group rests on the action, not on the speaker's words.

Games in Other Sections

These games allow spontaneous contributions to an ongoing story:

"Because" (p. 116)

"Fortunately, Unfortunately" (p. 30)

"I Was Present!" (p. 119)

"Letter Relay" (p. 41)

"You're Shaking Me Up" (p. 31)

"Guess the Voice" (p. 17) requires the player in the circle to tell a brief story. Attention is focused on disguising the voice, not on telling the story.

The following games elicit other brief contributions from players:

"Daddy Shot a Bear" (p. 128)

"Old Doc Jones" (p. 121)

"Would You Believe?" (p. 66)

※ ※

WOLF, ARE YOU READY?

Grade levels: Preschool through grade 2.

Space needed: Area for chasing, plus a "safe place" (such as an empty expanse of wall) large enough for the entire group.

Complexity: Low.

Game type: Chase, with improvised dialogue.

Quick summary: The Wolf stands far from the Safe Place. The group approaches the Wolf and asks a series of questions ("Wolf, are you ready? It's *one* o'clock"). The Wolf improvises answers ("No, I'm putting on my pajamas"). The final answer ("Yes, and I'm coming to get you") is the signal for the Wolf to chase the group to the Safe Place.

Directions: Point to the section of open wall (or other "safety area"), saying,

This is the Safe Place. The Wolf can't touch you if you're touching this wall. Everyone come over to the Safe Place!

Choose a volunteer to be the Wolf, saying,

You are the Wolf. You stand over here [at the opposite end of the chasing area] in the Wolf's Cave.

Join the group of children at the wall. Say,

If we're feeling brave, we can go over to the Wolf's Cave.

Walk toward the Wolf's Cave, joined by any who wish, and speak these lines (or chant them like a taunt, or sing them loosely to the tune of "It's raining, it's pouring, the old man is snoring," or sing them to the tune given on p. 153):

Wolf, are you ready? It's one o'clock.

The Wolf responds with a spoken, improvised description of what she or he will do at that time, such as:

No, I'm eating lunch.

Say or sing with the group:

Wolf, are you ready? It's two o'clock.

Encourage the Wolf to improvise another excuse, such as "I'm watching TV" or "I'm getting ready for bed."

Repeat for "three o'clock." At "four o'clock," tell the Wolf to say,

Yes, and I'm coming to get you!

Say, "Run to the Safe Place! The Wolf is chasing us!" The Wolf chases the other players to the wall. Choose a new Wolf and begin the game again.

Hints: If you are playing this game with preschoolers, try to get the Wolf to chase you instead of chasing the other children. As soon as the Wolf says, "Yes, and I'm coming to get you," say, "Oh, no! The Wolf is going to touch me!" Then back away from the Wolf toward the Safe Place, giving a running commentary: "Oh, oh! She's catching me now. She got me!" This makes it less scary for the others and guarantees that the Wolf will get the satisfaction of tagging at least one person!

Variations: Instead of specifying when the Wolf must say "Yes, and I'm coming to get you" (at "four o'clock"), allow the Wolf to decide when to say it. This can create suspense for the other players. You can limit the length of the Wolf's turn by saying:

Wolf, you can say it whenever you want—but you have to say it by "five o'clock."

Have the Wolf tell a longer story about what she is doing, such as:

No, I'm looking for some sheep to shear, so I can spin their wool. I want to make yarn because I'm knitting myself some socks to put on.

Skills Reinforced

Communication: Practicing turn-taking.

Group: Saying chanted lines in unison.

Leader: Pronouncing cue phrase clearly to entire group.

Storytelling:

Leader: Improvising single sentences.

Curricular: Reviewing daily routines. Dealing playfully with fear.

JANEY JO

Grade levels: Preschool through grade 2.

Space needed: A clear area for a circle of players, with room for one player to walk around the outside. (Can also be played with a chase, requiring room enough for running.)

Complexity: Low.

Game type: Stationary tag, with improvised dialogue.

Quick summary: The Midder sits in the middle of a ring of standing players; Janey Jo stands outside and makes a series of scraping sounds. Each time, the players in the ring say, "Midder, Midder, what's that sound?" The Midder responds with a series of excuses, then finally says, "It's the ghost of Janey Jo!" Janey Jo tries to touch a player before they can all sit.

Directions: Have the group form a standing circle. Say, "The Midder gets to answer three questions in this game. Who would like to be the Midder, and stand in the middle?" Have a volunteer stand in the center of the circle.

Stand outside the circle, and say,

> *I'll be Janey Jo. When you hear me make this sound (make a scraping noise, perhaps with your foot), you say to the Midder, "Midder, Midder, what's that sound?" Are you ready?*

Make the scraping sound. After the group says, "Midder, Midder, what's that sound?" say to the Midder,

> *Now you say something like, "It's just the dog scratching to get in." Just say it's some normal sound, but you make up what normal sound it is. Okay? Let's ask the question again.*

Make the sound again, have the group ask the question again, and have the Midder make an answer.

Make the sound again. If necessary, prompt the group to ask the question again, and the Midder to make a different answer.

Say,

> *This time, you'll say, "It's the ghost of Janey Jo!" As soon as the Midder says that, I'll try to tag everybody before you can all sit down. If you sit down where you are, you're safe. Ready?*

Make the sound. After the group asks the question and the Midder answers, lunge toward players in the ring—especially toward any who forget to sit down. If necessary, remind players to sit by saying something like, "Tamara is still standing! I'll get you!"

Choose another volunteer to be the Midder, and another volunteer to be Janey Jo. Repeat as desired.

Hints: As Janey Jo, you can stand still; this makes it less confusing for young children to take the role of Janey Jo after you. Or you can walk around the outside of the circle, hovering behind those who seem most eager to be lunged at; this increases the sense of anticipation. If any player seems genuinely frightened, of course, hover at the other side of the circle!

Very young children may need to practice sitting down in place, before you practice trying to tag them. Otherwise, their first impulse may be to run away from Janey Jo.

The storytelling portion of this game resides in the answers improvised by the Midder. To increase the value for teaching storytelling, encourage new responses by each Midder. If desired, lead a discussion about scary sounds or about ordinary things that might make scary sounds—and then return to the game.

"Midder" means "mother" in Scots dialect. You can leave the term untranslated to avoid the reluctance some boys might have to volunteer to play the Mother. Or, if you desire, you can explain what the term means and encourage boys to try it anyway. After all, anyone can pretend to be anything! Alternatively, you can make a new term for the Midder's role, such as Baby-sitter, Parent, or Teacher.

Variations: The Midder can become the next Janey Jo. This variation is especially effective if many volunteer to be Janey Jo but few want to be the Midder.

Change the number of questions allowed before the Midder must answer, "It's the ghost of Janey Jo!" Or allow the Midder to choose how many answers to improvise before giving the final answer.

If space allows, introduce the traditional ending, in which Janey Jo chases all the others (instead of trying to tag them before they can sit). The person caught first becomes the new Janey Jo.

Skills Reinforced

Communication: Practicing turn-taking. Saying chanted lines in unison.

Storytelling:
Leader: Improvising single sentences. Noticing character of various sounds.

Curricular: Reviewing household sound sources. Dealing playfully with death.

Movements

Movements communicate powerfully. Without using any other forms of oral communication, we could give the broad outlines of most stories through movements alone. Further, movements can often express fine shades of emotion.

In written communication, the qualities of movements are difficult to describe. We have only a few dozen verbs and adverbs to describe an infinite number of ways to pick up an object or to touch a person's face. The feelings and meanings that might be conveyed through movement have to be approximated through creative use of phrasing and analogy.

In oral communication, on the other hand, movements can be presented in all their direct power. It becomes much less important to use a more precise word than

"touch" if the movement can show exactly *how* "I touched her face."

To master oral communication, therefore, we need fluency in the endlessly expressive qualities of movements. These games help nurture that fluency.

Games in This Section

"Aunt Dinah" uses imitation to allow players to expand their repertoire of movement possibilities. This game lets players explore abstract movements in a nearly pure form. The game's slightly irreverent tone seems to increase the vitality of movements used in it.

Rather than encourage such abstract movements, on the other hand, "Walks of Life" attaches movements to their associations in society. The players must associate different movements and movement qualities with different occupations. The leader must find a movement that corresponds to a given occupation; the others must seek an occupation to fit the movement.

If "Aunt Dinah" expands the possibilities of pure movement, "Walks of Life" explores the world of applied movement.

Games in Other Sections

These games focus on the quality of movements:

"Do It Your Way" (p. 84)

"Monster Rumble" (p. 35)

"Rakan-san" (p. 23)

"The Back Speaks" (p. 25)

In the following games, listeners respond with movements to cue words in a story:

"Flying" (p. 106)

"Letter Echoes" (p. 39)

"Spaceship" (p. 114)

These games create stories about movements:

"Squabble Body" (p. 94)

"You're Shaking Me Up" (p. 31)

※ ※

AUNT DINAH

Grade levels: Preschool through grade 5.

Space needed: Enough for all players to make movements while standing in place.

Complexity: Low.

Game type: Imitating posture, with dialogue.

Quick summary: Leader repeats a fixed dialogue and assumes an improvised dramatic position; the group imitates. Then all dance in unison to a chorus.

Directions: Stand in front of the group (or circle) of standing players. Speak the following four lines yourself. As you say the word "this," strike a dramatic pose (e.g., raise one hand over your head):

Aunt Dinah died!

How did she die?

She died like this!

She died like this!

Begin again, saying:

Aunt Dinah died!

Say, "You say, 'How did she die?'" Pause while the group responds. Continue, striking a pose at the word "this":

She died like this!

Say, "You say, 'She died like this!' and do what I did." Pause while the group responds, imitating your pose as they speak.

Repeat the entire dialogue again, but strike a different pose (e.g., hold your arms up at your sides as though shrugging).

Repeat the entire dialogue another time or two, each time with a different pose; then go on to demonstrate the refrain. Say:

Aunt Dinah's still living!

Where is she living?

Without a break, put your hands on your hips and begin a "cross-step" sequence (first, stand with feet spread wide; second, jump slightly and come down with feet crossed, left foot in front; third, jump again and come down with feet spread wide; fourth, jump again and come down with feet crossed, right foot in front). Perform this whole sequence twice, while saying:

She's living in the country, gonna move to town;

Gonna dance that dance till the sun goes down.

Next, say, "Do it with me!" Speak the first line of the refrain:

Aunt Dinah's still living!

Then say, "You say, 'Where is she living?'" Pause while the group responds. Say, "Say it and do it with me," then perform the cross-step sequence while speaking the final two lines.

Hints: This traditional game gives players a chance to experiment with outlandish postures and gestures. Model a variety of poses, representing a wide variety of emotional states: jubilant, dejected, defiant, terrified.

Think of the refrain as punctuation after a series of challenging poses. Use it after every three or four poses, or as needed to add variety.

About Mentioning Death. "Aunt Dinah" refers to death in a playful way. If this is uncomfortable for you or your group members, please use a different rhyme. (See "Change the Rhyme," under "Variations.")

Consider, though, that until a few centuries ago children experienced death as a natural part of rural life. In the years following the Industrial Revolution, children were still spoken to about death, but usually within a religious context that emphasized the punishments or rewards of an afterlife. Still later, any mention of death was kept from children. More recently, it is considered permissible in some circles to mention death to children, provided that a somber tone is maintained.

All forms of taboo about death prevent children from coming to terms with the reality that people die. Kept from any symbolic treatments of death, children are left unprepared to face death when it enters their life.

Of course, if "Aunt Dinah" were the only mention of death to children, it would certainly be a strange choice. Along with a range of other songs and stories of varying tones, however, "Aunt Dinah" provides one end of the spectrum: a chance to take death lightly, even to laugh at it. In fact, this game takes death so lightly that many children don't associate it with death at all.

Variations: Have players take turns as leader. You might have one player model two or three poses, then lead the refrain. Have another player lead the next pair of poses and refrain.

Alternatively, go around the circle (or down the line), having each player lead one pose. After every third player's turn, lead the group in the refrain.

Change the rhyme. Here's an alternative rhyme, if you prefer. These four lines are used just as the first four lines given above, striking a pose at "nilly":

Leader: *Billy got silly.*

Group: *Billy got silly.*

Leader: *He did it willy-nilly.*

Group: *He did it willy-nilly.*

These two lines correspond to the lines "Aunt Dinah's living! Where is she living?"

Leader: *Never again!*

Group: *Not for a while!*

These final lines are chanted as all clap the beat:

All: *Till I say when,*

He won't even smile!

At the word "smile," all freeze until the leader starts again: If desired, substitute "Tilly" or "Milly" for "Billy."

Skills Reinforced

Communication: Practicing turn-taking. Imitating dramatic postures and gestures.

Storytelling: Trying out dramatic gestures and postures without having to describe them. Expressing physical impulses.

Curricular: Dealing playfully with the usually taboo subject of death.

※ ※

WALKS OF LIFE

Grade levels: Grades 3-7.

Space needed: An area that the whole group can see, and that's large enough for one to five players at a time to walk across.

Complexity: Medium.

Game type: Guessing a movement.

Quick summary: Players imitate the walk of a member of an occupation; the group tries to guess the occupation.

Directions: Speak this chant:

Here we come from Botany Bay,

Got any work to give us today?

What can you do?

What's the pay?

Show your stuff, and then we'll say.

Say, "You say part of what I just said. Your first line is 'What can you do?' Try saying that!" Pause while the group responds. Say, "Your second line is 'Show your stuff, and then we'll say.'" Pause while the group responds again.

Say, "Let's try the whole rhyme. I start. I'll point to you for your lines." Repeat the chant, cueing the group to join in on its two lines.

Say,

Now I'll pretend to be a kind of worker. I could be a movie star, a fire fighter, an office worker, or anything. You have to guess what I am, just from the way I walk across the room.

Walk across the room, imitating a distinctive walk (such as the bow-legged walk of a cowpoke). After you have walked across the room, say, "Who can guess what my occupation is? What kind of a worker am I? What's my job?"

Call on players to guess what you are. Validate each guess, pointing out, if possible, an element in your walk that is similar to what the player guessed. For example, you might say, "I *did* walk slowly, like an astronaut. But no, I was pretending to be something else."

If no one guesses correctly, walk a second time, adding more nonverbal clues such as adjusting your imaginary spurs or twirling your imaginary lariat. If no one guesses this time, then you chose an occupation unfamiliar to your group, or else this game is too hard for them and should be dropped.

If desired, remain the leader once more, walking as a member of another occupation (e.g., an underwater scuba diver). Let the group guess again.

Then say, "Is there a group of three or four people who want to try walking across and letting us guess?" Choose a group of volunteers, then give them a few moments to select an occupation. When they are ready, bring them in front of the group, and help them lead the rhyme.

After they have walked across the room, have them call on a series of players who wish to guess. If necessary, have the volunteers repeat their walks once. If no one guesses correctly the second time, have them tell the occupation.

Choose another group of volunteers and repeat as desired.

Hints: The storytelling value of this game depends on players becoming more sensitive to the expressive components of posture and movement. You may be able to heighten the educational value of this game by pointing out players' successes at imitation and at guessing. For example, you might say, "Great job, Darnell! You puffed out your chest and held out your arms—I could just see your bulging muscles!" Or you might say to a successful guesser, "How did you know she was a baseball player? Can you remember exactly what she did that tipped you off?" As with all such interventions, a cheerful, approving tone will help prevent turning the game into a lesson. At the first sign of resentment or boredom, return to playing the game without comment.

If players have a hard time thinking of occupations that are easy enough to act out, prepare slips of paper with the names of individual occupations. Then have each team draw one slip of paper.

Suitable occupations (and clues) include:

◆ astronaut (floating in space, bouncing on the moon)
◆ baseball player on way to bat
◆ beachcomber on beach (dodging waves, looking for shells)
◆ body builder
◆ clown
◆ cowpoke
◆ explorer at the North Pole
◆ fashion model on runway
◆ flight attendant on turbulent flight

- police officer on beat
- roofer on slanted roof
- sailor on rolling deck
- scuba diver
- soldier marching
- spy
- tight-rope walker
- window washer on narrow scaffolding

Variations: After each team's turn (whether the occupation was guessed successfully or not), you may want to allow all the players to try walking as a member of the chosen occupation.

Walking in teams is usually less intimidating, but some players may prefer to walk individually. Of course, your group may have already shed its fear of solo performance, and may be ready for the greater challenge of solo turns.

If desired, play with two teams, as in charades. Let each team choose a player or small group of players to receive the name of an occupation from the opposing team, then act it out for their own team to guess.

Alternatively, play as a chasing game, like the traditional "Lemonade." Each team has a goal line or "safety wall." The Walking team approaches the goal line of the Guessing team. All the members of the Walking team walk back and forth. When a member of the Guessing team shouts out the correct occupation, the Walkers shout "That's right," and the Guessing team chases the Walking team back to its goal line. If desired, have any players who were caught in the chase switch teams. The team that walked now guesses, and vice versa.

Change the subject from occupations to animals, sports, or the eating of various foods. You can adapt the second and third lines of the rhyme to say, for example, "Want any food from us today? What do you have?"

Skills Reinforced

Communication:
> *Group:* Decoding movements.
> *Leader:* Moving in a way that communicates a concept.

Storytelling:
> *Leader:* Choosing movements that characterize an occupation.

Thinking:
> *Group:* Translating from movements to concept.
> *Leader:* Translating from concept to movements.

Curricular: Reviewing occupations.

Eye Contact

"Eye contact," as used here, refers to the ways that people direct their eyes while interacting. The term includes avoiding gaze-to-gaze contact as well as making it. Defined this way, eye contact is part of every interaction between two people.

Like all elements of communication, eye contact is used in all cultures—and has different meanings, depending on the culture in which it is used. Within a culture, the meaning of eye contact is dependent on who is speaking, who is listening, and their attitudes toward each other.

In the dominant Anglo-American-derived culture in the United States, seeking eye contact is tantamount to asking permission to speak, and returning eye contact is a way to grant permission. Thus, it's a sign of respect for both speaker and listener to make eye contact. Therefore, a public speaker is expected to make brief, regular eye contact with listeners.

In other cultures, however, the meaning of eye contact differs. In some cultures, the speaker is expected to look directly at the listener's eyes, but it is a sign of respect for the listener to avert her eyes. In some cultures, the roles are reversed. In still other cultures, it is considered invasive for either speaker or listener to make eye contact.

Problems arise, of course, in intercultural situations. Without knowing why, the listener might take the speaker to be "shifty eyed," while the same speaker takes the listener to be "aggressive."

For effective communication, the speaker must sense the listeners' expectations and be able to provide the expected eye-contact behavior.

Games in This Section

In the game "From Me to You," making eye contact is used as a way of selecting the next leader. This gives players an opportunity to notice the power of eye contact and—whatever its cultural meaning for the player—to notice how it feels to seek, allow, or avoid eye contact.

FROM ME TO YOU

Grade levels: Kindergarten and up.

Space needed: Enough to form a circle of all players or a line of all players, with the Leader in front.

Complexity: Low.

Game type: Choosing the next player.

Quick summary: The Leader stands in front of a line or group of standing players and recites a short chant. By the end of the chant, the Leader must make eye contact with another player—who changes places with the Leader and becomes the next Leader.

Directions: As Leader, stand in front of the group members, who should be standing (in a line, if the group is small enough). Speak this chant rhythmically:

From me to you,

From me to you,

The story goes

From me to you.

As you speak the chant, stand as though you are about to tell a story or make an announcement to the group. Scan the group with your eyes, then lock eyes with one player (for example, Terry). As soon as the chant is finished, say,

My job is to make eye contact with another player by the end of the chant I just said.

I'm making eye contact with Terry, so we change places now.

Walk toward Terry, motioning her to take your place. When you are standing as part of the group and Terry is facing everyone, say,

Now we'll say the chant again. Terry, it's your job to make eye contact with someone who hasn't had a turn to stand in front of everyone.

Repeat the chant. At the end, say,

Terry, make sure you're looking someone in the eye. Now you and that person change places.

Once players understand the game, you won't have to speak at all, except for joining the chant.

Repeat as desired, or until every player has had a turn to be Leader.

Hints: Players who don't look the Leader in the eyes. Most players will cooperate with the Leader by looking up. If a few individuals prefer not to make eye contact with any Leader, it's usually best to allow them their preference. Allowing players not to play creates added safety for everyone.

If you think that some players might not understand the nonverbal cue in this game, you can ask them, saying, for example, "Jorges, did you want a turn?" If Jorges says yes, then you can help him know how to get a turn:

In this game, you have to look the Leader in the eyes to get a turn. Do you want to try it?

Cultural differences. Each culture makes its own rules about eye contact. In most European cultures, speakers are expected to look in the eyes of a listener, who is expected to reciprocate. In many other cultures, however, such as some West African and Native American cultures, one or both participants in a conversation are expected to avert their eyes.

The rules allowing eye contact may vary depending on the social status of the participants, too. An adult may be permitted to look a child in the eye, while a child may be expected to avert eyes from an adult.

If you notice players having different reactions to this game, you can ask,

How does it feel to look each other in the eyes like that? Is it different to look me in the eyes? Let's hear from different people how it felt.

If some players feel uncomfortable—whether for personal or cultural reasons—you can explain that different situations call for different kinds of eye contact. As discussed earlier, in most public speaking in Western countries, the speaker is expected to make eye contact with the listeners. Failure to make eye contact is interpreted by most audiences as shyness or even "shiftiness."

Variations: If your group is large, you may prefer to play this game in small groups of eight to twelve players. One subgroup at a time can come in front of the others to play. Or several subgroups can play simultaneously.

Form a circle with the Leader in the middle. Or keep the Leader within the circle; when a player has locked eyes with the Leader, the two will change places in the circle. Alternatively, let players stay in their place within the circle; each new Leader will not change places with the old Leader, but will immediately repeat the chant.

Vary the chant. Substitute a quote from curriculum, such as a poem, a quote from history or literature, or a principle that you'd like your group to memorize. Or use a sentence in another language, or in gibberish.

Skills Reinforced

Communication:

Group: Consciously allowing eye contact.

Leader: Consciously initiating eye contact.

Storytelling:

Group: Acknowledging the leader through eye contact.

Leader: Making eye contact with group members, with feedback.

Curricular: Discussing culturally based experiences of initiating and allowing eye contact.

Sound Imagery

Modern culture tends to keep sound subservient to sight. This keeps the power of sound unconscious for most of us; we watch the film screen while the soundtrack, unnoticed, manipulates our emotions.

As a sensory mode, sound has characteristics that distinguish it from sight and kinesthetic experience. Like sight, sound is instantaneous. Unlike sight, however, sound is omnidirectional. In other words, we don't have to face a sound source to hear it. In fact, it is a learned skill to focus on a particular sound against a background of other sounds.

Games in This Section

Both games in this section use closed (or blindfolded) eyes to force players to rely on sound rather than sight.

"Knocking" helps players distinguish the quality of a sound and its direction, then associate the sound with its visible source.

"Guess the Voice" helps players focus on the quality of their voices. Players also experience ways to disguise their voices and the difficulty of disguising a voice—in spite of changing it in various ways. "Guess the Voice" prepares the way for more advanced vocal work and the development of character voices.

Games in Other Sections

"Janey Jo" (p. 6) features the making of sounds and improvising verbal explanations for them. This focuses attention on everyday sources of sound.

"You're Shaking Me Up" (p. 31) includes sounds in a story. The story highlights humorously how difficult it is to screen out sounds, and gives players a chance to imitate sounds that accompany various activities.

KNOCKING

Grade levels: Kindergarten through grade 3.

Props needed: Any common objects hard enough to make a sound when knocked on.

Complexity: Low.

Game type: Guessing a sound.

Quick summary: One player knocks on an object in the room, while the others listen with closed eyes. The others guess the object.

Directions: Speak the following lines (or chant them like a taunt, or sing them loosely to the tune of "Twinkle, Twinkle, Little Star," or sing them to the tune given on p. 148). In place of the words, "knock, knock," knock on a table or any handy object:

I woke up in the middle of the night.

I heard a sound and it gave me a fright.

I said, "Who's there?" (knock, knock)

I said, "Who's there?" (knock, knock)

A knock was all I heard.

A knock was all I heard.

Say, "Did you hear the knocking sound? It was me knocking on the table, right? In the middle of the night, it seemed to me I was hearing the voice of the table! This time, I'll let you hear the voice of something else—and you'll try to guess what I'm knocking on. Ready? Close your eyes!"

Repeat the lines above, this time knocking on another object, such as the wall or a chair. (The ideal object would be one that makes a sound that's easy to distinguish from your first sound.)

Say, "Open your eyes. Raise your hand if you think you know what I knocked on." Call on a volunteer. Validate each answer. If several volunteers guess incorrectly, repeat the chanted lines and the knocking. If they still guess incorrectly, try another object.

Repeat as desired.

If you wish, say, "Is there someone who would like to do the knocking? You can choose any object in this room to knock on. I'll help you with the chant." Call on a volunteer to choose an object and knock on it at the appropriate time in the chanted lines.

Hints: If your group has trouble guessing the object you knocked on, remain standing near the object when the players open their eyes. Conversely, make it more challenging to guess by returning to your starting location before asking players to open their eyes.

Variations: Instead of knocking on an object, make a different kind of sound with it by scraping it or shaking it. Change the last two lines of the chanted words to:

A sound was all I heard.

A sound was all I heard.

The chanted lines can provide two things: something to say while the leader walks over to an object and back, and an element of fantasy. If the chant seems to get in the way for your group, however, omit it. Omitting the chant can also allow the leader to knock on the object more times, or in a longer rhythmic pattern, or as though the object is "angry," "happy," or "asking for help."

Skills Reinforced

Communication: Saying chanted lines in unison. Associating sounds with objects.

Storytelling: Noticing the character of various sounds.

Leader: Knocking on objects in rhythm with the chanted lines.

Curricular: Exploring the sound production of available objects. Experiencing the environment without sight.

※ ※

GUESS THE VOICE

Grade levels: Kindergarten through grade 4.

Props needed: Yardstick, cane, umbrella, or other long stick. Blindfold *(optional).*

Complexity: Medium.

Game type: Guessing a sound. Combining elements.

Quick summary: Players (who know each other) circle the blindfolded Guesser, who holds a stick. When the Guesser taps on the floor, the circle stops. The Guesser holds the stick out; an unknown player in the circle grabs the other end of the stick. The Guesser says, "Tell me how a ____ helped a ____" (naming two unrelated objects). The player in the circle must improvise a brief fantasy story about how the first object helped the second one. After the story, the Guesser must guess which player told the story.

Directions: Form your group into a circle. Say, "Who would like to be the Guesser in this game? You will be the one to wear the blindfold and point the stick." Choose a volunteer to be the Guesser.

Put the blindfold on the Guesser (or instruct the Guesser to keep eyes closed), and give the Guesser the stick to hold. Direct the Guesser to the center of the circle. Join the circle, then say,

> *We'll walk around the circle for a while. When you want us to stop walking,*
> *Guesser, tap the stick on the floor. Ready? Let's move our circle!*

Walk around the circle with the group. When the Guesser taps, stop walking. Say,

> *Guesser, your job is to point the stick at another player in the circle—but you*
> *won't know who you're pointing at. The person you point at will grab the*
> *other end of your stick, so you'll know someone is there. Go ahead, point!*

If necessary, gesture to the player who's being pointed at to hold the other end of the Guesser's stick. Say,

> *Guesser, your job now is to get the person on the other end of that stick to tell*
> *you a story, so you can hear that person's voice.*

Here's how you'll get that person telling a story. Think of two objects that have nothing to do with each other. What are two objects you can think of?

If the Guesser answers, "A spoon and a paper cup," say,

Great! So the question you ask is, "How did the spoon help the paper cup?" Go ahead, ask that question.

After the Guesser asks the question, speak to the player holding the other end of the stick.

*"Now **you** are the Storyteller. Tell a little story about how a spoon helped a paper cup. Go ahead, just make up anything!"*

Perhaps the Storyteller will say,

There was once a dry, empty paper cup. The cup said, "I'm so thirsty!"

The spoon dipped itself in the dishwater, flew over to the paper cup, and dumped a spoonful of water in the cup.

After the Storyteller finishes the story, say,

"Okay, Guesser! You heard the Storyteller speak. Can you guess whose voice that was?"

After the Guesser names a player, say,

"Okay, take off the blindfold and see who it was!"

Have the Storyteller become the next Guesser.

Repeat as desired, or until each player who wants a turn has had one.

Hints: This game requires players who already know each other.

If the story told is very short, or if the Guesser seems puzzled, you might allow the Guesser to ask "And then what happened?" This gives the Guesser a chance to hear the Storyteller speak longer. You can limit the Guesser to one or two such requests.

If the Guesser points the stick at a player who has already had a turn to be Guesser, you can guide the stick with your hand to another player, or else gesture to another player to grab it.

The blindfold can create great interest and drama, but it can slow the game as players put it on and off. If the blindfold would make the game less fun, have the Guesser simply close his eyes.

If the group is small or players know each other well, you might suggest that the Storyteller try to disguise her voice.

Variations: Instead of always asking the Storyteller to ask how one object helped another, the Guesser can improvise a different question or demand a sound, such as:

How did you get to school this morning?

What was the most embarrassing thing that ever happened to you in school?

What was the third object Jack brought down the bean stalk?

Who was the writer of the Declaration of Independence?

Make a sound like a rooster.

If the questions call for short answers, allow the Guesser to ask two or three.

If desired, you can require the Guesser's question to relate to a subject of your curriculum. For example, require that the question be about the Industrial Revolution or other historical subject, about a particular work of literature, or about agriculture or another topic from social studies.

Skills Reinforced

Communication: Practicing turn-taking.

Leader: Associating the sound of a voice with its owner.

Storytelling:

Group: Improvising a fantasy story using two objects and the verb "help."

Leader: Improvising the names of two unrelated objects. Improvising questions to extend the story.

Thinking:

Leader: Choosing sets of objects that will require longer stories.

Curricular:

Leader: Reviewing the names of group members. Experiencing exploration of the environment without sight.

Visual Imagery

The visual mode has great power. Through it, we can quickly receive enormous amounts of information. In addition, we can easily direct our focus to a specific region or detail within our visual field.

Unlike kinesthetic data, however, visual data give very little direct evidence of the experience of another person. Visual images show us the surface in great detail but cannot penetrate. This combination of answers and questions can make visual images very evocative.

Games in This Section

The games in this section focus on the evocative power of certain visual images. For all the rich, detailed information that visual images convey, they leave unanswered most of our questions about why, how something feels, and what might happen next. These games use visual imagery as starting points for creating answers to such questions.

"Cross-Picture Puzzles" uses specially chosen photographs to evoke stories. To help players make mental connections quickly, the game requires players to create a story that combines two or more photos. To help players develop alternative explanations for what they see, the game requires players to use the same photos in multiple stories. This also serves to develop the ability to create multiple hypotheses to explain visual data.

"They Tossed It High" works more abstractly. It uses the words (and melody, if used) of a song to create a visual image in players' minds. The game encourages players to imagine what comes next. To do so, players must allow the visual image to become dynamic. Finally, the game asks players to describe orally their mental image, sharing it with the others. This requires the listening players to make their own images even more dynamic; they must continue to change their original image to reflect the imaginings of other players.

Games in Other Sections

These games give players the opportunity to add visual imagery to a sound:

"Guess the Voice" (p. 17)

"Janey Jo" (p. 6)

"Knocking" (p. 16)

"Old Doc Jones" (p. 121) requires players to imagine changes in an object that they can see at the moment.

※ ※

CROSS-PICTURE PUZZLES

Grade levels: Grade 1 and up.

Props needed:
1. At least 16 evocative photos from magazines, calendars, or curriculum kits. (These work best when glued individually onto 8.5" x 11" pieces of oak tag or cardboard.)
2. A place to display at least a four-by-four grid of the photos: a bulletin board, a blackboard, or an open space on the floor. (It's not necessary to mark the lines of the empty grid, although it's fine to do so.)
3. A way to hold the photos in place during the game: thumbtacks for a bulletin board, or masking tape (or "E-Z-Up Clips") for a blackboard.

Complexity: High.

Game type: Combining elements.

Quick summary: A player draws random photos, then places them on the grid, in the manner of a crossword puzzle or crossword game. The player must then tell a story that includes images from all the photos in the row (or column) of the grid.

Directions: Prepare the pile of photos and the place to display them. Say, "I'll start this game with two photos from the pile." Draw two photos at random, then show them to the class. Say, "My job is to put these on the board, then make a story that uses them both."

Place them in the order you prefer on the board (or floor). Say, "I put this one first, so I'll start my story with it." Tell a story that involves both images, in the order (left-to-right or top-to-bottom) in which they appear.

For example, if you drew a photo of a submarine from the pile followed by a photo of a child riding a bicycle, you might say,

> *One day, deep beneath the waters of the Atlantic, a submarine was sailing on a top-secret spy mission. Suddenly, it struck a rock. The hull was breached! Water began streaming in! The submarine was forced to surface. It grounded itself safely on a beach. But the radio had been damaged by the water; they had no way to call for help.*

> *One sailor said, "I'll go looking for help." The sailor found a girl on a bicycle, and said to her, "Can you do a favor for your country—and keep it a secret? Dial this phone number and tell them this secret code!" The girl rode off, dialed the number, spoke the code, and went home. One week later, she got a letter in the mail from the Secretary of the Navy, thanking her for her help.*

Say, "Who would like to choose the next photo and make the next story?" Select a volunteer. Have the volunteer choose one photo at random and show it to the class. Say,

You can add the photo to the first two, anywhere you want. You can put it before them, after them, above one of them, or below one of them. But you have to make a new story using this photo and the others you put in line with it.

Have the volunteer place the photo on the board and tell a story using the new photo and the one or two it falls in line with. (For example, if the first two photos are in a horizontal line and the new photo is placed to the left of the other two, the volunteer must make a story using all three photos, starting with the new one.)

Repeat with another volunteer.

If a subsequent photo is placed where it touches other photos both horizontally and vertically, the player must make up separate stories for each horizontal and vertical line that uses the newly placed photo.

Continue as desired, or until 16 photos have been placed in a four-photo by four-photo grid.

Hint: I usually require the images to be used differently in each new story. For example, if the volunteer's story uses the submarine photo, the new story should not involve the submarine striking a rock and needing help. Instead, it might be the vehicle for escape, or a way to find the diamond ring that fell into the ocean.

Variations: Use a bigger grid. Allow rows and columns of five (or more) photos each. Or let the grid be unlimited. (In this case, the game will end when all photos are placed.)

Instead of professional photos, use the players' photos or their drawings. Alternatively, use drawings of symbols, Tarot cards, or one of the commercially available decks of symbol cards (for an example, see Star+Gate, in the Bibliography).

Use photos or drawings that relate to a subject of the curriculum. For geography or multiculturalism, use photos or drawings from one or more countries or regions. For history, use old photos or period drawings. For literature, use illustrations from a written story. For science, use pictures or drawings from a physical or biological environment.

Use cards with single words (or sentences) written out instead of photos.

Have each player place two, three, or a variable number of photos (the best numbers are one, two, or three). For a variable number, roll dice (dice with one, two, or three pips are available) or use a spinner. Alternatively, write the numbers 1, 2, and 3 on the board. Spell the player's name, pointing to a different number as you say each letter. The player chooses the number of photos indicated by the last number pointed to.

Skills Reinforced

Communication:
> *Leader:* Causing others to see a picture as you do. Maintaining the sequence of images in a story.

Storytelling: Connecting two or more visual images in a story.

Thinking: Retaining multiple meanings for the same visual image. Imagining the past or future of a scene.

Curricular: Operating on a two-dimensional grid.

THEY TOSSED IT HIGH

Grade levels: Grade 3 and up.

Complexity: Low.

Game type: Alternating solo stories with group chant.

Quick summary: Players listen to an evocative stanza, then tell what they imagine will happen next.

Directions: Say, "Imagine the scene in my verse."

Speak the lines listed below. (Or you may chant them like a poem, or sing them to the tune given on p. 152. You can also sing them loosely to the first four lines of the tune for "God Rest Ye, Merry Gentlemen"; the tune will seem unfinished, which may be a helpful effect for this game.)

They tossed it high, so very high,

They tossed it high and low;

They tossed it into a dusty garden,

Where none was allowed to go.

Say, "Imagine the scene again. In your mind, what were they throwing? Who were they? Where were they? What did the dusty garden look like?" Speak or sing the lines again.

Say, "Can you imagine what comes next? Who will share with us what you imagine?" Call on a volunteer player.

After each player describes as much or as little as he desires, repeat the spoken or sung lines. Each new player describes a different story or story fragment inspired by the lines of verse. Repeat as desired.

Variations: Add movements while chanting. For example, the group might join hands and circle left during the first two lines, then circle back to the right for the last two.

Use the first verse or two of a different song (or rhyme) to start your players' imaginations. Some commonly known possibilities include "Streets of Laredo," "Hickory, dickory, dock," "Oh, Susannah," and "Old Mother Hubbard."

Use an evocative stanza from a poem (or the first paragraph from a picture book, short story, or novel) appropriate to the players' interest and comprehension.

If players desire (and they often will!), allow them to continue a scene that one player has imagined. In this case, you will hear episodes in a single story rather than a series of beginnings to different stories.

Skills Reinforced

Communication:

Leader: Causing others to see a scene as you do.

Storytelling:

Group: Retaining multiple meanings of a scene.

Leader: Imagining the continuation of a scene, and describing it.

Thinking: Retaining multiple meanings for the same scene. Imagining and explaining the past or future of a scene.

Kinesthetic Imagery

The kinesthetic sense is based on our muscular sensations of stretching and contracting, tension and relaxation, and effort and release. Little recognized in modern culture, the kinesthetic sense is not even rated among "the five senses." Yet it is vitally important in oral communication.

Unlike visual and sound data, kinesthetic data are based primarily on the status of our own bodies, not of the outside world. We feel the strain of lifting something, the tense alert of being in danger, or the sag of disappointment.

Secondarily, however, we can take in kinesthetic data about other people's bodies. By watching posture and movement quality, by listening for signs of tension and ease in voice quality, we can form an internal image of someone else's kinesthetic state. This image usually takes time to form, rendering kinesthetic data slow to register. Yet the information so gathered is unavailable in any other sensory mode.

Unconsciously, we respond continuously to the kinesthetic state of people around us. The posture of our listeners can tell us a great deal about how well we are communicating. If our listeners are "on the edge of their seats," for example, we know they are not "holding back," that we are not "having trouble reaching them." As listeners, on the other hand, we open ourselves to a speaker who is "approachable," but neither "pushy" nor "a pushover."

Games in This Section

"Rakan-san" allows the simple imitation of posture, as does "Aunt Dinah" (p. 8). In its more advanced variations, however, it requires players to remember one posture while assuming another. This encourages players to "remember postures in advance," to create and access data in kinesthetic form.

In "The Back Speaks," one player tries to communicate a feeling through posture and movement alone. The others, deprived of cues such as words, vocal inflection, and facial expression, try to apply labels to the kinesthetic qualities they observe. In this way, players practice correlating verbal and kinesthetic information.

Games in Other Sections

The section on Movements (p. 7), of course, contains games based on kinesthetic experience.

"Monster Rumble" (p. 35) applies kinesthetic imagery (along with tone of voice and other communicative elements) to the characterization of a monster.

In "Do It Your Way" (p. 84), players apply labels such as "sleepy" or "scared" to movements that a leader performs.

※ ※

RAKAN-SAN

Grade levels: Preschool through grade 5.

Space needed: Enough for all players to make movements while standing in place. (In one variation, enough for a circle of players.)

Complexity: Low.

Game type: Imitating posture, with rhyme.

Quick summary: At the end of the rhyme, each player assumes the leader's pose. In one variation, the leader assumes a new pose while the players assume the leader's former pose. In the most advanced variation, each player assumes the pose formerly held by the player's right-hand neighbor.

Directions: Assemble players into a circle. Chant this rhyme:

Rakan-san, rakan-san

Come to life and pass it on.

Say,

> *In Japanese, "Rakan-san" means "the images," or "the statues." In Japan, they have many statues. Some of the statues are scary looking; others are happy; some look like they are dancing, or fishing, or maybe waiting for something. When I say the word "on," I'll change into a statue. Watch me!*

Chant the rhyme again, freezing into a statue at the word "on." (For example, you might bend your knees, raise your arms over your head, and make a terrible face.) Say,

> *Do you see what kind of statue I am? Notice how my legs are. Notice my arms. Notice my face. This time, when you hear the word "on," turn into a statue just like me. Ready?*

Chant the rhyme again, remaining in your pose as the players all attempt to imitate you. Repeat as desired, striking a different pose each time.

If desired, have a player become the new leader. Pass the leader's role around the circle.

Variations: One statue later. In this variation, you will change to a second pose while the players take on your first pose.

First, play the game as described above. Then, while holding a pose, say,

> *This time, you'll change to be like I am now—but I'll change to a new kind of statue. Don't let me fool you! Here we go!*

Repeat the rhyme. At the word "on," while each player assumes the pose you were just in, assume a contrasting pose. Remain in your new pose. Say, "Good job! This time, you'll turn into the statue I am now, and I'll turn into still another one! Let's do it!"

If some players change to imitate your current pose (e.g., hands over head) instead of your previous one (e.g., hands on knees), you can coach, "Hands on knees now! Stay with your hands on your knees, but watch what I'm doing now—you'll do that next!"

Continue as desired. If you wish, let a player take the leader's role.

Around the circle. In this more challenging variation, each player becomes a different statue, and all the different statues are passed around the circle. Say,

> *When you hear the word "on," pretend you are a statue. You can be frightening or sleepy or brave, but hold still until I tell you to move. When you hear the word "on," you have to freeze. Ready?*

Chant the rhyme, freezing into a statue at the word "on." Say,

Hold your statue, but try to look at the person on your right. Do you see what kind of a statue that person is? This time, you will change into the statue that you now see in the person on your right. Here we go!

Repeat the rhyme as each player assumes the position previously held by the "statue" on each player's right. If desired, give the players a moment to notice the new statue on their right; then repeat the rhyme again.

Continue as desired, or (with a small group) until the poses have traveled completely around the circle.

Skills Reinforced

Communication: Initiating and imitating postures and gestures. Practicing turn-taking. Saying chanted lines in unison.

Storytelling: Trying out gestures and postures without having to describe them. Acting on expressive physical impulses.

Thinking: Perceiving and replicating the multiple parts of a "statue." Holding one posture in memory while viewing another.

Curricular: Dealing playfully with emotions.

※ ※

THE BACK SPEAKS

Grade levels: Grade 2 and up.

Props needed: A chair.

Complexity: Medium.

Game type: Guessing a quality of movement.

Quick summary: A player, seated, facing away from the group, acts out an activity. The group guesses how the player feels about the activity from the posture of the player's back.

Directions: Arrange a chair in front of the group, with its back toward the group. Say, "I'm going to pretend to do something here—and all you'll be able to see is my back. You have to guess what I'm doing and how I feel about it. Ready?"

Sit in the chair, facing away from the group. Pretend to play the piano in a bored manner. As you are pretending to play, imagine to yourself that someone is forcing you to practice for two hours.

After a few moments, turn toward the group. Say, "Raise your hand if you can guess what I was doing." Call on a volunteer guesser. If the first guesser is incorrect, validate the guess, then call on another—until someone guesses correctly.

Then say, "Playing the piano! Yes! How did I feel about playing the piano?" Again, call on volunteers.

If no one guesses correctly, you chose too difficult an example—or this game is too difficult for your group and should be dropped. If someone guesses correctly, say,

Does someone want to try it? Think of how you might feel about playing the piano. Maybe it's your big chance to try out for a rock band, and you're scared. Maybe your neighbors kept you up half the night and now you're trying to repay them. Maybe you were just named best pianist of the year, and now you're playing to show the cheering crowd how pleased you are.

Have a volunteer sit in the chair and pretend to play. Have the volunteer call on group members who wish to guess.

Repeat with additional volunteers, as desired.

Hints: The storytelling value of this game comes from heightened sensitivity to the expressive powers of the back—and of posture and movement in general. Therefore, it makes sense to put less emphasis on what the player was doing, and more emphasis on how the player felt.

To help players learn from their experiences in this game, give brief appreciations of players who portray feelings well or notice feelings well. Alternatively, ask questions about successful play, such as: "How did you know what he was feeling?" or "What were you thinking when you were pretending to mend your shirt?"

Variations: Let each player choose a different action, as well as how the player feels about it.

To limit the possible activities (or to help players choose activities familiar enough to guess), write on slips of paper the names of various activities that can be performed sitting down. Let a volunteer draw a slip, then decide how he feels about the activity written on it, then act out the activity. Appropriate activities might include:

- changing TV channels
- dialing the phone
- doing homework
- eating
- opening a package
- picking up crumbs
- playing a video game
- playing the guitar
- playing the piano
- reading a book
- sewing
- typing
- writing a letter

Alternatively, write names of activities on white slips of paper, and ways of feeling on yellow slips. Have a volunteer choose one of each color, then act out the combination. Attitudes or feelings about the activities might include:

- afraid of being caught
- depressed
- delighted
- discouraged
- exhausted
- hopeful
- humiliated
- in ecstasy
- in pain
- proud
- shocked
- surprised

Choose an action appropriate to a historical event, work of literature, or social studies subject.

Skills Reinforced

Communication:

Group: Decoding movements.

Leader: Moving in a way that communicates a feeling or attitude. Using the back expressively.

Storytelling:

Leader: Choosing and executing movements that characterize a feeling or attitude.

Thinking:

Group: Translating from movements to feeling.

Leader: Translating from feeling to movements.

Curricular: Reviewing movements associated with an activity. Reviewing the names of feelings.

Improvising Plot

Most four- and five-year olds are happy to begin a fantasy story and keep talking unselfconsciously for at least several minutes. Few older children and adults, on the other hand, are as willing to improvise, perhaps for fear of judgment. Although many people decry our "loss of creativity" as we mature, the change might actually result from a "gain in self-censorship."

A game can help circumvent the internal censor by being playful, by taking attention off the result, and by providing a structure that reduces specific difficulties.

Games in This Section

One problem that any speaker has to face is, "What if I freeze up and can't think of what to say next?" Fear of freezing up can lead to freezing up, of course, and begin a vicious circle of anxiety and failure.

"Old Bloody Bones" solves this problem by providing the storyteller a phrase to say at any point to end the story.

"Fortunately, Unfortunately," on the other hand, gives a structure for each contribution to a story. When it is clear to players how easily a short contribution can meet the simple requirements of the game, the anxiety is likely to be reduced. Then the spontaneity can begin, the players can begin to build on each other's contributions, the story can start to take on a life of its own, and the group itself can become the creator, relieving individual players of any sense of risk.

Games in Other Sections

The majority of games in chapters 2, 3, and 4 give players an opportunity to improvise plot.

"Old Doc Jones" (p. 121) asks for a silly lie, a relatively unthreatening requirement.

These games encourage small contributions to a group plot:

"Because" (p. 116)

"I Was Present!" (p. 119)

"You're Shaking Me Up" (p. 31)

The following guessing games make it easy to focus on the process of concealing and guessing; therefore they make it easy to become unselfconscious about creating plot:

"Guess the Voice" (p. 17)

"Hide the Words" (p. 43)

"Mish Mash Mush" (p. 63)

"Story Crambo" (p. 47)

"Towns and Counties" (p. 73)

In these games, a single player creates a plot, but the group participates by responding to cues within it; as a result, the plot seems secondary:

"Flying" (p. 106)

"Grouping Stories" (p. 104)

"Spaceship" (p. 114)

"The Sea Is Getting Stormy" (p. 112)

※ ※

OLD BLOODY BONES

Grade levels: Kindergarten through grade 5.

Space needed: Enough to form a circle. (A variation has no space requirement.)

Complexity: Medium.

Game type: Alternating solo stories with group chant.

Quick summary: One player tells a brief story, ending with the words "Old Bloody Bones." At these words, all speak the chant and perform the accompanying movements.

Directions: Think of a story you will tell, ending with the words "Old Bloody Bones." Have a second story ready, in case there are no volunteers the first time. Prepare enough space. Get the group into a single circle. (See "Variations" for a version that requires less space.)

Speak the lines of the following stanza, or chant them like a poem, or sing them loosely to the tune of "Michael Finnegan" (also known as "One Little Indian") or "Skip to My Lou," or sing them to the tune given on p. 150. As you say the first three lines of the stanza, walk the circle around to the left. During the final line, move your hands down in front of you as though pantomiming rain:

Old bloody bones, a-coming, a-coming,

Old bloody bones, a-coming, a-coming,

Old bloody bones, a-coming, a-coming,

Old bloody bones, a-coming on down.

Repeat, walking around to the right during the first three lines and pantomiming rain on the final line.

Say to the group,

Do you know what to do when you hear the words "Old bloody bones"? You do what we just did! Let's have a practice. Old bloody bones!

Repeat the entire stanza and activity, repeating the words twice while circling first left, then right. If desired, practice the activity again. (You might say a sentence or two this time before saying "Old Bloody Bones.")

Once the stanza is done, launch right into a simple story, such as,

One day I was lost in a new neighborhood. I heard someone whisper my name. I turned to look, but didn't see anyone. So I kept on walking.

A few minutes later, I heard my name again, but this time it sounded angry. I turned around and saw a white paper bag on the sidewalk behind me. It was coming toward me! I started to run away, but the white paper bag kept right behind me.

Finally, I was exhausted. I had to stop. I said, "Who's in that white paper bag?" The voice said, "Open it up!" I was too scared and too tired not to do what it said. And do you know what I saw inside? Old bloody bones!

Immediately after saying the last words of the story, begin the stanza and activity again. After the stanza, say,

Is there anyone who could tell a little story, the way I did? When you're done, all you have to do is say, "Old Bloody Bones."

If no one volunteers, tell another story.

If players volunteer, call on one to tell a story; end with the spoken or sung lines. Continue through as many volunteers' stories as desired. To end the activity, speak or sing these words in place of the final line of the stanza: "Everybody sit back down!"

Variations: Change the activity that goes with the stanza. For older children, for example, snap fingers as you walk. Or do a clapping pattern while seated.

Change the kind of sample story you tell. This will strongly influence the kind of stories that players tell back to you. If desired, also change the words of the stanza to match. For example, tell stories about things that have happened during the longest nights of the year, then say, "Winter solstice a-coming, a-coming, winter solstice a-coming soon."

Skills Reinforced

Communication:

Group: Listening for a cue. Moving the circle together in the same direction at the same time.

Leader: Pronouncing the cue phrase clearly to entire group.

Storytelling:

Leader: Improvising a story with a specific ending phrase in mind. Embroidering the story. Building mood and suspense.

Thinking:

Leader: Thinking backward from the cue phrase, to an image and to a situation; reversing this order when telling the story.

FORTUNATELY,
UNFORTUNATELY

Grade levels: Kindergarten and up.

Complexity: Medium.

Game type: Round-robin.

Quick summary: Players take turns adding to a group story. The alternate additions must begin "unfortunately . . . " and "fortunately . . . ." The story ends with three consecutive additions beginning with "fortunately . . . ."

Directions: Begin a story, such as this one:

> *One day, we decided to go to the zoo. So we got up, got dressed, ate breakfast, and left the house. We went to the bus stop to wait. But unfortunately . . . [pause].*

> *What do you think happened that was unfortunate or unlucky?*

Call on a volunteer group member to add an "unfortunately," such as,

> *Unfortunately, it started to rain really hard.*

Interrupt, saying,

> *But fortunately . . . [pause].*

> *Who can add something fortunate or lucky?*

> Call on a volunteer group member to add a "fortunately," such as,

> *Fortunately, a big black limo pulled up to the bus stop. The driver rolled down the electric window and said, "Need a ride to the zoo?"*

Continue calling for alternating "unfortunately's" and "fortunately's" until ready to end the story. End the story by calling for three "fortunately's" in a row.

Variations: Insist that each player get one and only one turn (this can help draw out the shyest members of your group).

Insist that each player get two turns (or three, or another number) before the story ends.

Vary the opening as desired. Adapt it to the age and interest level of your group. If you wish, use the beginning of a work of literature. For an entire book of story beginnings, see *Storytelling: A Game* by Carolyn Mauk. (See Bibliography, p. 144.)

Skills Reinforced

Communication: Practicing turn-taking.

> *Leader:* Pronouncing a contribution clearly to the entire group.

Storytelling: Adding to a given story. Improvising an addition that creates positive action or negative action.

Thinking: Distinguishing positive from negative action. Maintaining the alternation between them.

Remembering Sequences

In any oral communication, the speaker will do well to present ideas or events in a logical order. Aware of this, many older children and adults are fearful of "forgetting the order" of a speech or story.

For centuries, speakers have shared tips about remembering. The two most powerful principles behind these tips are:

1. Understand the relationship among the events or ideas; or
2. Create an image of some kind that helps you remember the order.

The first of these principles is always preferable, when it applies. Once you realize that the three objects brought to harm Snow White go from external use (the bodice lace) to concealed in the hair (the comb) to internal (the poisoned apple to be eaten), you will remember their sequence easily.

In some stories or speeches, however, there is often no understandable principle ordering the events or ideas. In other stories, the principles are so complicated or detailed that you will not be able to reconstruct the relationships while continuing to speak. In these cases, it makes sense to create an image to remind you of the order.

A mnemonic (memory-assisting) image can involve any sensory mode. An ancient Greek orator suggested imagining (presumably, visually) a tour of your house, associating each successive part of your talk with a particular room. Kinesthetic mnemonics are also effective, hence the popularity of "finger plays" for children. Any image will be effective if it is easy for you both to remember and to associate with the events or ideas.

Games in This Section

In "You're Shaking Me Up," several players each suggest an activity with a corresponding gesture, thus creating a sequence of actions that are not in any logical order. The mnemonic used, however, fits the sequence naturally: the players who suggest each activity are lined up next to each other. To remember the next activity, you need only look at the next player, then remember what activity that player suggested.

※ ※

YOU'RE SHAKING ME UP!

Grade levels: Preschool through grade 4.

Props needed: Rhythm instruments *(optional, for variation).*

Complexity: High.

Game type: Filling in a plot.

Quick summary: A player tells an activity that he likes someone to do with him. Then the leader narrates the story of the player's attempt to get someone to do the activity. Players participate in the story by suggesting additional activities, joining in with appropriate movements as the activities are repeated cumulatively in the order in which they were suggested.

Directions: Say to the group, "What's your favorite thing to do with an adult?" Call on a volunteer.

Suppose Gail says, "Take a walk in the park with my father."

Then say, "Just for fun, let's make a story about wanting our father to take a walk in the park. Is that okay?"

If Gail agrees, begin the story:

One day, Gail said, "Dad, let's go for a walk in the park together."

But Gail's father said, "I'm asleep." So Gail had to wait.

Ask, "Gail, what's something you do when you're waiting for someone?"
Suppose Gail answers, "I play a video game."
Then say, "Gail, come stand where everyone can see you. Can you show us a movement for playing a video game?"

Direct the group to imitate Gail's movement. "Everybody pretend to play a video game, like Gail." Continue the story:

Gail played her video game.

From the bedroom, her father said . . .

Chant these lines, emphasizing the words in boldface:

*You're **shaking** me up,*

*You're **aching** me up,*

*You're **waking** me up!*

*Time to be **breaking** it up!*

Continue the story:

Gail said, "But I want to walk in the park!"

Her father said, "I'm asleep. Invite a friend over."

Say to the group, "Who wants to be the friend who came over?" Call on a volunteer. If you choose Jamal, have Jamal stand next to Gail. Then say,

So Gail invited Jamal over.

Ask Jamal, "What did you do when you got to Gail's house? It can be something you really do or something you *wish* you could do."

If Jamal says, "Play the drums," instruct everyone to join in. Continue the story (add or omit the encouragements in parentheses as needed):

So Jamal played the drums. (Everyone, pretend to play the drums!)

And Gail played her video game. (Everyone, pretend to play the video game!)

From the bedroom, her father said (Everyone, help me say this!),

*You're **shaking** me up,*

*You're **aching** me up,*

*You're **waking** me up!*

*Time to be **breaking** it up!*

Gail said, "But I want to walk in the park!"

Her father said, "I'm asleep. Invite a friend over."

Continue adding new friends, each of whom joins the line and suggests an activity with accompanying movement. After several more turns, your story might be something like this (add or omit the encouragements in parentheses as needed):

So Gabi was a cheerleader. (Everyone, pretend to be a cheerleader!)

So Charles drove his car. (Everyone, pretend to drive a car!)

So Annette brushed her teeth. (Everyone, pretend to brush your teeth!)

So Jamal played the drums. (Everyone, pretend to play the drums!)

And Gail played her video game. (Everyone, pretend to play the video game!)

From the bedroom, her father said (Everyone, help me say this!),

*You're **shaking** me up,*

*You're **aching** me up,*

*You're **waking** me up!*

*Time to be **breaking** it up!*

Gail said, "But I want to walk in the park!"

Her father said, "I'm asleep. Invite a friend over."

When your movement story has gone long enough, bring it toward an ending by substituting these lines:

Gail said, "But I want to walk in the park!"

Finally, her father said, "Okay, I'll take a walk with you in the park." And they did!

Ask Gail, "Did all your friends come with you, or go home then?"

Suppose Gail says, "Go home." Then end the story this way, having the group join in with each movement:

So Gabi went home, being a cheerleader.

So Charles went home, driving his car.

So Annette went home, brushing her teeth.

So Jamal went home, playing the drums.

And Gail and her father had a walk in the park together, all alone. As they walked, her father hugged her and said,

*I'm **glad** you were **shaking** me up,*

*I'm **glad** you were **aching** me up,*

*I'm **glad** you were **waking** me up!*

*It was **time** to be **taking** it up!*

Of course, if Gail says, "My friends came with us," then end the story with everyone joining the walk:

So Gabi came along, being a cheerleader.

So Charles came along, driving his car.

So Annette came along, brushing her teeth.

So Jamal came along, playing the drums.

And Gail and her father went walking in the park with everyone! As they walked,
her father hugged her and said,

*I'm **glad** you were **shaking** me up (etc.)*

Hints: It's easiest to remember the sequence of friends (and their movements) if the volunteers face the group, standing in the order in which they appear in the story. This arrangement allows you to point to each standing volunteer when her or his name appears in the story. To reinforce the left-to-right order used in reading English (from the group's point of view), have the additional players stand to the first player's left.

When your group is ready for a greater memory challenge, let the physical positions of the players be different in some way from the order in which they appear in the story. For one example, let the players remain seated where they were in the group. For another example, let the first player stand in the center; let the second player stand to the left of the first player; let the third player stand to the right of the first player; then continue to add players alternately to the right and left ends of the line.

Variations: Friends and peers. In the example given here, you ask the group, "What's your favorite thing to do with an adult?" You can vary the question by asking "What's something you like to do with someone?" or " . . . with a friend?"

Add sounds. To add sounds to the movements, have each volunteer make a sound using body sounds, or sounds made by common objects or rhythm instruments. For example, let Gail hum the song played by her favorite video game, and let Jamal clap his thighs to represent playing the drums. Alternatively, let Gail blow a whistle to represent the beep of a video game, and let Jamal play an actual drum.

Let players tell the story. After you have modeled the role of the storyteller one or more times, choose a volunteer to replace you.

Skills Reinforced

Communication: Pronouncing the name of an improvised activity clearly to the entire group. Saying chanted lines in unison.

Storytelling: Improvising descriptions of activities. Creating appropriate sounds and movements to match the chosen activities. Remembering a sequence of activities, with sounds and movements.

Thinking: Using the physical arrangement of players as a mnemonic device.

Curricular: Reviewing activities enjoyed by players. Dealing playfully with impatience and disruptive behaviors.

Creating Characters

Characterizations consist of a combination of oral language elements. A recognizable characterization may combine a way of speaking, a way of standing, and a way of moving. A way of speaking, in turn, may combine a vocal quality, a tempo or rhythm of speech, and the use of certain types of words or sentence structures.

Although actors create characterizations, they usually continue a characterization for an entire performance. Storytellers, comedians, lecturers, and conversationalists, however, may go from one characterization to another in the course of a few moments. Such characterizations may not need to be as detailed as an actor's, but they must be started and stopped distinctly.

For many people, the most reliable way to begin a characterization distinctly is through kinesthetic imagery. By finding a key muscular change that establishes how a particular character stands, walks, or feels, the oral communicator can use that muscular change to produce a rapid change in posture, which will produce a corresponding change in vocal tone, effort, and even pace of speech.

Games in This Section

"Monster Rumble" lets players explore the physical changes involved in characterizations. The game helps players go to a play-

ful extreme: the creation of a monster character. If you have ever spent a few seconds taking on the movement style of Frankenstein's monster or of Freddy Krueger, you know how easy and appealing this kind of transformation can be. The game structure allows players not only to experiment with creating their own monsters, but also to share their creations in an orderly way.

Games from Other Sections

By using movements to convey an attitude or feeling, the following games can contribute to creating characterizations:

"Do It Your Way" (p. 84)

"The Back Speaks" (p. 25)

MONSTER RUMBLE

Grade levels: Preschool through grade 3.

Space needed: A clear area for a circle of players, with room for one player to walk inside the circle. (A variation can be played with lines of five to ten standing players, requiring only enough room for one player at a time to walk forward a few steps.)

Complexity: Low.

Game type: Alternating solo movements with group chant.

Quick summary: Players pretend to become monsters. Accompanied by singing or chanting, the entire group walks as monsters in a circle. An individual monster walks into the center, turns around, then returns to the circle.

Directions: Before you teach this game, spend a few moments alone creating your "monster body." Find a way to walk like a monster that pleases you.

Assemble your group into a circle, then begin walking around the circle as a monster, speaking the following lines (or chanting them like a poem, or singing them loosely to the tune of "B–I–N–G–O," or singing them to the tune given on p. 149):

Monsters, on a rumble,

Monsters, in a jumble,

Monsters, number one:

One came over, looking tough,

Turned around and showed its stuff,

And then went back for more, of the

Continue walking as you begin the lines again:

Monsters, on a rumble,

Monsters, in a jumble,

Monsters, number one:

As you say "number one," stop walking around the circle, then face the center. Point to yourself, indicating that you are "monster number one."

If necessary, say, "This is my solo. Stand where you are and watch what kind of monster I am."

Walk a few steps into the circle, as a monster, as you say:

One came over, looking tough,

Turn once around in place as you say this line:

Turned around and showed its stuff,

Return to the circle as you say the final line:

And then went back for more, of the

Without pause, begin the lines again, gesturing the players to walk around the circle with you. When you reach the third line, change it to "Monsters, number two."

Using gestures (or words, if necessary), indicate that the player ahead of you should now take a solo turn in the center, as all speak or sing:

One came over, looking tough,

Turned around and showed its stuff,

And then went back for more, of the

Without pause, begin the lines again. Repeat as desired, or until everyone in the circle has had a turn.

Hints: If you feel shy about demonstrating a monster body, perhaps you can persuade a volunteer to take your place. You might even approach a player before you introduce the game to make sure the player understands what to do.

How to make a monster. Some groups will need no coaching about how to be monsters. Others will need help to be original, or else to respect the space of other players.

In most cases, coaching for originality will serve both purposes: players focusing on their internal sensations will be unlikely to purposely disrupt others. Most other problems can be solved by a reminder to "give the other monsters some space, too," by increasing the amount of space, or by decreasing the number of monsters walking at a time.

If your players need coaching to create original monsters, have them walk around the circle. Say,

> *You can each become your own kind of monster. Try to discover what it feels like to be a monster. Can you feel it in your body? Where do you feel it?*

After you ask a question of the group, give the players a few moments to explore, but don't expect verbal answers. If someone starts to answer with words, say, "Show me in how you move!"

If desired, ask more questions, such as these:

How big is your monster?

Does your monster scurry around like an imp, or walk slowly like a giant?

What part of your monster is dangerous?

What does your monster want from the world?

To form a circle using another game. To assemble your group into a circle, you can first play a game of "The Sea Is Getting Stormy" (p. 112). Once all are in line, omit the last line of the story. Instead, guide the leader to follow the last player in line, thus forming a circle. You can simply begin the monster chant at this point; no introduction is required.

Variations: To give more players a chance to have solo turns in less time, divide your group into smaller circles, each with the same number of players. When you are chanting "number one," the first player in each group will take a solo turn.

Alternatively, count off by sixes (or some other number) in your large circle. All the "number ones" will solo at once.

Line formation. If you do not have room for everyone to walk in a circle, have five to ten players at a time form a line. During the first three lines of the chant, players can walk in place as monsters. During the second three lines, an individual player walks a few steps forward, turns around, then returns to the line.

Once each of these players has had a turn to solo, you may choose to repeat the game with another group of five to ten players.

Skills Reinforced

Communication: Saying chanted lines in unison. Practicing turn-taking. Starting and stopping while walking in a circle (or in a line, or in an open space) together. Improvising combinations of posture and movements.

Storytelling: Creating the basis of a monster's character. Creating an original monster.

Curricular: Reviewing counting. Practicing the solo-chorus form. Dealing playfully with fear.

CHAPTER 2
Learning About Language

■ ■ ■

To improve language skills, we need to use language. All the story games in this book let us use language both to communicate and to play.

As essential as language-use experiences are, concepts of language structure can also be helpful, especially in analyzing problems in communication. Such problems are especially likely to arise when the context of communication changes—whether from oral to written language, from informal to formal language, or from private to public language. In attempting to solve such problems, a toolbox of identified concepts can be very useful—as long as the time spent learning concepts supplements, but does not replace, opportunities for voluntary, meaningful communication.

The games in this chapter combine the learning of language concepts with experience using language. They correspond to several classic language concepts as well as to a basic concept of transformational grammar.

Letter Sounds

Many children are forced to spend hours drilling letter sounds. Games can improve on drills in several ways: they can be more enjoyable, they can reduce the stigma on mistakes, and they can put children in the position of leader.

The easiest letter sounds to discriminate, of course, are the initial sounds of a word. Middle letters are less conspicuous, while final letters in English are often deceptive.

Games in This Section

"Letter Echoes" gives practice recognizing and using words with a given initial letter. It can be played as easily with a group of one or two as with a full auditorium. Played with too much attention to correct responses and too little attention to fun, to be sure, it can be as dull as any drill. Played in the spirit of creative silliness, on the other hand, it can be so much fun that players seek it out regardless of its educational value.

"Letter Relay" focuses on the final letter of a sentence, thereby giving practice in a more difficult arena of letter-sound recognition. At the same time, it relies less on a leader than does "Letter Echoes," and therefore has less resemblance to a drill. Since each letter that is decoded from the end of a sentence is also used for the easier task of beginning the next sentence, this game allows cooperation between players at different levels of sound-recognition ability.

※ ※

LETTER ECHOES

Grade levels: Grades 1-3.

Props needed: Blackboard or marker pad *(optional)*.

Complexity: Low.

Game type: Audience response to story cues.

Quick summary: Audience echoes words beginning with a chosen letter.

Directions: Say to the Group,

>*You know how I'm always telling you to listen quietly? Here's a game where you can listen loudly.*

>*Every time I say a word beginning with the letter "B," you say that word back. So if I say, "Ball," you say . . . (Group responds).*

>*Let's have a practice: Ball (Group: Ball!)*

>*Basket! (Group: Basket!)*

>*Throw! (Group should be silent; some will forget and echo)*

>*Oh, oh! I fooled you! Listen for the B-words.*

>*Are you ready for the story?*

Tell a story, such as:

>*Once, there was a big (Group: Big!) black (Group: Black!) bumblebee (Group: Bumblebee!). She woke up one morning, smelled the air, and got out of bed (Group: Bed!).*

Continue the story, allowing the Group to respond by echoing each word that begins with "B":

>*She said, I want to visit my friend, the blue butterfly. He is my best friend! Besides, he's so beautiful! But he lives far away.*

It was a long way to fly, but the big black bumblebee decided to try it. She began to fly. As she flew, she buzzed. She buzzed so loudly, she didn't hear someone calling her name.

"Hey, big black bumblebee! Where are you buzzing off to?"

It was the blue butterfly! "I was just heading to visit you."

"Well, I was bored, so I was coming to be with you. Here we are. Let's play basketball!"

So they did. First the bee was the basketball and a buttercup was the basket. Then the butterfly was the ball and a blackberry blossom was the basket.

Finally, it was time to say bye-bye. They were both so happy, they buzzed all the way back home.

Repeat as desired. Vary the story at will.

Hints: With young children, pause after each B-word, as a cue. After they have played for a while, pause after some words that don't begin with a "B," as well.

You can have the group help you make up a story. Say, "What are some words that begin with the letter 'B,' like 'bounce,' 'bike,' and 'bakery'?" Call on volunteers. Write about 10 of their suggestions where all can see them. Use all the words in your story. If you get stuck, ask group members for help. A sentence with several of the words in it makes an exciting grand finale.

Variations: Have players be the storytellers. They can tell the same story you told or a different one. If they create their own story, you can provide them with the letter and a list of words, or you can let them choose their own. Words whose second letter is a vowel may be easier to recognize as "B-words" than words beginning with a consonant blend, such as "blue" or "breathe."

Choose a different letter of the alphabet.

Have players echo any word that ends with (or contains) the given letter.

Let the echoing be accompanied also by a movement, such as clapping hands for each syllable; or by standing, echoing the word, then sitting down.

Omit the echo altogether, replacing it with a movement. For example, players can clap when they hear a cue word, or stand up and sit down, or stand up one time and sit down the next.

When I was eight, my cousin Roger (six years older) came to visit. He spent an hour lying on the floor with my younger brother and me sitting on his chest. He told an impromptu story about two boys and a very big baseball. Whenever he said a word with the letter "B," we were to bounce on him. You can play a similar version of this game with a child on your lap.

Skills Reinforced

Communication:

Group: Listening for cues; pronouncing words that begin with the chosen letter.

Leader: Pronouncing words clearly to the entire group (with immediate feedback).

Storytelling:

Leader: Maintaining coherence during audience participation; adjusting the rate of participation based on group response.

Thinking: Using arbitrarily selected words frequently in an improvised story.

Curricular: Recognizing letter sounds.

※ ※

LETTER RELAY

Grade levels: Grade 3 and up.

Props needed: Dictionary (*optional, for variation*).

Complexity: Medium.

Game type: Round-robin.

Quick summary: Create a story one sentence at a time. Each sentence must begin with the ending letter of the previous sentence.

Directions: Say to the group, "I'm going to tell you the first sentence of a story. Can you tell me the last letter of the sentence?"

As you tell the story, separate it from your instructions by changing places (e.g., take a step to the right) or by changing where you look or your tone of voice. Begin a story such as:

One dark, spooky night, I went walking in the woods.

Return to giving instructions (e.g., take a step back to the left, or return to your earlier direction of looking or tone of voice). Say, "Did you hear the last letter of that sentence?"

If the players respond hesitantly or incorrectly, repeat the sentence. When they respond correctly, say, "Yes, it ended with 's'! Now I have to start my *next* sentence with an 's.' What word starting with 's' could I use?"

Call on a player to suggest a word. If the suggested word is "suddenly," for example, you might respond, "That's an easy word to use at the beginning of a sentence. Okay, I'll keep going."

Return to telling the story, adding a sentence beginning with the suggested word, such as:

Suddenly, I heard a voice saying, "Why are you here?"

Say, "What letter did that sentence end with? That's right, 'e.' What word beginning with 'e' should I use to start my next sentence?" If, for example, the players say "excited," continue the story with their word:

Excited but scared, I looked around to see who was speaking.

Continue as desired. When you want the story to stop, bring it to an end. If you wish, say, "It's time to end our story, so I'm going to take a few turns in a row." Then create the next several relay sentences entirely yourself, to resolve the story.

Hint: If the players suggest a word that is awkward to use in the story at any point, ask for a change or for help connecting the word to the story.

For example, if the suggested word is "say," you might say, "I can't think of how to start my next sentence with 'say.' Can you help me?"

If the player does not have a suggested sentence, ask for another form of the word that will work. For example, you might say, "Can I use 'saying'?" Then continue with something like this:

Saying to myself that there must be some reason why no one else was in the woods, I walked cautiously.

Variations: To play the game without requiring a knowledge of letter sounds, have the next sentence start with the entire last word of the previous sentence.

Once your group seems at ease with suggesting appropriate words, ask them to suggest whole sentences as well. After the group suggests "suddenly," you might say, "'Suddenly' should be a good word to go on with. Who can think of a sentence that begins with 'suddenly' that would fit our story at this point?"

At a still more challenging level, omit the step of asking for a starting word that begins with the required letter; once you have explained the game, simply ask players to give the next sentence in the story.

If desired, play in small groups or in pairs.

Using two letters. To add much more challenge, use the last two letters of a sentence as the first two of the next. In other words, if the first sentence ended with the word "he*re*," the next sentence's first word would begin with "re" ("*Re*alizing she was in danger . . .").

By the way, a sentence ending in a word like "woods" is impossible to follow (no English words begin with "ds"), so you should ask a player who ends a sentence with such a letter combination to re-cast the sentence using a different ending word. If you wish, appoint a Lookup Manager to check suspect letter combinations in a dictionary.

Teams. Play as a game for two teams. One team suggests the initial word, and the second team must use it to start the first sentence of a story. Then the first team continues the story with another sentence (which begins with the final letter of the first sentence, of course). Continue until one team is stumped or until there is general agreement that the story is completed.

Skills Reinforced

Communication: Practicing turn-taking. Pronouncing a contribution clearly to the entire group.

Storytelling: Improvising a one-sentence addition to a given story.

Curricular: Imagining the spelling of a spoken word; naming its last letter.

Choosing a word beginning with a given letter. Creating a sentence beginning with a given word.

Words

Words are elemental building blocks of language. They are so fundamental that we often speak as though "language" and "words" are synonymous—we say, "his words cheered me," or "she had words with me."

Much of a student's learning in a new subject can consist of learning the terminology, the meanings of words used in a particular field. Indeed, certain words carry with them the associations of an entire activity or era. Think of "parasol," "bleachers," or "countdown."

As important as words are, though, they are by no means the entirety of language. The chapter "Mastering Oral Communication" describes some of the other important building blocks of spoken language. Even written language depends on elements of structure—such as sentence structure, repetition, and contrast—as much as it depends on words.

Many of the games in this book throw their focus—at least some of the time—on individual words.

Games in This Section

"Hide the Words" is a guessing game in which a series of words are hidden at different points in a story. It gives players an opportunity to pay attention to individual words within the context of an entire story. The players telling the story try to de-emphasize the words to be guessed, while the guessing players, of course, try to notice them.

Games in Other Sections

Several games in this collection have as their aim the guessing of one or a series of words:

"Fuddy Duddy" (p. 49)

"Proverb Guessing" (p. 60)

"Pun Puzzles" (p. 56)

"Story Crambo" (p. 47)

"Teakettle Stories" (p. 53)

"Towns and Counties" (p. 73)

In these next games, words are placed into existing sentences, creating new meanings:

"Places, Persons, and Things" (p. 67)

"Would You Believe?" (p. 66)

In the following games, players in the audience respond to individual words within a story:

"Letter Echoes" (p. 39)

"Spaceship" (p. 114)

In a variation of "Letter Relay" (p. 41), players use the last word of one sentence to begin the next sentence.

"Occupations" (p. 97) uses a series of words related to an occupation or sport, and substitutes them for certain of the original words in a familiar story.

HIDE THE WORDS

Grade levels: Grade 3 and up.

Props needed: Slips of paper and a writing implement for each player. Dictionary, book, or magazine *(optional, for variation).*

Complexity: High.

Game type: Guessing a word used in a story. Combining elements.

Quick summary: Each player writes a word on a slip of paper, then each chooses a slip at random. A team of three or four players creates a story together that incorporates all their chosen words. Each player on the team tells a section of the story, including the player's own word. The group tries to guess the chosen words.

Directions: Pass out one slip of paper (or a file card) to each player. Say,

> *We're going to play a guessing game. Write one word on your slip of paper.*

After each player has written a word on a slip of paper, collect the slips in a hat or bowl, then say,

> *Draw a slip of paper, but don't let anyone else see it.*

After all have chosen a word, say,

> *I need three volunteers to show how this game goes.*

Choose volunteers, then say to them,

> *Show each other your words. You have to make a story that uses all three words. Then each of you has to tell a part of the story, and your word has to be in the part you tell.*

Once the team creates a basic story-line and assigns a part of the story to each member, have the team members tell their story. One player will begin the story, the second player will continue it, and the third will bring it to an end.

After the team tells its story, say to the whole group,

> *Does anyone have a guess about what one of their words might be?*

Then say to the team of storytellers,

> *Each of you can call on two players who want to guess your word. Let the people you call on know if they guessed right or not.*

Allow team members to call on up to two guessers each. If two guessers both fail to guess one storyteller's word, say,

> *Congratulations! You stumped two people! Tell us what your word was.*

After all three original words have been divulged, say to the group,

> *Now you'll all get a chance to do what this team did!*

Have the group divide into teams. (For some ways to choose teams, see "Managing Turns and Teams," p. xvii.) After letting them have some time to prepare stories, have volunteer teams tell their stories to the whole group. Then have the group guess which words each team member drew.

Repeat as desired, or until each team has told its story.

Hints: Helping a team create a story. Sometimes a team will need help creating a story or dividing it into parts to tell. It's best to choose a sample team that is likely to succeed, since its successful playing will make the game clearer to the others than any explanation.

If your sample team has trouble, help the team members create a story and assign which parts will be told by which player. If they are stymied, involve the entire group in the process. Say,

> *Let's do this all together, so everyone can learn how this goes. James's word is "green," Samir's word is "bicycle," and Sonya's word is "book."*

First, you have to think of a story that could use those three words. Does anyone have an idea what one of those words could have to do with one of the other words?

Call on players to contribute ideas. Help them build on any connections they think of:

Good idea! Someone could have to ride a bicycle to a greenhouse to get flowers. Who could this person be getting the flowers for?

For her boyfriend? That makes sense. That takes care of two of our words already. That just leaves one. How can a book end up in our story?

Okay, we have part of the basic idea. Our hero is going to ride to the greenhouse to get flowers for her boyfriend, but along the way she loses her math book. Who do you suppose helps her find it?

Great! Her boyfriend helps her find it, and she gives him the flowers as a thank you. He's puzzled by how she got them so fast.

Once the sample team has the basic idea for a complete story, help the players choose a logical order in which to tell their individual sections of the story:

Now, James has to tell part of the story, using the word "green." Samir has to tell another part, using the word "bicycle." Sonya has to tell another part using the word "book." Who should tell the first part? Why?

That makes sense. If the story begins with our hero wanting flowers, then the greenhouse could be mentioned near the beginning. So James can go first.

Does it make more sense for the bicycle to come into the story now, or the book? Why the bicycle? Okay, that will be easy: first she wants flowers, then she decides to get them at the greenhouse. That will be the part that James has to tell.

Then she decides to take her bicycle to get the flowers. That's the part that Samir needs to tell.

Then she loses her book on the way back, and her boyfriend finds it. When he gives it to her, she gives him the flowers, and he's surprised. That's your part of the story, Sonya.

After the team tells its story, you can say,

Did they use the words they were supposed to? Did they tell their story? It's okay that the story changed some as they told it, as long as they get their words in.

If this had been the real game, you'd all try to guess those three words. Now the other teams can try it for real.

Few groups will need this much help creating and apportioning a story. But almost any group can succeed if you restate each of their ideas and patiently ask them the appropriate questions.

Accommodating groups of different sizes and abilities. If there are more teams ready to tell their stories than you have time to let tell, you can ask the teams to save their words, remember their stories, and return to them on a later day. (If they write down some key ideas from their stories, it might be easier for them to remember their thinking.)

Alternatively, teams can tell their stories to one or two other teams instead of to the entire group.

You can vary team sizes. Small teams make it easier to create stories, but often create stories that are more difficult for the group to guess.

If the sample group has difficulty dividing its story, it may be wise to have the rest of the players work in teams of two.

Each team member can call on more than two guessers. If many guessers fail to guess the words, it may be fun to have the team retell the story. To make each retelling easier for the guessers, require team members to abbreviate their sections of the story. You can say,

> *Congratulations! We have a stumper! Now tell the story again—but each part has to be half as long.*

If the group still fails to guess the words, ask the team to tell a third time, with each section of the story only half as long as the second time. This makes the hidden words increasingly obvious.

Encouraging strategies. When a group has mastered the basics of this game, you can suggest strategic word choices:

> *Write a word on each slip of paper. But be careful! If it's a word that stands out, it will be hard to hide if your own team draws it. But if it's too common a word, even you will never guess it if another team draws it. Try for words that aren't too hard or too easy to hide.*

When groups have used cleverness in creating stories, you can point out their successful strategies. For example, you might say,

> *That was very clever! You had to hide the word "rhinoceros," so you gave a whole list of animals. That sure fooled us!*

Variations: To make the game easier for those guessing, have each team choose just one slip of paper. Then the players on that team must incorporate that same word into each section of their story.

Instead of having players write words on slips of paper, you can use other methods to give each player a randomly chosen word. You can prepare slips in advance with spelling words on them. Or you can have players close their eyes and point to random words in a dictionary, a text, or other reading material.

You can require that the players write down words from a particular category. For example, you could say, "On your slip of paper, write down one action verb." Or you can ask for a word that has two syllables, that comes from a Latin root, that has to do with agriculture (or other social studies subject), that relates to the Age of Exploration (or other historical subject), or that is prominent in a particular work of literature. The smaller the class of possible words, the easier it will be to guess them.

Similarly, you can add a subject requirement to the story that each team creates. You might ask for a story related to the environment, to the history of Eastern Europe, or to inter-group relations.

Skills Reinforced

Communication:

Leader: Pronouncing a contribution clearly to the entire group.

Storytelling:

Leader: Creating a story that contains a given set of words. Coordinating a story with team members; maintaining the flow while telling a section of a story.

Thinking:

Leader: Including a word without drawing attention to it. Introducing other words as "red herrings" to which attention is deliberately drawn.

Curricular:

Group: Choosing and writing a word. Isolating words from a story context to find the hidden one.

Leader: Creating a story context and a sentence context for a given word.

Rhyming

Rhyming adds interest to many styles of poetry and song, of course, but it also helps beginning readers learn letter-sound patterns for whole groups of words.

Rhyming is more difficult than recognizing words with the same initial sound. In the first place, final sounds are less obvious to most people. Secondly, rhymes can involve not only single sounds (as in "too" and "do") but also a sequence of sounds (as in "tunes" and "dunes").

Games in This Section

The games in this section do not teach how to rhyme but allow playful practice for those who have already learned.[1]

"Story Crambo" gives an entire group extensive practice with rhyming. Each player tries to think of words that rhyme with the word given by the leader. Once a player has thought of a word and made a story clue for it, the leader must then guess which word is being guessed. In this way, leader and group get complementary practice in coming up with rhyming words.

Both games in this section use "marker words" to substitute in a story for the secret rhyming words. This adds challenge as well as a sense of playfulness.

In "Fuddy Duddy"—derived from the traditional game "Hinky Pinky"—the leader must think of a pair of rhyming words, the second of which must be a noun.

※ ※

STORY CRAMBO

Grade levels: Grade 2 and up.

Props needed: Blackboard or paper *(optional).*

Complexity: Medium.

Game type: Guessing a word used in a story.

Quick summary: One player chooses a secret word and announces another word that rhymes with it. The others must put their guesses in the form of brief stories, substituting "crambo" for the guessed word.

Directions: Your sample secret word is "sheet." Say,

> *I have a secret word for you to guess. My word rhymes with "beat." But you can't just say the word when you guess in this game. You have to tell a little story about it.*

> *Let's say you think the word is "seat." You tell a story about a seat, but instead of saying "seat" in the story, you say "crambo" instead. So you might make your guess by saying:*

> *"I came into class late, and went to my desk. But my chair was missing. So I just stood there by my desk. And then the teacher yelled at me because I wasn't sitting down. He said, "When you come into this classroom, I expect you to take a crambo right away!"*

> *I would hear that and think, "Oh, I expect you to take a seat. Crambo stands for 'seat' in that story." Then I would say, "No, it's not seat."*

> *Who wants to make a guess?*

Choose a volunteer. Perhaps your volunteer will say something like this:

> *"I was out on a farm looking at the crops growing in the fields. I saw the grain waving in the wind, and thought, 'We'll be able to make lots of bread when we harvest and grind all that crambo.'"*

Say,

> *Good crambo story!*

> *My job now is to guess what "crambo" meant in your story about the farm. If I don't know, I can say, "Tell me more about crambo!"*

> *This time I think I know what crambo is. No, my word is not "wheat."*

Ask for more guesses. After each crambo story, say either, "Tell me more about crambo," or "No, it's not _____." If a player tells a story about a crambo that was on his bed, or a crambo of paper that she wrote on, then say, "Yes, it's a sheet."

Repeat by choosing another word, telling a word that it rhymes with, and asking for volunteers to guess by telling crambo stories.

If you think one or more players are ready to take the role of leader, say, "Who would like to think of a word for us all to guess?" Then repeat the game with a volunteer as the new leader.

Hints: If the players have tried several guesses but haven't come upon the right word yet, give a hint (or ask the leader to give one). You might say, "My secret word is something you'd find inside a house," or "My secret word has to do with sleeping," or "My secret word begins with two consonants."

For younger players (such as second- or third-graders), you may need to brainstorm a list of rhyming words *before* the leader chooses one to be guessed. When teaching the game this way, start by saying a word, then having your group generate a list of five or more words that rhyme with the word you said. Then the leader chooses one word from the list as the new "secret" word. This way, the other players don't have to think of a rhyming word to guess but can simply choose one from the list.

Variations: To make guessing easier or to make a curricular connection, you can require the secret word to be from a given (large) category: items in the home, items in a supermarket, or things having to do with transportation. Alternatively, require the secret word to be a name, a noun, a verb, or an adjective.

To make guessing slightly easier or to give practice with counting syllables, require the word to have a given number of syllables.

Skills Reinforced

Communication:

Group: Pronouncing a contribution clearly to the entire group.

Leader: Attempting to understand a story in which one word is omitted. Inferring the meaning of a word from its context.

Storytelling:

Group: Creating a story that makes clear the meaning of a particular word.

Thinking:

Group: Using the marker word "crambo" in place of the word to be guessed; keeping track of the marker's meaning.

Leader: Decoding the marker word, "crambo." After a story clue, choosing a word from a given category. Thinking of appropriate hints if the group is stuck.

Curricular:

Group: Thinking of a word that rhymes with a given word.

Leader: Identifying the rhyming words thought of by group members.

※ ※

FUDDY DUDDY

Grade levels: Grade 3 and up.

Complexity: Medium.

Game type: Guessing a word used in a story. Guessing a phrase.

Quick summary: One player (or a team of two) thinks of a pair of rhyming words that describe an object or character. The player gives clues to the words by telling a story, substituting the words "fuddy" and "duddy" for the rhyming words. The group tries to guess the rhyming words.

Directions: Say,

> *This is a guessing game. I have to think of something I can describe with two words that rhyme, then I will tell you a story about it. You have to guess the two words.*

> *This time, I'll tell you my two words first, but usually you'll have to guess them. I'm thinking of a "hot pot." So I say, "I'm thinking of a fud dud." That tells you that my words have only one syllable.*

> *Now I have to tell you a story, using the words "fud" and "dud" instead of "hot" and "pot."*

My story might be like this. Once, I was in the kitchen cooking. I wanted to make some soup, so I looked for a dud to cook it in. But when I went to pick it up, I found out that someone must have been cooking in it already, because the handle of the dud was too fud for me to touch!

So that's my story. You'd listen to that and guess that when I said "fud" I meant "hot," and when I said "dud" I was talking about a pot.

If your players look puzzled, offer them another example, such as "fat cat" or "red bed." Give as many examples as they seem to enjoy. They may prefer guessing for several sessions before any of them wish to try becoming the storyteller.

When your group seems to understand the basic idea and to be ready to try the storyteller's role, say,

Let's try another one, but this time I'll help you make up the story. Let's make our two words be "big pig."

Who can make up a brief story about a big pig? What could happen to a pig because it was very big?

Choose a volunteer to comment on the possible fate of a big pig. If you elicit several answers, say them all and let the group choose which one to use:

Great! We could have a pig that couldn't fit in the barn because it was so big. Or we could use the idea of a pig that was bigger than its family and felt worried about being different. Or we can have our pig win first prize in the county fair because it was the biggest around. Those are all good ideas. Which one should we use in our story?

Once you have guided your group to constructing a story about a big pig (it can be a very simple story), help a volunteer tell the story with the word substitutions. If desired, you can write "big = fud" and "pig = dud" where the teller can see it. Your volunteer storyteller might end up saying something like this:

Once, I visited a farm, and I saw a fud building next to the barn. I said, "What's in that building?" They said, "Oh, that's where we keep our dud. It's a very fud dud."

In this case, the story doesn't provide much of a clue. You might say to the volunteer storyteller,

That's great! You used the words "fud" and "dud" in the right places. Now, can you give us a clue about what kind of an animal a dud is?

The storyteller might add:

So I said, "Why isn't the dud in the sty with the other duds?"

In this case, praise the teller's successful efforts! You might also ask for a clue about the other word, too:

Good storytelling! You used the word "sty," which gives us a very clear clue about a pig. Now can you also add a clue about what fud means? Can you describe the fud building somehow?

A successful response might be:

I looked at that fud building. The barn looked small next to it. The building was so fud, they could have put a whole football field in it.

Once your players understand both the rhyming-words part of the game and the story-clue part, you are ready to ask for volunteers to go through the entire process. Then you can say,

> *Is someone ready to try the whole game? Can you think of something you could name with two rhyming words, and then give us a story clue for it?*

Alternatively, you can ask players to form teams of two, preparing and telling their stories cooperatively. Each player will tell half of the story, and each can be responsible for including a clue about one of the two words.

Hints: Adding to your story clue. If any example stumps your players, say,

> *Did I stump you? When you are stumped you can ask me to tell more about the fud dud. Should I tell you more?*

Make your additional story clue more explicit and graphic, so that your players can guess successfully. For example, say,

> *Since my dud was too fud to pick up, I looked for another dud to cook my soup in. I opened the cabinet where I keep my duds and pans. There was a tea dud, but no more duds with a cover for cooking soup!*

> *I was starting to sweat. I thought, with the oven on, it's getting really fud in here. No wonder the handle of the dud was too fud. It must be 99° in here! That's fud enough to cook an egg on the sidewalk!*

Limiting the number of clue requests. If desired, limit the number of requests for additional clues. If your initial story clue stumps your group, say:

> *I stumped you! You can ask "What happened then to the fud dud?"*

If your second clue stumps them, say:

> *I stumped you a second time! This is your last chance. You can say, "Tell us the last chapter about the fud dud!"*

Avoiding explanation. If your group seems perplexed by your explanation of how to become the storyteller in this game, go back to being the storyteller yourself. After several sessions of playing this game as guessers, most groups can take the role of storyteller with very little instruction.

Multi-syllable rhymes. It's easier to guess multi-syllable rhymes if you change the words "fud dud" to reflect the actual number of syllables in the words to be guessed. You might say,

> *This won't be a "fud dud," because my words have two syllables. So this is a "fuddy duddy."*

Tell your story clue using "fuddy" and "duddy." For more syllables, use "fuddelly duddelly" and "fuddelary duddelary."

If the rhyming words do not have their accents on the first syllable, you may choose to use "baFUD," or "ubaFUD" or even "baFUDdy."

If the two words are of unequal number of syllables, substitute appropriately: for a "decider spider" use "bafuddy duddy."

If your players have trouble counting syllables, be sure to take the time to help them.

Realistic vs. fantastic. Some groups tend to limit themselves unconsciously to realistic or familiar subjects: a fat cat, a night light, or a metal kettle. You may need to encourage them (by example or by explicit suggestion) to explore fantastic, unfamiliar, unlikely, or silly subjects: a star car, a dragon wagon, or a sadder ladder.

These fantastic subjects make more demands on the guessers and on the story makers, but they add another dimension of imagination.

Variations: Require players to use two-syllable (or more) rhymes. (See "Hints: Multi-syllable rhymes," above.)

Introduce or require the use of a trio of rhyming words as the subject to be guessed, such as a "sick, thick stick." In the story clue, substitute "wud" (or "wuddy," etc.) for the third word.

Require that one of the words be taken from a particular category, such as animals, colors, places, cities in the Middle East, your vocabulary list for the week, or words relating to the life processes of a flowering plant. Imagine the story clue for a "crystal pistil"! Incidentally, if one of the two words is to be a place, it will probably be the first—as in "Rome dome" or "Missouri fury."

Skills Reinforced

Communication:

Group: Attempting to understand a story in which some words are omitted. Inferring the meaning of the words from their context. Practicing turn-taking.

Leader: Pronouncing a contribution clearly to the entire group.

Storytelling:

Leader: Creating a story that exemplifies a quality of an object or character.

Thinking:

Group: Decoding the marker words.

Leader: Using the marker words, "fuddy" and "duddy," in place of the words to be guessed; keeping track of which marker stands for which word.

Curricular:

Group: Guessing a pair of rhyming words.

Leader: Thinking of a suitable pair of rhyming words. In a variation, determining the number of syllables (and, optionally, the stress pattern) of the rhyming words.

Homonyms

Homonyms are words that sound the same but have different meanings. As used here, the term "homonym" can refer to words that are spelled the same (such as the animal, "bear," and the action, to "bear" a heavy load), or to words that are spelled differently, often called "homophones" (the cupboard was "bare").

It's an accident of language that one sound can stand for more than one word. In learning to read, therefore, homonyms can cause misunderstandings. As a result, it's easy to view them as nuisances. In these games, however, homonyms are desirable. Accidents of language, after all, form the basis for a wealth of language play!

Games in This Section

In "Teakettle Stories," the leader thinks of any homonym pair, then constructs a story that uses both words. As with the rhyming-word games in the previous section, marker words are substituted for the words to be guessed. This requires the leader to keep both meanings in mind simultaneously and requires the rest of the group to search for two unknown variables at once. This game makes it easy to find suitable homonyms but makes it somewhat difficult to create and tell a story and to guess the words.

"Pun Puzzles," on the other hand, makes it easier to tell and guess, but puts more demands on the exact homonyms that can be used. Players must brainstorm a list of terms related to a profession or sport, then choose several homonyms from this limited list. Those who guess, however, are not seeking a homonym but the profession or sport that the terms apply to. As a result, this game makes more demands on the lead-

ers' knowledge of homonyms, but, in a group of mixed ages, it may allow successful intuitive guessing by players who aren't necessarily able to define a homonym.

Games in Other Sections

In two games from other sections, homonyms can be used to make guessing more difficult. In "Proverb Guessing" (p. 60), a player who, for example, uses "gathers" as a noun rather than a verb makes it more difficult for the group to guess "A rolling stone gathers no moss." In "Towns and Counties" (p. 73), use of homonyms can sometimes make the clue syllables less obvious: "knew" stands out less than "new" in a clue story for "New London."

In two other games, the use of homonyms can add playful possibilities for the story maker. In "Daddy Shot a Bear" (p. 128), the multiple meanings of "shot" allow many new interpretations. "Questions and Answers" (p. 87) is a much more whimsical game if a player can make a story about "The first (movie) star I see to knight," rather than the literal line on the player's card, "The first star I see tonight."

※ ※

TEAKETTLE STORIES

Grade levels: Grade 4 and up.

Complexity: Medium.

Game type: Guessing a word used in a story.

Quick summary: A player chooses a pair of secret words that sound the same (homonyms). The player tells a clue story that uses both words, substituting "teakettle" for the words. The group tries to guess the secret words.

Directions: Say,

> This is a guessing game. I'm going to think of two words that sound the same, like "so" in "It was so big, you couldn't see the top of it" and "sew" in "I learned to sew my own clothes."

> Can you think of some other pairs of words that sound the same?

Call on volunteers to brainstorm some homonyms. Here are some common ones:

- ate—eight
- beat—beet
- buy—by—bye
- C—sea—see
- cents—scents—sense
- chili—chilly
- dew—do—due
- die—dye
- for—fore—four
- foul—fowl
- hear—here
- hoarse—horse
- main—Maine—mane

- missed—mist
- oar—or—ore
- one—won
- pail—pale
- peak—peek
- pole—poll
- rain—reign—rein
- son—sun
- stair—stare
- steal—steel
- T—tea—tee
- to—too—two
- way—weigh—whey
- weak—week

After the group names some homonyms, say,

The clue I'm going to give you is a story that uses both of the sound-alike words. But I won't say the words in the story. Instead, I'll say "teakettle."

If the word is "so," and "sew," my story clue might be like this.

Tell the following sample story. Whenever you say "teakettle," be sure to preserve the speech inflection that would be usual for "so" or "sew." Say,

*I wanted to learn to **teakettle** my own clothes. My mother said it was too hard for me. **Teakettle**, I asked my father to help. He said it was too hard for me, too. **Teakettle**, I took a course in **teakettling**. They showed us how to use a pattern, how to cut fabric and thread, and how to **teakettle** by hand and with a **teakettling** machine. It was very hard to learn. My parents said it would be hard, but I didn't know it would be **teakettle** hard!*

Say,

From that story, you would have to guess that "teakettle" meant "so" and "sew." Do you want to try guessing a different pair of words?

Tell the following story:

*I was camping out in the woods one morning. The sun was getting warm enough that I decided to take off my coat. Just then, crashing through the woods came the most enormous **teakettle** I ever saw.*

*I dropped my coat and climbed a tree. From up in the tree I saw the **teakettle** pick up my coat and put it on! I thought to myself, that's the first time I saw a **teakettle** that wasn't completely **teakettle**!*

Ask the group,

Does anyone have a guess about what "teakettle" stands for in my story?

Call on a volunteer. If your group seems lost, repeat the story, adding more clues (see "Hints"). If your players seem clear that "teakettle" means "bear," but not that it also means "bare," you can state both meanings:

*So I saw a **teakettle** who was wearing clothes. The **teakettle** was not **teakettle**!
The bear was not . . . bare!*

If desired, repeat the entire process with other sample stories. When you think your players are ready to create their own clue stories, say,

Is there someone who can think of two words that sound the same, for us to guess?

Once you choose a pair of words, you need to make a little story with both words in it. Tell us the story, but say "teakettle" instead of your secret words.

If necessary, confer privately with a volunteer, to help the volunteer create a story. You may need to ask questions such as,

How could you get a trunk that you pack clothes in, in the same story with an elephant's trunk?

What could a clothes trunk have to do with an elephant?

Where would an elephant have to be, to come across a clothes trunk?

Repeat with other volunteers, as desired, or until each player has had a turn.

Hints: Giving more hints. If your group seems lost after hearing a story once, then continue or rehash the story. Incorporate clues that are even more obvious, while you watch for signs of recognition in players' faces. Say,

Let me tell you more of the story.

*You see, I had only seen **teakettles** that weren't wearing clothes. They had no clothes, so they had to go **teakettle**.*

*And this **teakettle** had big paws and brown fur. It looked like it just got out of its cave after sleeping all winter. A least it didn't have the grayish fur that marks the most dangerous **teakettle**, the grizzly **teakettle**.*

Say,

Do you know what my story's about?

When someone says "a bear," say,

What did the bear do in my story?

After players retell your story, focus on the other meaning of "teakettle":

*Now, do you know what I meant by saying that the bear was wearing a coat, so it wasn't **teakettle**? It had no clothes, so it had to go **teakettle**.*

Using the term "homonym." It's not necessary to use the term "homonym" to play the game. If your group knows the term, this can be a chance to reinforce it. If your group doesn't know it, you can omit using it.

Once your group has played this game, you have an opportunity to introduce the term: "By the way, there's a term for 'teakettle' words, two or more words that sound the same. They are called homonyms."

Variations: Team teakettle. Have players form teams to create and tell clue stories. Each player continues the story, using "teakettle" at least once. If desired, form teams with as many players as words with the same sound (a team of three might choose "so," "sew," and "sow"); have each player continue the story, adding a new meaning.

Round-robin teakettle. Give a team of three or four players a pair of homonyms, but don't have them prepare a story. Instead, have them improvise a round-robin story. The first player will begin a story using "teakettle" for the homonyms. Each subsequent player must continue the same story, including both of the homonyms in each segment.

Join-in teakettle. Play this as a "join-in" guessing game. Start a "teakettle" story, stopping after you've given enough clues about at least one of the group of homonyms. Ask,

> *Raise your hand if you think you know what "teakettle" means in this story. But don't say it aloud!*

If you want to be sure a player is correct, have the player whisper the secret words in your ear. If few players raise their hands, continue the story, then ask again for a show of hands. Once enough players raise their hands, say,

> *One of you can add to my story. Remember, you have to say "teakettle" for the secret words. Who will tell what happened next?*

Choose a volunteer to add a small segment to the story. Then call on another to add yet another segment. You may need to remind the players to use more than just one of the homonym pair: "Don't forget that teakettle can also be part of an elephant!"

Skills Reinforced

Communication:

Group: Attempting to understand a story in which some words are omitted.

Leader: Pronouncing a story clue clearly to the entire group.

Storytelling:

Leader: Creating a story that contains both words of a homonym pair.

Thinking:

Group: Allowing the marker word "teakettle" to be understood with two meanings.

Leader: Using the marker words "teakettle" in place of the word to be guessed; keeping track of the marker's dual meanings.

Curricular: Reviewing homonyms; exemplifying their dual meanings.

❈ ❈

PUN PUZZLES

Grade levels: Grade 5 and up.

Props needed: Paper and pencil or blackboard *(optional)*.

Complexity: High.

Game type: Guessing a word used in a story. Guessing a topic. Combining elements.

Quick summary: A team of five players chooses a secret sport, profession, or other subject, then creates and tells a story with no apparent relation to the subject. Each player's segment of the story must include one homonym of a word associated with the subject. The others guess the subject.

Directions: Divide the players into teams of five. Say,

> *This is a guessing game. I'm going to think of a subject that has a lot of special words used with it, like a sport, a profession, or a type of place. What's a subject we could use for this game?*

Call on a volunteer. If someone suggests, "the ocean," say,

> *The ocean! Good idea! Normally, your job would be to guess "the ocean," but this time we'll make the puzzle story together. What are lots of words that have to do with the ocean?*

Write down or try to remember the list of words that the players generate, such as: wave, crest, sand, surf, beach, lifeguard, boat, ship, sail, fish, shark, whale, sun. Say,

> *Which of those words has another meaning, or another word that sounds just like it?*

Circle or repeat aloud the words that players mention as having homonyms. It may help for you to clarify the second meaning or word of each homonym pair:

> *Wave! So, we can have a wave at the ocean, and we can wave goodbye to someone.*

> *What's another word from that list that has another meaning or another word that sounds the same? Sand! What's the other meaning of "sand"? Sure, we can sand something with sandpaper.*

You'll end up with a list, such as: wave, crest, sand, beach (beech), ship, sail (sale), whale (wail), and sun (son). Say,

> *We need to choose five of those words that we want to put in our story. Which five should we choose?*

Call on five volunteers to name words, or allow a consensus to develop among the players. Once you have a list of five words, say,

> *Now we have to make a story using the five words "wave," "sand," "ship," "wail," and "beech." What could those five things have to do with one another?*

Call on volunteers for ideas. If one says, "We could sand something out of the wood from a beech tree and then ship it out," say,

> *Great! How can we fit "wave" and "wail" into that story?*

If someone else volunteers, "When we ship it out, we wave goodbye to it, and then we're sad, so we wail," you might say something like:

> *So this will be a story about something we make from the wood of a beech tree. What could we make?*

Perhaps a volunteer will say, "a statue." Complete the sample story:

> *So, here's our story.*

> *One day, we got an order in the mail. A customer wanted us to make a statue out of wood. We went right to work. We got three logs, one of oak, one of **beech**, and one of maple. We carved the statue carefully, and then it was time to **sand** it.*

*When the statue was finished, we liked it so much, we wanted to keep it. But we had promised to **ship** it to our customer, so we called the delivery service. When the delivery person put it on her truck and drove off, we tried to **wave** goodbye to our statue. But we were so sad, all we could do was stand there and **wail**.*

Say,

In the game, I would tell you that story, and you'd have to hear "beech," "sand," "ship," "wave," and "wail" and think, "the ocean" or "being at the beach," or another way of naming the same subject.

Are you ready to try guessing one?

Give a sample story, such as:

*One day, I didn't have time to shop for my groceries, so I tried to go during my lunch hour. I thought, if I do everything right, I have just enough **time out** of the building, if I **rush**.*

*I drove to the store and parked my car. I went running into the store, and then remembered the parking meter. So I went **running back** to the car, put a **quarter** in the meter, and ran back to the store.*

*I bought everything I needed, ran out, and fell **down**. The **sack** broke and everything I bought was ruined. So I got up and rushed back—and I was still late getting back to work!*

Say, "Can anyone guess what my subject was?" If someone says, "football," say, "Why did you say football?" Let the player identify as many of the pun words as the player noticed. To help the players who might have missed the puns, repeat each word, mentioning both of its meanings. If the player missed some, ask, "Were there other football words in my story?" When all the football words have been identified, say, "Yes, you guessed it! My subject was football!"

If desired, tell another sample story. Easy topics include baseball, basketball, computers, the library, and sewing. When the group seems ready, ask,

Would you like to think of your own secret subjects? Each team can think of one subject together, and tell a story together.

First, choose a subject. Second, make a list of words that have to do with it. Third, choose five of those words that have two meanings or other words that sound the same, to use in your story.

Then make up a story using those five words. When you tell the story, each one of you will tell part of your story, and each one will have to use one of the words.

So, if this team was telling the story about football, Hussein would start, and work in the words "time out." Chi Ling would continue the same story, and work in the word "rush." Each would tell part of the same story, and each would use one of the five words.

Are you ready to try it? I'll help you if you get stuck.

Help any teams who need it. When all teams have prepared their stories, ask for a volunteer team to tell its story while the others guess.

Repeat as desired, or until each team has had a turn to tell its story.

Hint: If you or a team tells a story and no one guesses correctly, repeat the story as many times as necessary, making it shorter in subsequent tellings. Shorter stories make the pun words more obvious, thus making it easier to guess.

The first time that no one guesses correctly, say, "Listen to the story again," and repeat it. If no one guesses correctly the second time, say, "I stumped you! When I stump you in this game, I have to tell the story again, even shorter." Tell the story again, about half as long. The football story might come out like this:

> *I thought: I have just enough **time out** of the building to get groceries, if I **rush**.*

> *So I drove to the store and parked. But I forgot the meter, so I went **running back** and put a **quarter** in it.*

> *On my way back, I fell **down** and broke the **sack**. Everything was ruined, and I was late!*

If no one guesses correctly this time, say, "We have a double stumper! I have to tell it again, even shorter." This version of the story might be:

> *I had enough **time out** of the building if I would **rush**.*

> *I went **running back** and put a **quarter** in the meter.*

> *I fell **down** and broke the **sack**.*

If no one guesses this time, repeat once more. You can also add two forms of hints. First, you can say, "The subject is a sport." Second, you can emphasize the pun words as you tell the story. If no one guesses this time, you may have chosen a game too difficult for your group. Drop it for now and go right into a game they already love.

Variations: Teams of four or fewer members (with one word hidden by each player) make it easier for teams to create stories, but more difficult for listeners to guess the subjects. In a very small group, let individuals make their own stories; this makes guessing even harder. Teams of six make creation more difficult, but guessing easier.

You can require that the subject be chosen from curricular topics: a period in U.S. history, a craft or art medium, a theory of the nature of light, a historical period in English poetry, or a type of industry. Choose any type of subject that will have at least a dozen plain-English terms associated with it.

Skills Reinforced

Communication:

> *Leader:* Pronouncing a clue story clearly to the entire group.

Storytelling:

> *Leader:* Creating a story that contains a given set of words. Coordinating a story with team members; maintaining the flow while telling a section of a story.

Thinking: Maintaining dual meanings of homonym pairs.

> *Leader:* Including a word without drawing attention to it. Introducing other words as "red herrings" to which attention is deliberately drawn.

Curricular: Reviewing homonyms; exemplifying one of their dual meanings. Reviewing a sport, profession, or other category.

Group: Isolating words from a story context to find the hidden ones; identifying the category from a hidden set of words.

Expressions and Proverbs

Some sentences do not mean what they seem to say. Their meaning is metaphorical, based on popular culture or folklore. "Hit the road" does not mean to strike the pavement, nor does "Don't cry over spilt milk" have to do with grieving for a breakfast drink.

Because these sentences and phrases cannot be deciphered word by word, they present a particular problem for newcomers to a particular language community. A New Yorker in London will be just as surely perplexed by local expressions and proverbs as will a Cambodian 10-year old newly arrived in New York.

Games not only help players notice the discrepancies between literal and metaphorical meanings, but they also motivate players to comb their mental repertoire for the proverbs and expressions they already know. If a game is played regularly, players may even seek to learn additional expressions, just to use them in the game!

Games in This Section

"Proverb Guessing" uses the hallowed category of proverbs. To play, your group must have a working knowledge of a dozen or more proverbs. This game does not teach what a proverb is, but gives practice in selecting and recognizing proverbs.

"Mish Mash Mush" relies on nonliteral expressions such as "hit the hay," "blow a gasket," or "throw your hat in the ring." Not only must a player recognize an expression to use it in a story, the player must also present both the literal and nonliteral meanings within the same story. This requires a clear understanding of both meanings.

※ ※

PROVERB GUESSING

Grade levels: Grade 5 and up.

Props needed: Slips of paper on which you have written individual proverbs *(optional)*. A blackboard is handy for teaching the game to a new group *(optional)*.

Complexity: High.

Game type: Guessing a word used in a story. Combining elements.

Quick summary: A player (or group of players) hides the words of a proverb in consecutive order in a story. The other players must guess the proverb.

Directions: Say, "You know what proverbs are, right? Let's name some." (If the group is not familiar with proverbs, stop this game now. The group needs to know what a proverb is, and to have a substantial repertory of familiar proverbs.)

Say,

> *I'm going to hide a proverb in my story. This first time, I'll tell you what the proverb is before I start. The proverb will be "A rolling stone gathers no moss."*

Write the proverb on the blackboard. Then continue, saying:

I have to tell a story that uses those words, in order. You have to listen to the story, and guess "A rolling stone gathers no moss." Now, the little words "a," "the," "is," and "it" don't count, so we can cross off "A." But I'll have to hide the other five key words in my story. Ready for the story?

Cross off the "A." Then tell a story using the individual words in the proverb, such as:

*One day, my friend and I are out walking. We come to a big, grassy hill. My friend says, "Let's go **rolling** down it!"*

I say, "Are you crazy? My mother yells at me for getting my clothes dirty!"

But my friend says, "Don't worry so much. She won't even know you were in the woods."

*I'm still not sure this is a good idea. So I say, "She punished me last weekend for just getting a **stone** in my good shoes. Can you imagine what she'll do if I get grass stains on my trousers?"*

*But my friend just **gathers** her skirts around her legs and starts rolling like there's **no** tomorrow. So I join her.*

*Sure enough, when I get home, my mother says, "You'd better have a good reason why you have **moss** on your shirt!"*

I had a good reason, but my mother didn't see it that way. I was grounded for a whole weekend!

Say, "Did you hear the word, 'rolling'?" If no one remembers it, say the first lines again. Then say, "Did anyone hear the word 'rolling' this time?"

Continue asking about each word. If the group looks perplexed, give another sample story. Here are some common proverbs you might use:

- A stitch in time saves nine.
- A watched pot never boils.
- All's well that ends well.
- Birds of a feather flock together.
- Don't count your chickens before they hatch.
- If at first you don't succeed, try, try again.
- Make hay while the sun shines.
- One good turn deserves another.
- Out of sight, out of mind.
- People in glass houses should not throw stones.
- Strike while the iron is hot.
- The pen is mightier than the sword.
- Too many cooks spoil the broth.
- Two heads are better than one.
- Two wrongs do not make a right.

When the group seems ready to go on, say, "Is there a group of four who would like to try to fool us?"

With the four volunteers in a line off to the side, whisper to them, "Your proverb is 'The early bird gets the worm.'" Assign each one of them, in order, one of the four key words, "early," "bird," "gets," and "worm." Say, "Start thinking about a story that could use those four words."

Then speak to the whole group again. Say,

They each have one word to work into their story. So Jerry will have to use the first word in his part of the story. Then Anina will have to work her word into her part of the same story. Do you get how it works?

Have the four volunteers tell in order their four parts of one story. At the end, say, "Did anyone guess the proverb they had?" If so, review where each key word occurred.

If no one guesses correctly, say, "That means we have a stumper! Tell your story again!"

If no one guesses this time, ask each volunteer to make his or her part of the story half as long. Repeat, if necessary, shortening each part until someone guesses.

After a sample story or two, you can divide the whole group into groups of four (or three, or five) and have each group choose its own proverb. If a proverb has more key words than a group has players, have the players take second turns as needed. (For example, have the first player continue the story with the fifth key word, after the fourth player works in the fourth key word.)

Hints: This game is much easier with teams of storytellers than with a single storyteller. Like many similar guessing games, most children find it easier than most adults do.

Before turning the game over to small groups, it may be wise to post the list of little words that don't count: "a," "an," "the," "is," and "it."

Variations: Pass out a slip of paper to each group on which you have written the proverb to use.

If desired, choose proverbs first, then ask for groups of the appropriate sizes. For example, if you choose the proverb, "A word to the wise is sufficient," call for four players; for "People in glass houses shouldn't throw stones," call for seven players.

Instead of proverbs, use quotations from history or literature, or scientific principles (e.g., "An object in motion remains in motion . . . ").

Skills Reinforced

Communication:

Leader: Pronouncing the clue story clearly to the entire group.

Storytelling:

Leader: Creating a story that contains a given set of words. Coordinating a story with team members; maintaining the flow while telling a section of a story.

Thinking: Thinking of the hidden words as parts of a proverb and simultaneously as parts of the story.

Leader: Including a word without drawing attention to it. Introducing other words as "red herrings" to which attention is deliberately drawn.

Curricular: Reviewing proverbs.

Group: Isolating words from a story context to find the hidden ones. Identifying the proverb from the hidden words.

MISH MASH MUSH

Grade levels: Grade 6 and up.

Complexity: Medium.

Game type: Guessing a word used in a story. Guessing a phrase.

Quick summary: A player tells a story in which a character acts out the literal meaning of an idiomatic expression. In telling the story, the player substitutes the phrase "mish mash mush" for the expression. The group guesses the expression.

Directions: Say,

> *This is a guessing game. I think of an expression like "pull my leg"—which means to tease me by saying something that isn't true. It doesn't mean to grab my leg and pull it!*

> *So I tell a story about someone who hears "pull my leg" and thinks it means to actually grab my ankle and pull. But I say "mish mash mush" instead of "pull my leg" and you have to guess what "mish mash mush" means.*

> *Let's try a sample, and see if you can guess this one. I'll tell the whole story; wait for the end to guess what expression I'm thinking of.*

Tell the following sample story:

> *My older brother and our mother used to fight all the time. He was always threatening to leave home, and since he was old enough, he knew our mother couldn't stop him.*

> *One morning, they had a big fight over breakfast. My mother finally said, "You've been threatening to mish mash mush for months. Do it now!"*

> *So my brother went down to the basement, and got a boxing glove. He put it on one hand and came up to the street. He knelt down, and began to punch the asphalt. My mother came out and said, "What are you doing?" He said, "You told me to mish mash mush!"*

Say, "Can anyone guess what expression I meant by 'mish mash mush'?" Call on a volunteer.

If the volunteer guesses correctly, summarize your story. Say,

> *Yes, I was thinking of "hit the road." My mother told my brother to hit the road, meaning to leave home. My brother got a boxing glove and went outside and hit the road—he punched the road with his boxing glove.*

> *I had to tell the story without using the words "hit the road," so I said "street" and "punch the asphalt."*

If, on the other hand, no volunteer has guessed "hit the road," amplify the part of your story in which the character acts out the expression literally:

> *Let me tell you a little more about what happened.*

> *When my mother said, "Mish mash mush," my brother said, "Really? You really want me to mish mash mush?"*

My mother said, "Yes."

My brother looked puzzled, but he got on a boxing glove. Then he went outside to the street. He looked down at the pavement and spoke to the street: "I don't want to hurt you, but my mother told me to do this." He smacked the pavement, hard. Then he called to my mother, "Do I have to mish mash mush again?"

If no one guesses at this point, you have chosen an expression that is unfamiliar to your players, or this game is too hard for them at present. You can say, "I was thinking of 'hit the road.'" If your group still looks puzzled, just drop the game without comment by immediately starting a familiar activity.

When the group has guessed "hit the road," tell another sample story or say, "Would someone like to try one for us to guess?"

Repeat as desired, or until every player has had a turn to tell a "mish mash mush" story.

Hints: Here are some other expressions to use for sample stories:

◆ chew the fat
◆ don't let the cat out of the bag
◆ keep it under your hat
◆ turn the tables
◆ weigh your words carefully

Make sure your sample stories include two uses of "mish mash mush." The first part of your sample story should describe a situation in which the phrase is used idiomatically (the brother is asked to leave home). The second part of your sample story should describe the acting out of the literal meaning.

Before your group begins to tell their own stories, you can make sure they are familiar with a common body of expressions by eliciting a list of expressions they know (or by providing a list of expressions that you then teach them).

If a player tells a story that befuddles the group, have the player repeat the story with added clues. Sometimes a player's story will not make clear the situation in which the expression is used idiomatically. More often, the player needs to describe more fully the literal actions; these may be difficult to describe without using the words of the phrase. You can help by asking, "Can you tell us more of what your brother did with the boxing glove?" After the expression has been revealed, you might also ask, "How could she have made it clearer to us?"

Variations: If your group has the specialized knowledge required, you can require players to use expressions derived from a particular era or activity, such as:

◆ sports, or a particular sport
◆ Greek myths
◆ farming
◆ computers

Adapt this game for guessing idioms that a group is learning in a second language. Players can tell the story in their first language, or in the language of the idiomatic phrase. As a middle ground, the narrative can be in the first language, while the dialogue is all in the second language.

Skills Reinforced

Communication:

> *Group:* Attempting to understand a story in which some words are omitted.

> *Leader:* Pronouncing a story clue clearly to the entire group.

Storytelling:

> *Leader:* Creating a story that contains an idiomatic phrase used first idiomatically and then literally.

Thinking: Maintaining the dual meanings of the idiomatic phrase.

> *Group:* Decoding the marker words.

> *Leader:* Using the marker words, "mish mash mush," in place of the phrase to be guessed; keeping track of the marker's dual meanings.

Curricular: Reviewing idiomatic expressions.

Grammar

If someone were to return now to a language arts classroom after a 50-year absence, the biggest surprise might be that the theory of grammar has changed. Where analyzing parts of speech and sentence diagrams once reigned supreme, new ideas from the science of linguistics have created a fundamental rethinking of the grammar curriculum.

One of the new concepts derives from the theory of "transformational grammar," the idea that we learn to create sentences by discovering how to transform old sentences into new ones.

We learn *words* by hearing them first from others, but we say *sentences* that we have never heard before. We create new sentences by following certain principles for changing sentences we have heard, ending up with sentences just as proper as the ones we started with. Thus, we know that we can substitute any concrete noun for "bicycle" in the sentence "I saw the bicycle," and still have a sentence that makes sense. In fact, we can transform "bicycle" into a noun phrase, as in "I saw the bicycle my brother used to own" or "I saw the seat from the bicycle my brother used to own."

Interestingly, the stories of very young children frequently consist of a series of transformations of a simple sentence.[2] Such stories, in fact, are the basis for one of the games in this section.

Story games can allow players to experience the transformation of sentences in a playful context. In the normal course of events, we create sentences to convey specific meanings. In games, however, we can extend the boundaries of expression by transforming sentences just for fun—and then noticing the meanings we have created.

Such games have been used for recreation, of course. But artists and poets have used similar games for stimulating ideas and for breaking out of deadening habits of expression.[3] At the very least, such games give us an opportunity to notice our own grammatical power: the power to create unlimited meanings through simple sentence transformations.

Games in This Section

"Would You Believe?" sets up a series of simple sentences that can be transformed by substituting action verbs. Based on the spontaneous stories of young children, this game is essentially a formula that makes it easy for players to create humorous images.

"Places, Persons, and Things," on the other hand, makes greater demands of two kinds. First, it asks players to contribute three different kinds of nouns (corresponding to the three parts of the classic definition of a noun), which are then substituted in a simple sentence. (In variations, other parts of speech are also used.) Second, it asks players to make sense of the silly sentence that results—by creating a story. The sentence comes first, followed by the meaning, followed finally by the story that explains it.

Games in Other Sections

These two games give one player a chance to make a series of substitutions in a simple sentence:

"Janey Jo" (p. 6)

"Wolf, Are You Ready?" (p. 4)

These games involve transforming a whole story through simple substitutions:

"Occupations" (p. 97)

"You're Shaking Me Up" (p. 31)

In "Guess the Voice" (p. 17), the leader transforms a simple sentence ("How did the _____ help the _____?"), leaving another player to create a story that answers the resulting question.

"Janey Jo" (p. 6)

"Wolf, Are You Ready?" (p. 4)

"Occupations" (p. 97)

"You're Shaking Me Up" (p. 31)

❈ ❈

WOULD YOU BELIEVE?

Grade levels: Preschool through grade 2.

Complexity: Low.

Game type: Filling in a plot.

Quick summary: Players substitute verbs in a one-stanza story designed to produce non-sensical images.

Directions: Say, "This is a very silly, little story about a ball, a tree, and a dog. But we can make it even sillier. Are you ready to hear it?"

Speak these lines (or chant them like a poem, or sing them loosely to the tune of "Reuben, Reuben," or "Red River Valley," or sing them to the tune given on p. 153):

Would you believe that I threw the ball?

Would you believe the ball threw the tree?

Would you believe the tree threw the dog?

Would you believe the dog threw me?

Say, "Did you hear what I did to the ball?" Unless your group is certain that you threw the ball, say "Listen again!" and repeat the chanted lines. When your group responds "you threw it," say, "What else could I do to the ball?" Call on a volunteer.

Suppose the volunteer says, "You could kick it."

Then say, "I'm going to say the lines again, but this time I'll say 'kicked' every time I said 'threw' before. You can say it with me if you like." Speak or sing again:

Would you believe that I kicked the ball?

Would you believe the ball kicked the tree?

Would you believe the tree kicked the dog?

Would you believe the dog kicked me?

Say, "Try to say it with me this time." Repeat again.
Repeat as desired.

Hint: If your players do not seem to be enjoying the silly images in this story/verse, they may need help imagining them. Share your enjoyment of their silliness by saying something like, "Can you imagine a tree kicking a dog? I think that's silly."

Variation: After exploring a few transitive verbs that work with "ball" as their direct object, substitute another word for "ball." For example, substitute the word "car," and let your players explore another family of verb possibilities:

Would you believe that I drove the car?

Would you believe the car drove the tree?

Would you believe the tree drove the dog?

Would you believe the dog drove me?

Skills Reinforced

Communication: Saying chanted lines in unison.

Leader: Pronouncing a one-word contribution clearly to the entire group.

Storytelling:

Group: Imagining the objects mentioned in the chanted lines to be performing the action suggested by each verb.

Curricular: Experiencing the category of transitive verbs. Experiencing word substitution.

※ ※

PLACES, PERSONS, AND THINGS

Grade levels: Kindergarten through grade 5.

Props needed: Three slips of paper (or file cards) and a writing implement for each player. Three hats, boxes, or bags in which to collect the slips (*optional*).

Complexity: High.

Game type: Combining elements.

Quick summary: A player selects at random three words or phrases (a place, a person, and a thing), then puts them into a sentence framework: "I went to (the place) to ask (the person) for (the object)." The player creates a story that explains the sentence.

Directions: Pass out one piece of paper (or one file card) to each player. Say,

To play this game, everyone writes the name of a place on this piece of paper. It can be a place on a map, like "Chicago," but it's usually more fun if it's a general place, like "my living room" or "a riverbank" or "a laundromat." Write the name of any general kind of place on your paper.

After each player has written the name of a place, collect all the pieces of paper and put them in a hat or box. Pass out another piece of paper (or a file card of a different color) to each player. Say,

On this piece of paper, everyone writes a kind of person. You could write someone's name, but this game is more fun if you write "my sister" or "the world's best basketball player" or "a truck driver."

After each player has written the name of a person, collect these pieces of paper and put them in a second hat or box. Pass out a third piece of paper (or a file card of a third color) to each player. Say,

On this last piece of paper, everyone writes the name of a thing, such as "the boot" or "my father's handkerchief," or "a pack of gum."

After each player has written the name of a thing, collect these pieces of paper and put them in a third hat or box. Say,

I'll play first. I draw one piece of paper from each hat. Let's see what I got.

Draw one slip of paper from each hat or box. Read them aloud to the group. If the slips say "the laundromat," "my favorite rock star," and "a glass of orange juice," say,

Each of us gets a sentence that says, "I went to a place to ask a person for a thing." But we use the words we draw for the place, the person, and the thing.

My sentence works out to be, "I went to the laundromat to ask my favorite rock star for a glass of orange juice."

My job now is to make a story that explains that sentence.

Create a simple story that ends in or explains the sentence made from the papers you drew. For example, you might say,

One day, my little sister was sick. I asked her if she wanted anything, and she said she just wanted a glass of orange juice.

I said, "No problem!" I went to the refrigerator. But we were out of orange juice. I said, "No problem! I'll just go to the store." It was late, but the store would be open for a few more minutes. So I went out on the street.

I was walking by the laundromat, and inside I saw someone who looked just like my favorite rock star. I couldn't believe it! I just stood there looking at her for half an hour. She was just sitting there on top of a dryer.

Suddenly, I remembered the orange juice. Oh, no! The store had already closed. The only place left to get orange juice was the juice machine inside the laundromat.

I went inside, and saw that it really was her! I just stood there looking at her. Finally, she said, "Can I help you?"

I stuttered, "Uh, uh, uh. I want some orange juice for my sister. She's sick."

The rock star smiled. She had a pile of quarters on the dryer. She took some, put them in the juice machine, and punched the button for orange juice. Then she handed me the can that came out and said, "Here. Tell your sister it's my treat."

I grabbed the orange juice and ran home. But my sister never believed who bought her the orange juice!

Say,

Do you get the idea? Who wants to try it?

Choose a volunteer to draw a slip of paper from each hat or box and make a story from the resulting sentence.

Repeat as desired, or until each player who wants a turn has had one.

Hints: It may help to have everyone draw slips of paper before asking for volunteers. Players may be more willing to volunteer after they have seen their slips of paper and realize that they do, in fact, have an idea for a story.

It may help to write out the basic sentence so that all players can see it: "I went to _____ to ask _____ for _____."

If you don't have hats or boxes for the three piles of papers, just use three desk tops or counter areas, or have three volunteers hold them in their arms or laps. If you use three different colors of paper or file cards, you can place them all in one hat or box or pile; then each player can take one of each color.

If a player can't think of a story to explain a sentence, ask questions that explain an element or relate any two of the three elements, such as,

- ◆ What are some reasons you might desperately need a glass of orange juice?
- ◆ What are some things a rock star could be doing in a laundromat?
- ◆ What are some ways you could get a glass of orange juice in a laundromat?

If your players might have trouble thinking of or writing down the names of places, persons, or things—or if they might have trouble knowing what you mean by a "general place" or a "kind of person" or a "thing"—you can play this game with slips of paper you fill out yourself in advance. Some suitable places might include:

- ◆ the school cafeteria
- ◆ the kitchen
- ◆ my bedroom
- ◆ the local playground
- ◆ a video arcade
- ◆ a fire station
- ◆ our baseball field

- ◆ a deserted beach
- ◆ a spooky forest
- ◆ a fancy restaurant
- ◆ a haunted house
- ◆ an abandoned rowboat
- ◆ a crowded bus station
- ◆ the biggest circus tent I ever saw

Here are some people:

- ◆ my mother
- ◆ a police officer
- ◆ a teacher
- ◆ the principal
- ◆ a baby
- ◆ Michael Jordan
- ◆ President Lincoln
- ◆ a famous model

- ◆ the baker
- ◆ my brother
- ◆ the football coach
- ◆ a grouchy neighbor
- ◆ a stranger
- ◆ the woman in the scary-looking hat

Finally, these might be suitable things:

- a magazine
- my t-shirt
- a basketball
- a pencil
- half a glass of milk
- a bicycle
- a page of stickers

- a 20-dollar bill
- a fork
- a pizza
- a handful of buttons
- some thumbtacks
- the newspaper
- the secret password

In these sample lists, each written item is a noun phrase. Young players may just write a single word; older ones can be encouraged to write longer, more descriptive phrases, such as "the last dock still not underwater," "a tiny gnome who was holding a huge basket on his shoulder," or "a bicycle without any tires."

Variations: Require that the place be a geographic location (or even a kind of geographic location, such as a place within a desert or a river system, the name of a place within a specified region, or a place important to a particular historical subject).

Require that the person (or object) be from a specified historical period or event, or from a specified work of literature.

Require that the object be from a particular category, whether chosen from social studies or science. Examples include objects made of artificial material, objects that require water in their manufacture, objects found in the home, objects that float, or objects commonly associated with a specified sport or occupation.

To play this game with kindergarten students or others who can't write easily, gather the three nouns as oral suggestions from the whole group. Then guide the group in creating a story to explain the resulting sentence.

Write three lists of 13 items (one each of places, persons, and things) on a blackboard or other writing area visible to all players. Have each player draw a playing card for each list, and use the item in the list suggested by the number of the card (e.g., the player who draws an ace uses the first item, the player who draws a king uses the thirteenth). Or use shorter lists, with the appropriate portion of the deck of cards. Or create your own deck of number cards, to use with lists of any length you choose.

Divide your group into three equal groups. To each player in the first group, whisper a phrase describing a place; to each player in the second group, whisper a phrase describing a person; to each player in the third, whisper a phrase describing an object. Have the players form teams of three, each team including one member from each of the three groups. Each team must then create a story explaining the sentence which is formed by using the team's three whispered words.

Create a new basic sentence that uses the same three elements, such as:

- I went to (a place) to get (an object) for (a person).
- I went to (a place) to sell (an object) to (a person).
- When I was in (a place), (a person) asked me to give (the person) (an object).
- I followed (a person) to (a place), dragging along (an object).

Create a new basic sentence that uses different elements, such as:

- I tried to stop (a person) from (transitive verb)-ing (an object).
- The first time I ever (verb, past tense), I was afraid (a person) would (transitive verb) me.

- I was supposed to (transitive verb) (an object), but it was (spatial preposition) (an object).
- (Article) (adjective) (object) (transitive verb, past tense) (number) (objects) (adverb).

Skills Reinforced

Storytelling:

Leader: Improvising a fantasy story explaining the arbitrarily generated sentence.

Thinking:

Leader: Finding connections between the three randomly selected words.

Curricular: Reviewing three categories of nouns. Experiencing word substitution.

Group: Choosing and writing a noun from each of three categories.

REFERENCES

1. For musical activities that teach rhyming, see Doug Lipman, *We All Go Together.* Phoenix, AZ: Oryx Press, 1994. Pages 115–20.
2. Sutton-Smith, Brian. *The Folkstories of Children.* Philadelphia: University of Pennsylvania Press, 1981. Pages 8, 48–50, 54, 69–72, 82.
3. Brotchie, Alastair, comp. *Surrealist Games.* Boston: Shambhala, 1993. Pages 10–12.

CHAPTER 3
Exploring Places, Periods, and Peoples

▨ ▨ ▨

SECTIONS IN THIS CHAPTER

The subjects treated in this chapter are geography, history, literature, multiculturalism, and social studies. They represent the study of humans: our distribution over our planet, our past, our literature, our cultural diversity, and our institutions.

Story games can support such studies in three major ways. First, they can help reinforce the details of these subjects: the names, dates, categories, and slogans. This kind of learning requires repetition—and repetition might as well be fun.

Second, story games can encourage players to make connections between a subject and their own lives, to remember and tell relevant stories from their personal experience.

Third, story games can reinforce the principles of these disciplines: the concepts, structures, patterns, and relationships. A story game may not be the ideal way to introduce such a principle, but it can be an ideal way to give practice in it. In playing a game like "Inventions" or "Squabble Body," for example, a player becomes an active wielder of the tools of history or multiculturalism.

Geography

Geography is rich in facts. There is such a fascinating abundance of "who," "what," and "where" in geography, that we often neglect the equally fascinating "why?"

The geography games in this book, like most geography education, work more on the level of details than of ideas. Some games give players a chance to remember and recognize geographical names; others also allow players to incorporate their knowledge of a place's characteristics.

One variation of "Cross-Picture Puzzles" (p. 21), however, allows players to apply their imaginations to the stuff of geography, rather than use the details of geography to generate the stuff of imagination.

Further, any game that uses place names can involve some geographical concepts if you require that the place names be chosen from a particular category—such as places on peninsulas, or places with a relationship to a major river.

Game in This Section

"Towns and Counties" lets players practice their knowledge of the most common details of geography: place names. Like most guessing games, it encourages players to review facts apart from the facts' original context.

Games in Other Sections

In the rhyming-word game "Fuddy Duddy" (p. 49), you can require players to use a place name as the first word of the rhyming pair, as in "Seattle battle" or "Bahamas pajamas." This variation is challenging, because not every place name rhymes with a common word. A player who has thought of a rhyming pair, however, will have created something memorable. Fifteen years after playing a form of this game in Rhode Island one day, for example, I still remember being stumped by "Woonsocket moon-rocket."

The following two games have variations that allow players to use their knowledge about a place, not just its name:

"Occupations" (p. 97)

"Places, Persons, and Things" (p. 67)

If you use photos from a particular geographic area in "Cross-Picture Puzzles" (p. 20), players can make stories based either on their emotional associations with the places or on their accumulated knowledge about them. Players will, therefore, have an opportunity to apply their imaginations directly to their geographical knowledge.

※ ※

TOWNS AND COUNTIES

Grade levels: Grades 4-9.

Props needed: A blackboard or other visible writing medium is helpful for teaching the game the first time *(optional).*

Complexity: Medium.

Game type: Guessing a word used in a story.

Quick summary: Players break a place name into syllables, then "hide" the individual syllables as words in a story.

Directions: Say, "This is a guessing game. You have to guess the name of a place. This time, I'll tell you the name of the place you're going to guess, first: 'Boston.'"

Write "Boston" on the board. Say, "I'm going to hide the word 'Boston' in my story. First, I'll chop 'Boston' into syllables." Draw a line between the "s" and "t."

Say, "We'll chop 'Boston' into 'boss' and 'ton.' I'll tell you a story that has the word 'boss' in it first, and then later has the word 'ton.' You'll hear them, and put them together to get 'Boston.' Are you ready? Here's my story."

Tell the following story, or something like it:

> *I quit my job today. You know why? I'm mad at my boss. Every day, she gives me too much work. Yesterday, I complained. So today, I walked in, and she gave me more than ever! I mean, there was a ton of work for me to do. So I quit!*

Say, "Did you hear the word 'boss'? Where was it?" Call on a volunteer, who might say, "You said you were mad at your boss!" Say, "Good! Did you hear the word 'ton'?" Call on another player, who might say, "You had a ton of work to do."

Say, "Okay, this time I won't tell you the answer ahead of time. This will be another two-syllable place name. Are you ready?"

Tell the following story, or something like it:

> *One day, I decided I wanted some new shoes. So I went to the mall. The shoe stores were all closed, so I decided to have lunch, instead. I didn't want Burger King or Papa Gino's, so I ate at York Steak House. I walked home, and got blisters from my same old shoes!*

Say, "Does anyone have any guesses?" Call on someone. If, as usually happens, someone guesses "New York," say, "Did you hear the word 'new'? Where was it? What about the word 'York'? Where was that?"

If, on the other hand, the group is stumped, say eagerly, "Good! We have a stumper! I'll tell it again, but shorter." Tell it again, something like this:

> *I went to get some new shoes, but all I did was eat lunch at York Steak House.*

Repeat this shorter version, if no one guesses. If no one guesses again, make it even shorter:

> *I wanted new shoes. I ate at York Steak House.*

If necessary, repeat, emphasizing the words "new" and "York," until someone guesses correctly.

Give another sample story, if desired. Local place names are the easiest to guess.

Divide the players into groups of two (or three). Say, "Your job is to think of a two-syllable (or three-syllable) place name, then hide it in a story. Each person in your group will get one syllable. So, if Carla and I are partners and we chose 'New York,' she could get the word 'new.' She'd start off a story, maybe about getting a new bicycle. Then I'd finish the same story she started, working in the word 'York.' Maybe I'd say I rode my bicycle to get a York Peppermint Patty. Are you ready? Get in your groups and choose a place name."

After giving the groups a few moments to choose a place name and then create a story from it, ask for a group of players to volunteer to tell its story to the entire group. After the story has been finished, have the others guess the hidden place name. If the group is stumped, have the tellers repeat their story. If the group is still stumped, declare a "double stumper!" Have the tellers repeat their story, but half as long. If necessary, have them repeat again, but one-quarter as long.

Continue with as many stories by players as desired.

Hints: Most children find this game much easier than do most adults.

Make yourself available privately to help groups of players brainstorm place names. Many players get stuck because they try to evaluate an idea before they say it aloud. If this seems to be the case with a group, encourage the players to say many place names out loud without pausing to decide whether the names have the correct number of syllables or would make good game words. After the group has listed five or ten possible place names, then encourage group members to go back over their list and choose which ones might be suitable.

Once groups have agreed on a place name and a way to divide it into syllables, repeat the syllable-words to them (e.g., "How could we make up a story about someone who wants to win something and a chess game and someone who will stir something?" for "win-chess-stir"—Winchester). Once group members come up with a story concept, help them agree which player will take each syllable.

If a group of three comes up with a four-syllable place name, the first player can have a second turn in the story, after the third player's turn.

Variations: Have players tell solo stories. This makes guessing more difficult, because the story is not broken up into segments that each have one syllable of the place name.

Choose a different body of proper nouns instead of place names. Use names of people from the Bible (e.g., "Eye-sick" for Isaac), or names of characters from Greek myths (e.g., "Hair-uh" for Hera). Alternatively, limit the place names to those from a particular part of the world or to those with a particular geographical feature.

Skills Reinforced

Communication:

Group: Listening for multiple, separated clues.

Leader: Pronouncing the clue words clearly to the entire group.

Storytelling:

Leader: Creating a story that contains a given set of words. Coordinating a story with team members; maintaining the flow while telling a section of a story. Embroidering the story as desired.

Thinking:

Leader: Including a word without drawing attention to it. Introducing other words as "red herrings" to which attention is deliberately drawn.

Curricular: Reviewing place names. Isolating one-syllable words from the story context to find the hidden ones. Identifying the place name by assembling the hidden words as syllables of a longer word.

Maintaining the declined form of a cue word (e.g., if the word is "go," the teller can't say "he went," but must recast the sentence: "he decided to go.")

History

Many of the games in this book can be used in the study of history. The gamut is well represented, from games that require knowledge of simple facts to games that allow the imaginative application of historical principles.

Games in This Section

"History Mystery" lets players work with the implications of a historical fact. The storyteller works from the fact to the implications, while the group is given the implications and must infer the fact. Unlike most history exercises, it lets players apply their knowledge of history by thinking about what is historically impossible rather than what is historically correct.

"Inventions" puts broad principles of history into action. In this game, players describe an unreal invention and then imagine its historical consequences. As a result, the game allows players to apply the historical principles of technological change.

Games in Other Sections

These games have variations that make use of simple historical facts, quotations, or lists of words:

"Guess the Voice" (p. 17)

"Hide the Words" (p. 43)

"Proverb Guessing" (p. 60)

"The Sea Is Getting Stormy" (p. 112)

In variations to these games, players can replicate actions from a historical event:

"Do It Your Way" (p. 84)

"The Back Speaks" (p. 25)

Variations of these games allow players to ask questions about a historical event, or to create altered versions of an event:

"I Was Present!" (p. 119)

"Questions and Answers" (p. 87)

In playing the historical variations of these games, players apply their knowledge of historical concepts:

"Occupations" (p. 97) (Use an occupation from a historical period or unit of study.)

"Spaceship" (p. 114) (Use a multi-part object or process from history.)

In "My Mother, Your Mother" (p. 99), players can be required (in a variation) to tell how a historical conflict was resolved. To do so, players must identify the conflict and resolution in the historical event.

In a variation to "Because" (p. 116), players make a statement about a given historical period. Even if the statement is whimsical, players must call on their knowledge of history to give a "because" statement and a "therefore" statement.

If you use photos or drawings from a particular historical period in "Cross-Picture Puzzles" (p. 20), players can make stories based either on their emotional associations with the period or on their accumulated knowledge about it. Players will, therefore, have an opportunity to make imaginative use of their historical knowledge.

HISTORY MYSTERY

Grade levels: Grade 5 and up.

Complexity: High.

Game type: Filling in a plot. Guessing a fact.

Quick summary: Starting with a historical fact, a player creates a mini-mystery story featuring a fraudulent, historically impossible object. The group tries to identify the historical contradiction implied by the object.

Directions: To solve this sample mystery, your players need to know that the first Spanish expedition to North America and the Caribbean was Columbus's voyage in 1492. (If they don't know that, use a different sample story based on facts they do know.)

Say,

I'm going to let you solve a History Mystery.

My cousin doesn't know much about history. People are always trying to sell him things that they say are old and valuable.

Just last week, he was all excited about a treasure map someone wanted to sell him. He said, "It's a map of treasure that was buried by Spanish pirates in the Caribbean. No one has ever found it. I'll be rich! And I can buy this map for only $1,000."

I said, "How long has the treasure been lying there?"

He said, "This map is a thousand years old!"

I said, "Don't waste your money. The map is a fake."

How did I know?

Call on a volunteer to solve the mystery. When someone correctly solves it, say,

Good detective work! You knew that Columbus sailed in 1492, and that his voyage was the first Spanish expedition to North America. That meant that no Spanish pirates could have been in the Caribbean a thousand years ago. So they could not have buried the treasure that long ago.

If this deductive reasoning does not seem comprehensible to your group, this game is too hard for them. Drop the game without comment by starting a familiar activity.

If the group seems to follow this reasoning, however, say,

Would you like to make up your own History Mystery? Let's make one up together.

First, we need a history fact. Who knows a fact we could use for our mystery?

Call on a volunteer. If the volunteer says, "George Washington was the first president of the United States," say,

Great! George Washington was the first president of the United States. That's our history fact.

To make up a mystery, we need to think of an object—like the treasure map—that's impossible because George Washington was the first president. What object could not possibly exist, because George was our first president?

Call on volunteers for ideas of impossible objects. To facilitate brainstorming, accept all ideas enthusiastically. Some ideas might be:

◆ a coin with the inscription, "Thomas Jefferson—Our First President."
◆ a letter to George Washington saying, "I hope you will be president some day," signed, "The President of the United States of America."
◆ an election poster saying, "Vote for a change! Let's get a different president. Vote for George Washington!"
◆ A letter from Martha Washington saying, "I'm sad that my husband never lived to see the Constitution ratified."

Choose one idea to work with, or have the group choose one. You might say, "Which of these ideas should we use for our mystery?" If the group chooses the election poster, say,

Great! Now we have an impossible object. All we need now for our mystery is to make a little story about our cousin wanting to buy this election poster.

To stretch out the mystery, let's make it sound like a possible real poster, first. We could ask our cousin a question, and then learn what makes this poster impossible. For a change, let's make our cousin female this time.

Tell the story yourself (unless you think someone in your group could tell it successfully at this point):

My cousin doesn't know much about history. People are always trying to sell her things that they say are old and valuable.

Just last week, she was all excited about an election poster someone wanted to sell her. She said, "It's an authentic poster from George Washington's first election campaign! And I can buy this antique poster for only $1,000. It's worth much more than that. I'll be rich!"

I said, "What does the poster say?"

She said, "It says, 'Vote for a change! Let's get a different president. Vote for George Washington!' It's the only poster like it still existing!"

I said, "Don't waste your money. The poster is a fake."

How did I know?

Call on a volunteer to restate the answer: George Washington was the first president, so he couldn't have been running against someone who was already president. Say,

Do you see how to make this kind of mystery? We start with a fact, then we make up an impossible object, and then we make a story about our cousin wanting to buy the object. At the end, we say, "It's a fake! How did I know?

If desired, stop for the day at this point. Or create another sample story with the group. Or ask a volunteer or group to create another mystery:

Is there someone who would like to make up your own History Mystery?

Repeat as desired, or until each player or team has had a turn.

Hints: Don't be afraid to remain in the storyteller role for several sessions. Create your own mysteries using facts your group is likely to know.

Making up a History Mystery requires the coordination of several types of thinking: the ability to remember a historical fact, the ability to make deductions from that fact, the ability to imagine an object that sounds plausible but is contradicted by the previous deductions, and the ability to construct a story based on all that previous thinking. As a result, your group may need to learn this game over a period of days, weeks, or months. Depending on the age and sophistication of your players, they may learn better by example than by being told what deductive steps to follow.

If you tell a sample mystery that stumps your group, add hints in story form. For example, you might add hints to the pirate story this way:

*When my cousin said the map was 1,000 years old, it made me suspicious.
So I said, "Are you saying that Spanish pirates buried this treasure in the
Caribbean 1,000 years ago?"*

My cousin said, "Yes! Imagine how valuable the treasure must be by now!"

*I said, "So what year does that mean the treasure was buried? 1994 minus 1,000.
Wait a minute! If that map is real, then Spanish pirates were in the Caribbean
in the year 994!*

*"But when did the Spanish arrive in the Caribbean? Let me remember my
history. The first Spanish voyage to the Caribbean was by Columbus. That was
in . . . .Oh, oh! That map is a fake!"*

Variations: Require that the historical facts come from a particular area of historical study: a period in history, the history of trade or technology, or the history of democratic institutions.

To make the mysteries more challenging to solve, allow the objects to be either possible or impossible. Then the group must evaluate the object without knowing in advance whether it is possible or not.

To make the mysteries even more challenging to create and to solve, specify that your cousin wants to know which of three objects to buy. Let one or two of the objects described in the story be possible historical objects. Now the group must deduce which objects are possible, and which are certainly fraudulent.

Let the stories become more elaborate. Add one or more of the following elements:

◆ a description of the object's supposed history (e.g., it was unearthed after a tragic fire destroyed a French cathedral, revealing a secret vault below ground.)

◆ a description of the person offering the object to your cousin and the situation in which the offer was made (e.g., my cousin helped an old man cross the street and get home in a rainstorm; when they arrived at the old man's run-down mansion, he said, "You are so kind, I will make you an offer of this heirloom.")

◆ a description of the detective who solved the mystery (e.g., my cousin called on Pompei Khan, the great history detective; she had to wait outside Pompei's office for three days while a constant stream of history professors and politicians came and went, but at last, she was admitted to Pompei's incredibly messy office. . . .)

◆ a crime committed by one of several suspects; the guilty suspect is identified via the impossible object

Skills Reinforced

Communication:

Leader: Pronouncing a story clearly to the entire group. Maintaining a sequence of facts to reveal.

Storytelling:

Leader: Improvising a story presenting the chosen mystery.

Thinking:

Leader: Starting with a true statement, producing a statement that is implied to be false.

Curricular: Reviewing historical facts and their implications.

INVENTIONS

Grade levels: Kindergarten and up.

Props needed: File cards or slips of paper, plus pencils *(optional)*.

Complexity: High.

Game type: Filling in a plot.

Quick summary: A player contributes an idea for a fantastic invention. The others create a story detailing what the invention would make easier in the world, what difficulties it would create, and how society would change as a result.

Directions: Say,

> *This is a game about wonderful inventions. Who can think of an invention that doesn't really exist yet, but maybe you wish would be invented?*

Call on a volunteer. If the volunteer says, "Beaming people from one place to another," say,

> *Great! Can you tell me how it would work?*

If the volunteer adds details, restate them for the whole group. Continue:

> *First, let's imagine what this invention would make easier. Any ideas?*

Call on some volunteers. Their ideas might include:

◆ People could go on vacation anywhere in the world.
◆ If your friends moved away, you could still see them every week.
◆ People could commute to work anywhere in the world.
◆ We wouldn't need as many stores, because people could go to one big store in New York or Los Angeles just as easily as one by their house.

Validate all ideas. Then say,

> *Great! Now, let's imagine what this invention might make harder in the world. Who can think of something?*

Call on other volunteers. Their ideas might include:

◆ People would get tired out because they'd keep going to everything they ever wanted to see.
◆ If there was just one big store of each kind, it might get so crowded it would be terrible.
◆ If people lived on a mountain top and their beamer broke down, they'd be stuck.
◆ People would probably start to live on top of Mt. Everest and it would get crowded and wouldn't be pretty anymore.
◆ Robbers could use beamers to steal from your house if you were gone for just five minutes, and you couldn't keep them out.

Validate all these ideas, too. Summarize the thoughts that have been given. Then say,

> *Now let's imagine how the world will change because of this invention. What will change physically? Will people act differently? Will there be changes at home? At work? Will the world be more peaceful, or less?*

Call on volunteers, especially those who may not have spoken yet. They may say things such as,

- People won't live in cities anymore. They'll spread out evenly over the whole world.
- We won't need cars, so we won't need roads anymore, either.
- People will carry their valuables with them at all times, because robbers could get them so easily.
- People will stay friends for their whole lives.

Now, form all these ideas into a simple story. Say,

Let's tell the story of the beamer invention. We'll start this way:

Once, in the year 2,000, someone invented a beamer. This meant that people could travel anywhere in the world, instantly.

As soon as people had this invention, they saw that some things were much easier.

For example, one thing that was easier was. . .

Who will say one thing that was easier?

Call on a volunteer to continue the narrative, rephrasing one of the thoughts already spoken (or stating a new thought). The volunteer might say,

One thing that was easier was that people could go to any store in the world to get exactly what they wanted.

Call on two more volunteers to add things that became easier. The second volunteer might say,

And then people didn't have to commute for long hours. They could live far from their jobs and still get to work instantly.

And the third might add,

Soon, people were living in places where no one had lived before. All they needed was a beamer, and they could live on Mt. Everest or on a desert island.

Resume the narrative yourself:

But in time, people noticed some disadvantages of the beamer. For example . . .

Call on three more volunteers to provide narrative of three disadvantages. Their three contributions might be:

For example, there was no excuse for not going everywhere. People got exhausted going to Disneyland after work one day, and skiing on the Alps the next morning before beaming to the office.

. . . And some places got so crowded, it was a three-hour wait to get beamed back out. The most beautiful places in the world were always crowded.

. . . And thieves got richer and richer. Robbers could beam into bank vaults. They could beam into jewelry stores at night. They could go into anybody's home without opening a door. No place was safe.

Begin the final section of the story:

Fifty years after the invention of the beamer, the world was different in many ways. For example . . .

Call on three final volunteers to add how the world changed. They might say,

For example, there were no cities anymore. People built houses in the desert, on mountain tops, on tropical islands.

. . . And people stayed in touch with all their friends, because they could always beam over for a quick video game.

. . . And everyone always carried huge backpacks of all their money, their jewelry, and their important papers. They never knew when someone would beam into their house and steal everything. They were always scared, because someone might beam up behind them and hurt them. The world was a nervous place.

If the final player does not give the story what sounds like an ending, you can add a one-line ending, or call on a volunteer to "wrap it up."

If desired, repeat. Or break into teams (see "Variations") and let players create their own Inventions stories. Since these stories take time to develop, one story a day may be enough.

Hints: Some groups may need you to suggest an invention, at least the first time. Try one of these:

- ◆ a machine that can turn a book into a sandwich
- ◆ a car that could drive itself wherever you want to go
- ◆ a house that you could shrink down and carry in your pocket

Encouraging brainstorming. Inventions Stories require considerable speculation, so it's important to give players a chance to think out loud. Give extra time and attention to the brainstorming aspect of this game (i.e., imagining what would get easier, what would get harder, and how the world would change).

In general, your role is to help players discover their own differing ideas, not to get players to think like you do.

Noticing differing concepts. While players are brainstorming, you may notice that different players have different concepts about the invention under discussion. For example, Yusef may say, "robbers will be able to beam into any house," and Deirdre may say, "every neighborhood will have a receiving station." You might respond to this contradiction by saying something like this:

That's interesting! Yusef, are you imagining that the beamer lets you go anywhere? Deirdre, are you imagining that you need another beaming machine to beam to?

You have several options for responding to these different concepts. You can ask for clarification from the player who thought of the invention; you can allow the group to decide which version they want to use in the story; or you can have different teams or individuals pursue separate stories about the different versions of the invention.

Stimulating brainstorming through questions. If the brainstorming lags, you may be able to stimulate discussion by asking additional questions, such as:

- ◆ Would this invention require energy to run? What form of energy? How much? What would be the effect on the world economy of this energy demand?
- ◆ Would this invention be free? Or could only some people afford one? How might people who couldn't afford one respond to those who have one? Would some countries have them while others did not?
- ◆ What laws might get passed controlling the use of this invention?
- ◆ What new inventions might people try to make in response to problems or opportunities created by this invention?

Variations: Have each player write a brief description of a future invention on a file card or piece of paper. Put all the descriptions in a hat, and have each player (or team of players) pull out one invention to make a story about.

Divide the group into two teams. The first team will decide on an invention and describe it aloud to the other team. The second team will agree on three things that the invention would make easier. Then the first team will agree on three things that the invention will make harder. Finally, the second team will agree on three changes in society that will result. Repeat, reversing the roles of the two teams.

Divide the group into three teams. Have players write descriptions of inventions on paper. Select one piece of paper randomly. Have the first team agree on three things the chosen invention would make easier; the second team, three things that would be harder; the third team, three resulting changes in society.

Divide the group into teams of three. The first player in each team will select a written description of an invention from the hat, then say what the invention would make easier. The second player will say what it would make harder, and the third will describe the resulting changes in society.

Alternatively, use teams of nine players. Each team will choose an invention (by a chance selection of a written description or by agreement). The first three players will each say one thing that the invention would make easier; the second three will each say one thing that would be harder; the final three will each say one change that would result in society.

Instead of an invention, describe some other technological change in society. What would happen if we suddenly discovered an unlimited source of low-cost energy? What if all metal were suddenly to disappear from the earth? What if a new discovery allowed people to memorize in a week all the information they could possibly need in a lifetime? Use the same structure of things made easier, things made harder, and changes in society.

Alternatively, describe some other change and its effects. What if a new continent emerged in the Pacific? What if gold were discovered in the Antarctic? What if the birth rate among humans suddenly became one-quarter of its current rate? What if it quadrupled?

Skills Reinforced

Communication:

Leader: Pronouncing a story clearly to the entire group. Coordinating a story with team members; maintaining the flow while telling a section of a story.

Storytelling:

Leader: Improvising a story that chronicles the creation and effects of a fantasy invention.

Thinking:

Group: Thinking of the advantages and disadvantages of an imaginary invention. Thinking of its implications for society.

Leader: Summarizing the contributions of several players in a story.

Curricular: Reviewing and applying knowledge of social change mechanisms.

Literature

Story games make it easy for players to review works of literature. Several games in this collection start with a familiar story—which can be a folktale, short story, illustrated book, novel, epic, or poem—and change it playfully, thus making review enjoyable.

The deeper study of literature deals with meaning—with making personal connections to a story, with speculating on an author's intentions, and with learning how meanings are communicated through form and content. Since so many of the games in this book involve the creation of stories, players gain firsthand experience as authors. Many of the games encourage players to experiment with particular story forms.

Games in This Section

In "Do It Your Way," players act out the actions within a piece of literature, thus gaining personal, kinesthetic experience of the literary work.

In "Questions and Answers," on the other hand, players review a piece of literature by diverging from it. To create even the most whimsical question (or answer) about a piece of literature, players must remind themselves of the work's content.

Games in Other Sections

In a variation to "Guess the Voice" (p. 17), players answer a straightforward question about a work of literature.

In a variation to "The Back Speaks" (p. 25), players perform an action from a literary work.

In variations to these three games, players choose a character, expression, or quotation from a piece of literature:

"Mish Mash Mush" (p. 63)

"Places, Persons, and Things" (p. 67)

"Proverb Guessing" (p. 60)

In "Occupations" (p. 97), a player retells a familiar story, making substitutions for individual words within it.

In these two games, players tell altered versions of familiar stories:

"Grouping Stories" (p. 104)

"I Was Present!" (p. 119)

In variations to these games, players improvise additions to beginnings from works of literature:

"Fortunately, Unfortunately" (p. 30)

"They Tossed It High" (p. 22)

❋ ❋

DO IT YOUR WAY

Grade levels: Kindergarten through grade 4.

Space needed: An area that the whole group can see, and that's large enough for one player at a time to perform movements.

Enough room for all players to make movements *(optional).*

Complexity: Low.

Game type: Guessing a quality of movement.

Quick summary: One player chooses a Way to perform actions. The group tries to guess the Way, which is a feeling or an adverb. Group members get clues by asking the player to perform particular actions from a familiar story, in the Way the player has chosen.

Directions: Before you demonstrate this game, select a story that is familiar to the group and select your Way to do things. A Way is a quality of movement, a feeling, or an adverb, e.g., sleepily. (For more examples of stories and Ways, see "Hints.")
Say,

> *This is a guessing game. You have to guess what my Way of doing things is.*
> *But the only things I'll do are movements from the story, "The Three Little*
> *Pigs." What action would you like to see me do from that story? Raise*
> *your hand if you have an idea of what action you'd like to see me do.*

Call on a volunteer group member. Perform the suggested action in the Way you have chosen.

For example, if the volunteer suggests "Be the wolf blowing down the door to the straw house," and you have chosen "sleepily," then you might walk sleepily up to an imaginary door, inhale while stifling a yawn, exhale a few perfunctory puffs, close your eyes and pretend to fall asleep.

Say, "Can anyone guess what my Way of doing things is?" Call on volunteers. Validate each response. Accept synonyms.

If the first guess is incorrect, ask for another action to perform. Perform it, then ask for another guess. If, on the second or third guess, a group member describes your Way with approximate accuracy, treat it as a correct guess. You can say, "Bored? I'd say that's very close. I was thinking of sleepy. Good guessing!" Repeat with an even easier example, to be sure the group understands their goal.

Once the group has guessed your Way, say, "Is there someone here who would like to do what I did, and choose a Way for us to guess?"
Choose a volunteer. Say,

> *Your job is to choose a Way. Mine was "sleepy." Yours can be any feeling,*
> *or any way of doing things. Let us know when you've chosen one, but*
> *don't tell us what it is.*

Allow the volunteer to call on group members for movement suggestions and guesses. Usually, you will want each suggested action to be different. You can say, "Who can think of another action from the story?"

If the group has trouble guessing the volunteer's Way, it may help if you have the volunteer whisper the Way in your ear. Then you can judge if the problem is in the acting, the guessing, or the volunteer's rejection of near guesses.

Repeat as desired.

Hints: Examples. Like most games, this one is more easily demonstrated than explained. Before you demonstrate it, you may want to practice doing a particular movement from a story in a particular Way.

Some easy choices of Ways to move include angrily, with fear, enthusiastically, and sleepily. Some familiar stories that include easy actions are "Jack and the Beanstalk," "Cinderella," "Little Red Riding Hood," and "Goldilocks and the Three Bears." It's easiest to guess Ways that contrast with the expected attitudes of the characters. For example, if Jack is eager to go up the beanstalk, we may not notice, but if Jack is embarrassed, it will stand out humorously.

Let all try the actions. After a correct guess has been acknowledged, offer the group a chance to try doing the specified action in the volunteer's Way. This gives everyone a chance to experience each Way.

Declining. If the group asks you to perform an action you're not clear on, physically unable to perform, or uncomfortable doing, feel free to decline. It may help if you suggest a substitute action:

> *Actually, I don't think I can figure out how to be a stagecoach turning into a pumpkin. How about if I'm the fairy godmother waving her wand to set the spell, instead?*

Synonyms. If desired, introduce the term "synonym" to your group, by saying something like this:

> *If my Way is "frightened" and your guess is "scared," I think your guess should count. After all, "frightened" and "scared" mean almost the same thing. Words that mean almost the same thing are called "synonyms." In this game, synonyms count as correct guesses.*

Variations: Change the story from which the actions are chosen. Allow the group to select a story, or allow the volunteer who will be doing the acting to select one. Change to a new story for each Way, or keep one story for several turns. Obviously, the story should be familiar to the group. If desired, quickly review the story chosen.

Choose a story from your curriculum, such as a work of literature, the life of a historical figure, a historical episode, or the daily life of a particular time and place (e.g., choose a movement from the daily life of a Roman senator).

Instead of individual volunteers, call on a small group to choose a Way and act it out together. If preferred, divide the entire group into teams of four or five. Then each team can present its Way to another team or to the whole group.

Skills Reinforced

Communication:

Group: Pronouncing a movement request clearly. Decoding movements.

Leader: Moving in a way that communicates a feeling or quality of movement.

Storytelling:

Group: Choosing actions from a story.

Leader: Performing actions from a story, with a specified feeling.

Thinking:

Group: Translating from movements to an adverb or feeling.

Leader: Translating from an adverb or feeling to movements.

Curricular: Reviewing actions within a story or other work of literature.

QUESTIONS AND ANSWERS

Grade levels: Grade 4 and up.

Props needed: Two slips of paper or file cards for each player; pencils. Two hats, boxes, or bags in which to collect the slips (*optional*).

Complexity: High.

Game type: Combining elements.

Quick summary: A player makes up a story that answers a randomly drawn question about a well-known work of literature and also mentions a randomly drawn line from a nursery rhyme. (Another genre or work of literature can be substituted for the nursery rhymes.)

Directions: Hand out one slip of paper to each player. Then say,

> *On this slip of paper, write a question about the story "Cinderella." Your question could be a serious question, such as "Where did Cinderella get her beautiful dress?" or it could be a silly question, such as, "What did Cinderella and the prince name their first child?"*

After each player has written a question about "Cinderella," collect all the pieces of paper and put them in a hat or box. Pass out another piece of paper (or a file card of a different color) to each player. Say,

> *On this slip of paper, write a line from a nursery rhyme, or the name of a nursery-rhyme character. You could write a name like "Little Jack Horner" or a line like "What a good boy am I!"*

After each player has written the name of a nursery-rhyme character or a line from a nursery rhyme, collect these pieces of paper and put them in a second hat or box. Say,

> *I'll play first. I draw one piece of paper from each hat. Let's see what I got.*

Draw one slip of paper from each hat or box. Read them aloud to the group. If the question is "What did Cinderella and the prince name their first child?" and the nursery-rhyme character or line is "Little Jack Horner," say,

> *My job is to make up a story that answers the question I drew, and that mentions the nursery-rhyme line or character. So I have to make a story that tells what Cinderella and the prince named their first child, and that mentions Little Jack Horner.*

Create a simple story that answers your question and uses your nursery-rhyme quote. For example, you might say,

> *Once, there was a little boy named Jack. His parents were a prince and princess. Now, in that kingdom, the favorite form of music was the shoe band. Everyone played the shoe.*

> *The problem was that little Jack couldn't join the band, even though he was a prince. Why not? His mother wouldn't give him a shoe to play, since her only extra shoe was too fragile to beat on, being made of glass.*

One day, Jack came upon a ram's horn lying in a field and blew into the end of it. He became the first horn-player in the modern world! That's why Cinderella and the prince called their first child Little Jack Horner.

Say, "Do you get the idea? Who wants to try it?"

Choose a volunteer to draw a slip of paper from each hat or box and make a story that answers the question while mentioning the nursery rhyme character or quotation.

Repeat as desired, or until each player who wants a turn has had one.

Hints: If you don't have hats or boxes for the two piles of papers, just use two desk tops or counter areas, or have two volunteers hold them in their arms or laps. If you use two different colors of paper or file cards, you can place them all in one hat or box or pile; then each player can take one of each color.

It may help to have everyone draw slips of paper before asking for volunteers. Players may be more willing to volunteer after they have seen their slips of paper and realize that they do, in fact, have an idea for a story.

If you create a sample story that is silly (like the one given about Jack Horner the musician), it may give permission to other players to create humorous stories, too. Don't hesitate to make your examples even more far-fetched. For example, you could create a pun on your nursery-rhyme line:

There was a glass-slipper repairer named Oola Jaa, whose son was also named Oola Jaa. The father (known as Big Jaa) ran a small store at a crossroads, but the son turned it into a complete shopping mall, which he named "Oola Jaa, Jr., Intersection," after himself.

The queen (previously known as Cinderella), a frequent customer, was so impressed that she named her first child after the shopping mall's popular nickname, "Little Jaa Corner."

Such silly stories can draw on just as much knowledge of the original story ("Cinderella" in this case) as a serious story might. Informed silliness might be especially valuable if your group is tired of a story after a long unit of study.

When asked to create a story for this game, many players will have an idea that seems to them to be too short or inconsequential to tell. If they actually begin to tell it, however, they will find that their brief idea turns into a substantial story. As leader, you can help a player who says, "Well, I don't have much of an idea," by encouraging the player to tell the story anyway. It may also be helpful to say, "Your story can be very short in this game—just tell it and don't worry."

Variations: Change the story. Change the story about which the questions are asked. Let it be another folktale, a short story, a film, a book, an author's (or director's or artist's) life work, or even a genre (cowpoke movies, Romantic poetry, soap operas, Greek drama).

A historical event or period will also serve as a replacement for "Cinderella." This turns the game into history review: "Write down a question, serious or facetious, about the First World War." Or: ". . . about the military tactics of the First World War." Or even: ". . . about the use of trenches in military tactics in the First World War." The subject can be defined broadly or narrowly (but keep in mind that narrow subjects are sometimes easier to get ideas about!). Players will need to draw on their knowledge of the First World War, of course, to make even playful questions and answers.

Change the second element. The second element, nursery rhyme lines, can also be varied. Any familiar canon of poems, songs, lines from a play, etc., will do, as will any cast of characters. Characters or quotations from a novel make an ideal curricular tie-in, as do characters or quotations from a historical period, or from a genre or period of literature. Characters from popular culture, TV, or ads work well. From folklore, use fairy tale characters or figures from Greek myths, or even motifs from a folklore motif index. (See MacDonald, in the Bibliography, p. 144.)

For nonreaders. If your players cannot read fluently, form them into a circle. Have each player think of a question about Cinderella and a line from a nursery rhyme, then tell the question to the player on the left, and the nursery rhyme line to the player on the right. Then each player makes a story based on the question received (from the player to the right) and the line received (from the player to the left).

Alternatively, create a stack of photos from magazines or calendars, and have each player draw two and make a story combining them. Or have a second stack containing words; let players choose one from each stack and create a story that starts with the photo and incorporates the word.

Skills Reinforced

Communication:

Group: Choosing and writing a phrase and a question.

Leader: Pronouncing a story clearly to the entire group.

Storytelling:

Leader: Creating a fantasy story that answers an arbitrarily selected question while using an arbitrarily selected phrase.

Thinking:

Group: Creating a question about the given story.

Leader: Finding a connection between the arbitrarily selected question and phrase.

Curricular: Reviewing a story or another work of literature; reviewing nursery rhymes or another area of literature or history.

Multiculturalism

Multiculturalism seeks to respect and incorporate the various cultures that constitute our society. Just as children grow to expand their early self-oriented view to include the viewpoints of others, so has our educational system grown toward acknowledging and celebrating cultural diversity.

Two important concepts help us recognize and value our diversity. First, our differences can be seen in the context of our similarities. Second, our differences are valuable.

Humans are infinitely different from each other. At the same time, the similarities among humans are overwhelmingly obvious—at least when contrasted with other forms of life. Some people focus only on the differences among people—whether racial, religious, physical, or gender-based— while ignoring the similarities. Others can't seem to acknowledge the differences, but insist on seeing only the similarities. A broad view, however, can accommodate differences without losing sight of similarities.

Humans are different from each other—fortunately! Differences are not only to be tolerated, they are to be celebrated. We are all richer because of individual and cultural differences. Biologists have demonstrated the survival value of having diverse genetic backgrounds within a species. Indeed, every possible difference among people—including difference in culture—represents a potential strength that can benefit all people.

It is valuable to study these concepts. The most important application of these principles of multiculturalism, however, is concrete and immediate: applaud the diversity that exists within your own group. No matter how similar your group members might seem to each other, they are unique individuals. Your first job in multicultural education is to make it safe to be different right here, right now.

Story games help honor diversity by encouraging individual responses, by focusing on creative responses to playful problems, by encouraging cooperation, and by discouraging attempts at ranking, correcting, or evaluating performance. If the principles of multi-culturalism are not applied in your group's daily life, no amount of ethnic celebrations or slogan-carrying banners will convince students to value the uniqueness of others or to dare to reveal their own uniqueness.

Several games in this collection represent the folklore of several cultures, thus giving evidence of the contributions of diverse peoples.

Games in This Section

"People Are Different" gives players a chance to notice differences that they have experienced—in a context where the differences are likely to be valued. The game asks us to tell of a time we learned something from someone who is different from us in some way. Because the different person is one who helped us learn, we are likely to value the difference.

"Squabble Body," on the other hand, uses fantasy stories to speak directly to the value of difference. By helping players construct stories in which a part of the body loses its uniqueness—with disastrous results—this game gives whimsical but clear examples of the value of differences. This game demonstrates the way in which differing abilities can complement each other, as well as the value of cooperation.

Games in Other Sections

These two games elicit personal experience stories, encouraging your players to share the variety of their experiences:

"Apple Tree" (p. 123)

"My Mother, Your Mother" (p. 99)

By describing the parts of a spaceship (or other entity) as they work harmoniously together, "Spaceship" (p. 114) gives examples of cooperation.

A variation of "From Me to You" (p. 13) stimulates discussions of culture-based feelings about giving and refusing eye contact.

"Sets in Conflict" (p. 108) deals not only with the desire to belong to a group, but also with ways to join a group without changing one's own essence.

The Cultural Background Index (p. 155) lists the cultures from which some of the games (or the rhymes or songs accompanying them) have been derived.

※ ※

PEOPLE ARE DIFFERENT

Grade levels: Kindergarten and up.

Complexity: Low.

Game type: Alternating solo stories with group chant.

Quick summary: One player answers the question: "Tell about a time when you learned something from someone who was different from you." The player ends the story with the words, "People are different." At these words, all speak the verse (and perform the optional accompanying movements).

In a variation, players retell a story told to them by another player, and the group guesses whose story the player told.

Directions: Speak the following verse. (Or sing it to the tune given on p. 151. Or, sing it freely to the tune of the fourth verse of "The Twelve Days of Christmas," stretching out "So many stories" to use the melody for "On the fourth day of Christmas," and singing "that makes them wonderful" to the melody for "three French hens.")

So many stories, so many people.

Stories are different, that makes them wonderful.

People are different, that gives them stories to tell.

Say, "Can you clap that verse with me?" Repeat the verse as all clap to the beat. Say,

When you hear me say, "People are different," do you know what to do in this game? What we just did! We say the verse and clap. Try it. People are different!

Repeat the verse, then say,

This is a game about times that you learned something from someone who is different from you.

Tell a true story about a time that you learned something from someone who was different from you. Or, if you prefer, tell the following story from my life:

When I was about eight years old, I had a friend named Jimmy. We rode our bicycles around the neighborhood together, played baseball together, and built "forts" together in empty lots.

My parents were both born in the United States. They spoke English. Jimmy's father, though, was born in Poland. He spoke English, too, but with an accent that was different from mine. I thought he sounded stupid. I was sure that I was smarter than him.

One day, I was over at Jimmy's. We started making fun of someone in the neighborhood. Every time I said something bad about that person, we both laughed. Then Jimmy would say something bad about that person, and we'd laugh again.

Finally, Jimmy's father heard us and came over to us, looking upset. I thought to myself, "He's too stupid to know how to make fun of people, the way we know."

Jimmy's father only said one thing to us. Speaking in his thick accent, he said, "If you can't say something nice about someone, don't say nothing."

When I heard him say that, I knew he was right. I realized that making fun of people felt good in some ways, but it also made me feel bad inside. I knew I'd rather be the kind of person who only said nice things about people.

Later, I realized that Jimmy's father was smarter than I was.

People are different!

Repeat the verse, with clapping. If desired, tell another story from your life. When you are ready to have other players tell stories, say,

Who will tell us a story of a time you learned something from someone who was different from you in some way? You can tell any true story. When you're done, just say, "People are different."

After each story, repeat the verse, with clapping. Repeat as desired, or until every player who wants a turn has had one.

Hints: Helping players understand this topic. It's relatively rare in our society to hear people talking about differences in positive terms. As a result, players may need extra help with this game.

To help players get the idea of what kind of story this game calls for, don't hesitate to give several examples. It may help to give examples from different areas of your experience (such as home, school, or vacation) or different circles of people (friends, family members, people acting in professional roles, or strangers).

If a player gives a story that mentions learning something from someone but doesn't mention a difference, ask, "How was that person different from you?"

If players give stories that don't seem related to the topic, just return to giving your own stories for a while. Ask them again later or another day.

If your group seems stuck on one kind of difference (a difference of age, for example), you can suggest some various kinds of differences. You can say something like this:

People can be different because they are older or younger. And they can also be different because they come from different countries, or have different religions, or are male or female, or have different kinds of disabilities, or look different in some way.

Or you can simply offer a story of your own that highlights another kind of difference among people.

Helping players describe differences in positive terms. If players state differences in negative terms, help them restate what they learned in more neutral or positive terms.

For example, if a player says, "My uncle helped me swim even though he's old," you can say something like this:

So your uncle is different from you because he's older. And you learned something from him: how to swim better. Great! People are different!

Then begin the verse immediately. The return to the verse and the clapping can help prevent your restatement from being taken as a reprimand.

If appropriate, you can also explore how the uncle's difference contributed to his ability to help:

How did your uncle know how to swim so well? Did his knowing how to swim have anything to do with his being older than you?

Variations: Changing the movements. Have each player try to find a unique way to clap (or walk) while chanting the verse.

Add movements to the verse. Movements can be performed while seated (e.g., three different ways to clap, one for each line of the verse) or they can be performed while standing or walking.

Telling to a partner first. If players seem uncertain about whether to share their experiences, give them a chance to tell the story first to a partner before sharing it with the entire group.

If desired, have players walk singly around the room during the verse. On the final word "tell," have them stop and find a partner. Give the first player from each pair one minute (or longer if you think your group needs or can use the extra time) to tell a story while the other listens. Then call "switch!" After both partners have told their stories, have two or three volunteers tell their stories to the entire group.

Using two circles for partners. Have players form two concentric circles with the same number of players. Have the circles rotate in opposite directions while all say the verse. At the final word "tell," have everyone stop. Each player is now the partner of the nearest player in the other circle.

Have players tell their stories to their partners. Afterward, if you wish, you can have a few volunteers share their stories with the entire group. Alternatively, have a few players share with the group the stories they were told by their partners.

If there are groups within your group who do not normally choose each other to talk to, you might choose to segregate the circles (e.g., have all the boys in the inner circle and girls in the outer). This structure guarantees cross-group storytelling.

Guessing whose story was told. Have players tell their stories to partners, as in the last two variations above. Let the players know that their stories may be shared with the group. Do not have volunteers share their own stories, however. Instead, after each player has heard stories from three different players, say,

> *Is there someone who will tell a story that you heard from one of the other players? Tell it without naming the person whose story it was, so we can try to guess who told it to you.*

After a volunteer (say, Rotita) has told a story, say,

> *Can anyone guess who told that story to Rotita? Raise your hand if you think you know. Rotita, you can call on someone to guess.*

Let Rotita call on up to three guessers. Then say, "Rotita, we were all fooled. Who told that story?" Once Rotita names the original storyteller, ask the teller if he would like to add anything to the story as Rotita told it.

If the players are unknown to each other, let Rotita tell who her three partners were before the guessing begins.

Repeat as desired.

Skills Reinforced

Communication: Saying chanted lines in unison.

Leader: Pronouncing a story clearly to the entire group.

Storytelling:

Leader: Telling a personal experience story.

Thinking:

Leader: Noticing how the person in the story is different from you, regardless of similarities.

Curricular: Reviewing experiences of learning from those who are different. Practicing the solo-chorus form.

SQUABBLE BODY

Grade levels: Kindergarten through grade 3.

Complexity: Medium.

Game type: Filling in a plot.

Quick summary: Players choose four random elements and use them to create a fantasy story using the following formula: the human body was changed to reduce the difference between two given body parts—this seemed to be an improvement at first but later was seen to be a disaster.

Directions: Say,

> *Here's a special way to make a story. We need two objects that don't have anything to do with each other. Who can think of an object—any object in the world?*

Call on two volunteers. If they suggest "a pair of glasses" and "a motorcycle," say,

> *Our story will have a pair of glasses in it, and a motorcycle.*

> *Now we need two parts of the body. What part of the body should we have in our story?*

Call on two more volunteers. If they suggest "fingers" and "head," say:

> *Good! Our story will use the fingers, the head, a pair of glasses, and a motorcycle.*

> *Here's how the story works.*

> *One day, the fingers said, "We are great! We can do so many things!"*

> *What can fingers do?*

Call on volunteers. Insert their suggestions into your narrative:

> *The fingers said, "We can push doorbells, and we can pick things up, and we can make music by snapping. Fingers are the best thing in the world!"*

> *Then they said, "You know, it's a shame that the whole body isn't as good at things as we are. Now, the head can't pick anything up much, and it sure can't ring a doorbell. We wish that the head was gone, and there were fingers in its place!"*

> *The fingers' wish was granted. Suddenly, the body had 10 fingers on the hands—just like before—and it had no head. It just had an 11th finger growing up from the neck!*

> *As soon as the body was changed this way, a good thing happened—having to do with a pair of glasses.*

Ask the group,

> *What could be a good thing that happened, having to do with a pair of glasses—that happened because the body had an 11th finger instead of a head?*

Call on a volunteer. If the volunteer says, "If there's no head, then glasses wouldn't fall off," say something like,

Yes! Up until now, the body had had a terrible time with its pair of glasses, because they kept falling off the head. A head can't grab anything! But now, the body had a finger growing instead of a head, so the finger could just grab the pair of glasses between the lenses. They never fell off, now.

One day, though, something terrible happened—having to do with a motorcycle.

Ask the group,

What could be a terrible thing that happened, having to do with a motorcycle—that happened because the body had an 11th finger instead of a head?

Call on a volunteer. If the volunteer says, "The body was riding a motorcycle but couldn't see because it had no eyes, and so it crashed," say something like,

Absolutely! One day, the body decided to ride on a motorcycle. That was one of its favorite ways to get around. But the body could not see, because it didn't have a head. So the body didn't see the curb coming up, and didn't steer the motorcycle away from it. When the motorcycle hit that curb, it crashed.

The body picked itself up from the ground. Luckily, it wasn't hurt, but the fingers said, "I think we might have made a mistake. Maybe it's better to have some fingers and a head than just all fingers. We wish the extra finger was gone, and the head was back in its place!"

The fingers' wish was granted. That's why, from that day to this, bodies have fingers on their hands, but on their necks, they have heads!

If you wish, create another sample story using two more objects and two more parts of the body.

When your group is ready, have groups of players create and tell their own "squabbling body" stories based on two new objects and two other parts of the body. If desired, one group can suggest objects and body parts for another group to use.

Hints: With some players—especially very young ones—you will need to remain in the storyteller role, turning their ideas into a continuous narrative.

Other players will be able to tell a story once you have led them through its content by summarizing their own ideas, or by asking them questions: "What could that have to do with not having a head?" "Then what happened?" or "What did the body try to do then?"

Still other players will need more help with thinking of story ideas than with turning their ideas into a story. It may help to begin by brainstorming the abilities of both body parts used in a particular story. Once these abilities have been brought to mind, it may be easier to think of an incident using one of them.

The structure of this plot. This game emphasizes the value of differences. To achieve this, players fit their own details into an invariant structure.

The plot could be described this way:

1. The first body part is proud of its abilities.
2. The first body part wishes the second part were the same as it, and the second part becomes the same as the first part!
3. A good thing happens as a result of this new arrangement, having to do with the first object.
4. Then a bad thing happens as a result of this new arrangement, having to do with the second object.

5. Having experienced the bad thing, the first body part wishes the body were back the way it was; that's why the body is as it is today.

Any story with this structure will contain the lesson that differences are valuable. It is not necessary to state the lesson aloud, however. If the game works, the players will gain the appropriate knowledge through creating and sharing their own Squabble Body stories—which will allow them to delight in their individual differences.

Variations: Instead of calling on volunteers to suggest the parts of the body and objects to use, you can make two piles of cards, one with the names or pictures of body parts, and the other with the names or pictures of objects. Or you can begin the game by passing out four slips of paper to each player, and asking each player to write on two slips the names of body parts, and on the other two the names of unrelated objects; players can put the "body-part papers" in one hat, and the "object papers" in the other, then draw two from each hat.

Have the players create stories in teams. If desired, each team can form into two sub-teams to prepare separately the "good thing that happened" and the "bad thing that happened."

Have players use their own body parts as "puppets" to tell their stories.

Instead of human bodies, create a story about the parts of an animal or insect's body.

Skills Reinforced

Communication: Pronouncing contributions clearly to the entire group.

Storytelling:

Leader: Improvising a fantasy story about parts of the body who come to recognize the value of their differences.

Thinking: Thinking of the abilities of body parts. Thinking of possible consequences of changes to the body.

Leader: Summarizing the contributions of several players in a story.

Curricular: Reviewing knowledge of the body. Creating examples of differences that are positively valued. Dealing playfully with differences, bragging, and intolerance.

Social Studies

Story games can further social studies by helping players review subject matter. They can also help players deal imaginatively with problems that arise in society.

Games in This Section

A classic topic for social studies is occupations—the variety of jobs, trades, and professions in the working world. "Occupations" requires players to draw on their knowledge of forms of work by first thinking of various occupations, and then thinking of many words associated with a particular occupation. Thus, this game helps review the study of a single occupation or of occupations in general.

"My Mother, Your Mother" helps players focus on the issue of conflict resolution, through telling stories of conflicts successfully resolved. In variations, the conflicts can be specified to come from the family, the school, or other social institutions—as well as from literature or history.

Games in Other Sections

These two games draw on players' knowledge of occupations:

"Pun Puzzles" (p. 56)

"Walks of Life" (p. 10)

"Guess the Voice" (p. 17) can require players to answer random factual questions from social studies.

In "Places, Persons, and Things" (p. 67), players think of a term that describes a role in society.

In a variation of "Mish Mash Mush" (p. 63), players use an expression derived from an occupation.

In "The Back Speaks" (p. 25), players demonstrate how a given human activity can be approached with different attitudes, depending on the interpersonal and social context.

In playing the appropriate variations of these games, players apply their knowledge of social studies concepts:

"Spaceship" (p. 114) Use a multi-part object or process from social studies.

"The Sea Is Getting Stormy" (p. 112) Use a category from a social studies topic.

※ ※

OCCUPATIONS

Grade levels: Preschool and up.

Space needed: An area that the whole group can see and that's large enough for a standing line of one to ten players *(optional)*.

Complexity: Medium.

Game type: Filling in a plot.

Quick summary: Several players each choose a noun relating to a particular occupation (or to another subject). The leader begins to tell a familiar story, stopping before a key noun. The leader points to a player, who says the noun chosen earlier, thereby substituting it for the noun in the story. The leader continues the story, stopping at each key noun, and pointing to each player in turn to supply a substitute noun that relates to the occupation.

Directions: Say,

> *This game uses an occupation, a type of work. Let's use a carpenter for an example. What are some things that have to do with carpenters and what they do?*

Call on a volunteer to provide the name of a thing relating to carpentry. If the volunteer says, "a hammer," say, "Good! Would you please remember the word 'hammer' for this game? Who else can think of a thing that has to do with a carpenter's work?"

Call on three more volunteers. If desired, have all the volunteers sit or stand in the order in which you called on them; this will make it easier to call on them in a consistent order during the story.

As an example, suppose the four suggested things are hammer, nail, apron, and table saw. Suppose also that your group is familiar with the story of "The Turnip." Then say,

> *I'm going to tell the story of "The Turnip." But I'll change it by having you put your objects into it. Are you ready?*

Begin the story:

One spring, Grandfather planted a . . .

Instead of saying the word "turnip," point to the first player, the one who suggested "hammer." If the player does not say "hammer," say, "Say the word you were going to remember." If necessary, say, "Say, 'hammer.'"

Continue telling the story. Pause at each principal noun in the story to point to a volunteer, who should say the single noun suggested before. Thus, your story will sound like this (the words in parentheses are spoken by the players you point to):

One spring, Grandfather planted a (hammer). It grew all summer. When the (hammer) was ripe, Grandfather went to pull it out of the ground, but the (hammer) wouldn't budge.

So Grandfather called to the (nail), "Help me!" The (nail) pulled, and Grandfather pulled, but the (hammer) wouldn't budge.

So the (nail) called to the (apron), "Help me!" The (apron) pulled, the (nail) pulled, and Grandfather pulled, but the (hammer) wouldn't budge.

So the (apron) called to the (table saw), "Help me!" The (table saw) pulled, the (apron) pulled, the (nail) pulled, and Grandfather pulled, and this time, the (hammer) came popping out of the ground. That night, every one had a hearty supper of (hammer) soup!

Repeat as desired. If you wish, have four more volunteers suggest four new things relating to carpentry. Have a volunteer take your place as the storyteller.

Hints: For young players, use familiar stories and keep the number of substitute words between one and twelve.

For older players, a story can be less familiar, as long as the players can understand its original sense. A larger number of words can be substituted. (See the variations for other ways to alter this game for the tastes of older players.)

With large numbers of substitute words, it can be challenging for the storyteller to keep track of the substitutions. If so, you may prefer to allow inconsistent substitutions: Grandfather planted a (hammer), but when he pulled, the (screwdriver) would not budge; finally, they all pulled together, and the (window) came up; that night, they all had (door knob) soup.

Variations: Use a different occupation, such as farming, teaching, fire fighting, or being a rock star. Use an occupation from a particular place or period of history.

Instead of an occupation, use words from a different social studies subject: a mode of transportation, a country or other place, a social unit (e.g., family, neighborhood, municipality), or a form of government. Or use words from a subject of a different kind: a sport, a hobby, an art form, a historical event, or a period of history. To maximize their interest in the game, allow your players to choose the subject.

Use a different story, whether a familiar story or a story or nonfiction paragraph from a newspaper, a textbook, or a summary of a movie.

Instead of asking the players to volunteer their words before the story begins, have them supply words in the course of the story. This can slow down the story (especially with young children) but can also add excitement.

Do not confine words to names of things; instead, also allow verbs.

Use a longer story, and have each player contribute multiple words. This also allows a further variation, in which each player chooses a different occupation. Thus, one player provides words from carpentry, another from baking, still another from auto mechanics. (This variation was a parlor game in the nineteenth century, known as "Trades.")

Skills Reinforced

Communication: Practicing turn-taking.

Leader: Pronouncing a story clearly to the entire group. Maintaining the sequence of the familiar story.

Group: Pronouncing a chosen word clearly to the entire group, on cue. Attempting to understand a story in which some words are substituted.

Storytelling:

Leader: Telling a familiar story. Giving nonverbal cues for participation. Maintaining coherence during audience participation.

Curricular: Reviewing an occupation or sport. Reviewing a familiar story. Experiencing word substitution.

※ ※

MY MOTHER, YOUR MOTHER

Grade levels: Grade 1 and up.

Complexity: Medium.

Game type: Alternating solo stories with group chant. Guessing true or false.

Quick summary: A player tells a purportedly true story about people resolving a conflict; after the story, the others guess whether it was true or false.

Directions: Point to individual players in turn, as though saying "Eenie meenie" or "One Potato, Two Potato," while saying this rhyme:

My mother, your mother,

Live across the way,

419 East Broadway.

Every night they have a fight, and this is what they say:

Icka backa soda cracker,

Icka backa boo.

Icka backa soda cracker,

Out goes you.

Point to yourself on the word "you." Say,

It fell on me. So my job is to tell a story about people having a conflict or an argument—and then solving it. The trick is that the story could be a "soda cracker story"—that's a true story. But it could also be an "icka backa story"—that's a made-up story. Your job is to guess which it is.

At the end, I'll take a vote. If you think the story is true—a soda cracker story—hold a hand out, palm up, as though you had a soda cracker resting in it. If you think the story is false, hold out your hand palm down, as though you threw something away that tasted "icka backa" bad.

Let's have a practice vote. At the count of three, everyone vote soda cracker—that's true. Ready? One, two, three, vote!

Look around at the group's hands. Each player should be holding out one hand, palm up. Say, "Now let's all vote icka backa—that's false. Ready again? One, two three, vote!" Look around again; hands should be held out, palm down.

Next, tell a story from your life. Choose a story that you think will interest your group and be within their comprehension. A mid-elementary group might appreciate this story from my life:

When I was little, my best friend was named Gary. One day, we were walking through tall weeds in an empty lot, and we saw something brown and black in the grass. It was a bushel basket full of old phonograph records—the kind they called 78's. Records are like an old-fashioned kind of CD.

Gary said, "I saw it first, so they're all mine." I believed him. Then he said, "Help me carry them to my house." He was my friend, so I did.

Every day I could, I went to his house to hear the records. I would say, "Play, 'Close the doors, they're coming through the window.'"

But he would say, "I want to hear 'Thumbelina.'" We would argue about what record to play.

One day, his mother heard us arguing. She made us both tell her the whole story. Then she said, "You found them together, so you should share. Doug, you take half the records home. Next week, bring them back to Gary, and he'll give you the other half to take home."

That way, we both got to play the records we wanted—half the time. So we stopped fighting about them.

And we both loved those records. In fact, I grew up to be a musician and a storyteller, and Gary grew up to be a disk jockey!

Now say, "On the count of three, everyone vote. One, two, three, vote!" The players should all hold out their hands, either palm down to mean "false" or palm up to mean "true." Look around, saying,

I'm looking around to see what people thought. Some thought "soda cracker true" and some thought "icka backa false." The story was . . . true!

Give a little time for reactions ("It sounded like it really happened to you." "Do you still know Gary?"); then say, "Who would be willing to tell a story about people having a conflict or a fight and solving it? It could be a true story or a made-up story. Hold up your hands, and I'll use the rhyme to choose." Saying the rhyme, count out among those volunteering. The player you point to at the word "you" will tell the next story.

Hints: A difficult subject. Conflict resolution is a difficult subject for most children—perhaps because it's a difficult subject for our society. Most TV shows, for example, show only a few ways of solving problems, and most of those ways are violent.

As a result, children may not come up with solutions to conflicts that seem clever or profound. They may be violent solutions, or they may rely on a few simple strategies, such as taking turns or sharing.

I believe that by telling these stories, however, players' awareness of how to solve a conflict will be heightened. As a result, I encourage players to tell their stories, even if they appear repetitious or stereotypical. In time, players will begin to notice how conflicts are resolved or are not resolved, and they will become interested in novel approaches. Eventually their true stories will show the effect of a broadened repertory of approaches to conflict resolution.

Example stories. The best example stories come from your own life. If, however, you decide to use one of mine, you can tell it as though it happened to you (making it a false story), or you can change it to be, "There was once a boy named Doug. . .," (making it a true story).

Using the counting-out rhyme. For hints about using the counting-out rhyme, see "Apple Tree" (p. 124).

Variations: Have players work in pairs or small groups to prepare a story to tell.

Tell a story, true or not, of a conflict, but don't tell how it was resolved. Have players (alone or in groups) create possible endings to the story that resolve the conflict. After each ending is told, have the entire group speak the rhyme, omitting the "true or false" guessing.

Omit the guessing of true or false. Have a player tell a story of people resolving a conflict, then immediately begin the chant.

Skills Reinforced

Communication: Saying chanted lines in unison.

Group: Using an agreed-upon gesture to "vote."

Leader: Pronouncing a story clearly to the entire group.

Storytelling:

Leader: Telling a personal experience story about resolving a conflict.

Thinking: Reviewing criteria for and practicing the determination of truth or falsehood.

Leader: Thinking of ways to resolve conflicts.

Curricular: Reviewing experiences of conflict resolution. Practicing the solo-chorus form. Experiencing a genre of folklore story, the "memorat"—the personal story told as true.

CHAPTER 4
Practicing Math, Science, and Thinking Skills

■ ■ ■

In the three areas of curriculum brought together in this chapter, thought processes have a central role. Facts, of course, matter in both math and science, and science depends greatly on observation. But the essence of each of these subjects undoubtedly lies in making connections, imagining structures, and discovering patterns and principles. The great moments in science and mathematics—from the invention of the zero to Gödel's proof, from Newton's apple falling in gravity to Einstein's $E=mc^2$—have all involved thinking in a new way about something already familiar.

Divergent thinking is the ability to look at the same data in more than one way. Only divergent thinking lets Newton see a falling apple differently from how generations of others have seen it. Critical thinking skills, in contrast, involve reacting to a statement. They let us evaluate an assertion in terms of the knowledge we have already. Such thinking skills are useful in all subjects.

Surprisingly, perhaps, these thought processes have many points in common with the thought processes involved in storytelling. Story games can make it easy to practice and apply these shared ways of thinking.

Mathematics

Mathematics is often thought of as the study of numbers and of arithmetical operations (addition, subtraction, multiplication, and division). Although arithmetic is part of mathematics, it's only a small part.

In the broadest sense, mathematics is the study of relationships between concepts. Mathematicians study how one concept implies or depends on another concept, and how systems of concepts relate to one another. Algebra, for example, studies how numbers (which are concepts) relate to operations, how operations relate to true statements (such as equations), and how one statement does or does not imply another (finding solutions and proofs for equations). Mathematics explores the trail of "if . . . " to "then. . . . "

Where is the common ground between mathematics and storytelling? On the surface level, stories can contain references to numbers or to mathematical puzzles; story games can even give experience counting and performing arithmetical operations. On deeper levels, however, stories also depend on relationships. Just as a mathematical proof shows an inescapable progression from an opening statement to a concluding statement, so a story shows a progressive unfolding from an opening situation or problem to a conclusion.

Once you know how to look, the correspondences between mathematics and stories appear frequently. Set theory, for example, is the study of like and unlike, of similarity and difference, of inclusion and exclusion; many story structures exemplify these concepts. Mathematics pursues the implications of relationships between concepts; stories pursue the implications of relationships between characters. Mathematics seeks the results of operations upon known and unknown quantities; stories follow the results of actions upon known and unknown people and situations.

Story games can give practice with a large range of math skills and thought processes, from simple counting to algebraic operations.

Games in This Section

"Grouping Stories" gives players a chance to practice counting the most interesting items in the world: each other. In the basic game, players hear a number in a story, then form groups of that size. Very young children will find it challenging to form groups of a specified size, especially until they have learned to count themselves in their group. Like the seven brothers in a famous numskull story, young children tend to omit themselves when counting their group. In variations, older players get a chance to practice additional arithmetical operations and even to create their own arithmetical "story problems."

"Flying" brings players into the world of sets. The leader must think of several members of a given set (such as "things that fly"), while the group must decide if each object mentioned belongs to the set.

"Sets in Conflict" requires more sophisticated manipulation of sets. In this game, players generate overlapping sets that include two out of three chosen objects—a potentially challenging exercise. Inclusion and exclusion is more than just a concept, however, since most of us have strong feelings about what groups we are included in or excluded from. "Sets in Conflict" lets players incorporate in a single story both the intellectual and emotional aspects of being part of a set.

Games in Other Sections

"Wolf, Are You Ready?" (p. 4) gives players practice in counting to four, from "one o'clock" to "four o'clock."

In "Cross-Picture Puzzles" (p. 20), players place pictures on a grid (like a crossword puzzle). This gives experience with the geometry of a two-dimensional array.

The following games use "marker words," which are the story-game equivalent of an unknown variable, "x," in an algebraic equation:

"Fuddy Duddy" (p. 49)

"Mish Mash Mush" (p. 63)

"Story Crambo" (p. 47)

"Teakettle Stories" (p. 53)

* *

GROUPING STORIES

Grade levels: Kindergarten through grade 3.

Space needed: Enough room for the group to stand in groups of two, three, etc.

Complexity: Medium.

Game type: Audience response to story cues.

Quick summary: As the storyteller, one player narrates a familiar story, adapting it to mention various numbers from two to ten. Each time a number is mentioned, the others arrange themselves into groups of the size mentioned. At the mention of the number ten, a new player becomes the storyteller. In variations, the others must perform a mathematical operation mentally before knowing what size groups to form.

Directions: This game can be played at many levels of mathematical difficulty, as well as with many stories. For more sophisticated versions, refer to the "Variations," below.
Say,

In this game, I will tell the story of Red Riding Hood. But I will sneak some numbers into the story. Whenever I say a number from two to nine, make yourself into groups that size.

So, if I say "two," you'll have to find a partner to stand next to. Let's try it. Red Riding Hood was wearing two red boots!

Pause while the group forms itself into pairs.
If one player is left over, either become that player's partner or say,

Don't worry if you don't have a partner this time. Choose someone right away the next time.

After all the other players are standing with partners, begin the story:

Once, there was a little girl who wore a cloak with a bright red hood. One day, her mother, said, "Take this basket of food to your grandmother, who lives in the woods."

So Little Red Riding Hood started out to her grandmother's house. But when she had gone a little way, she looked inside her basket. Inside, there were three cupcakes for her grandmother!

Pause while the players form into groups of three. Make sure that any player who was left out of a group before is now included in one. There may be one or two new players left over; if necessary, remind them that they can be part of a group soon. Then continue the story:

Little Red Riding Hood was hungry, so she ate two of the cupcakes.

Pause while the players form into groups of two. Continue the story, mentioning numbers from two to nine. When the players seem to understand the game so far, say something like this:

Little Red Riding Hood kept walking. Suddenly, she saw the wolf. She was so frightened that she closed one of her eyes.

If some players seem to want to form groups of one, say, "Don't move! The number has to be two or bigger!"

Continue explaining the game:

You've been doing great! I think you're ready to learn the rest of the rules for this game.

The rules are, if I say "one," you stay with your group. If I say a number bigger than ten, you stay with your group.

If I say, "ten," you still stay with your group. But if you want to be the next storyteller, then you raise your hand. I'll choose someone to keep the story going. Ready?

Little Red Riding Hood put all ten of her fingers in front of her face!

Don't move, but raise your hand if you want to be the new storyteller!

Change places with a volunteer. Say to the volunteer,

You're the new storyteller. Keep telling the story. Every time you say a number, we'll have to scramble to make new groups. When you want to stop, work in the number ten.

Continue as desired, or until the story has been concluded—or until each player who wants a turn has been the storyteller.

Hint: If players are having trouble knowing who is already in a group, ask players in groups to hold hands in lines or circles, or to link elbows.

Variations: Change the story. Use a different story that is familiar to your group. A story that does not mention numbers in its original version is less likely to confuse the storyteller. Thus, "Jack and the Beanstalk" is less likely to cause unexpected groupings than "The Three Little Pigs."

Let the storyteller improvise a story. If desired, provide a topic or opening sentence, such as "One day, we decided to go out on an adventure," or "The night was dark and stormy. Outside, we could hear the sound of the wind howling."

Change the cue for the changing of storytellers. Each time the storyteller uses a number in the story, choose a new storyteller.

Alternatively, each time the players form groups, note how many players are remainders (players left over after forming groups of the required size). Each time there is at least one remainder, change storytellers. This way, storytellers will come to notice the numbers that allow them to continue as storyteller (i.e., the factors of the group size). If the group size is a prime number, join in (or drop out) to change the group size to a composite number.

Change the formula for group size. In the directions above, the group size is the same as the number mentioned in the story, as long as that number is between two and nine. In the following variations, the group size is calculated in various other ways from the number mentioned in the story.

At the start, choose one number (e.g., three). Have players regroup only when the storyteller mentions a multiple of the chosen number.

Have players form groups equal to one more than the number spoken by the storyteller. Thus, if the storyteller mentions "four," the players will form groups of five.

Have players perform other mental operations on the spoken number, such as:

◆ subtract one
◆ add (or subtract) two (or three)
◆ subtract the spoken number from ten
◆ halve the number if it is even; otherwise, leave it unchanged
◆ find the square root if it is a perfect square; otherwise, ignore it

Have the players get into groups that are the size of any factor of the spoken number.

Have the storyteller express the number as a formula, followed by a command to "calculate." Thus, the storyteller might say, "Each of the three cupcakes had two candles on it; calculate candles!" Players would then get into groups of six (three cupcakes times two candles each). Similarly, the storyteller might say, "First there were five flowers along the path, but then Red Riding Hood picked two; calculate flowers left!" Then players would form groups of three (five flowers minus two flowers taken).

Skills Reinforced

Communication:

Group: Listening for cues. Responding by forming a group of the specified number.

Leader: Pronouncing number cues clearly to the entire group (with immediate feedback).

Storytelling:

Leader: Adapting a story to include various numbers. Maintaining coherence during audience participation; adjusting the rate of participation based on the group's response.

Curricular:

Group: Reviewing counting (and, in variations, other arithmetical operations). Experiencing the necessity of counting oneself in a group. Isolating number words from a story context.

Leader: Integrating numbers into a narrative (in variations, creating "word problems").

※ ※

FLYING

Grade levels: Kindergarten through grade 4.

Space needed: Enough room for the leader and several players to face the rest of the group.

Complexity: Low.

Game type: Audience response to story cues.

Quick summary: Players make a flying gesture whenever the storyteller mentions something that flies. Penalty for mistakes: join the storyteller in front of the room and make flying gestures to help mislead the remaining players.

Directions: Stand in front of the Group with your arms folded in front of you, held at shoulder level. (The fingers of one hand touch the elbow of the other arm.) Say, "All of you sit like this!" When all comply, say, "When I mention something that flies, everyone does this." Lift both hands, until your forearms are vertical, and wave them in front of you. This is the "flying gesture."

If desired, give a "training flight." For example, say, "So if I say, 'I saw a goose,'" we all do this, right?" Make the flying gesture. Say, "Now you do it whether I do it or not. So, I might say, 'I was out walking in the field, and overhead I saw a goose flying." Do not make the gesture at the word "goose," but check that the Group does. Continue: "Next to the goose [Group gestures] was a duck [Group gestures]. Then they landed, and began squawking at a turtle." Check that no one gestures at the word "turtle."

Say, "Good! You have the idea. If you make a mistake, you have to come up and help me—by doing it at the wrong time and trying to fool everybody else. Are you ready?"

Begin a story such as the one that follows. Interrupt whenever anyone fails to gesture at the right time or performs the gesture at the wrong time, saying, "You come up and join me. You can't say anything, but you can make the flying gesture anytime—or not make it when you should! You help me fool everyone else." As more players make mistakes, more and more players will be standing with you, and fewer will be sitting in their original places.

> *One day, I was riding on an airplane [Group gestures]. I looked out the window and saw something in the clouds [Group should not gesture]. Sure enough, it was an eagle [Group gestures].*

> *The eagle [Group gestures] had something on its back. First, I thought it was a backpack, but then I saw it was a puppy [Group should not gesture]. The eagle [Group gestures] had a puppy on its back! Then they did a loop-the-loop, dove down toward the earth, then headed back up toward the sun [Group should not gesture].*

> *Just then, my airplane [Group gestures] began to come in for a landing, and I lost sight of the puppy and the eagle [Group gestures]. But when I went to get my luggage, I looked back at the plane [Group gestures]. There, sitting on the runway [Group should not gesture] was the puppy. And high above it was a very large bird [Group gestures], getting smaller and smaller, until finally, the eagle [Group gestures] was nothing but a dot in the sky [Group should not gesture].*

Continue the story as desired. If some players have not been eliminated by the end of the story, announce, "These are our winners! Let's give them a hand!"

If desired, ask for a volunteer to tell another story.

Variations: Other categories. Change the category of word that cues the gesture. For example, players can make the gesture when the storyteller mentions something with teeth, an invertebrate, something with red on it, something commonly manufactured in Asia, or something made of metal.

Let the teller choose the category. Ask for a volunteer to tell a story. Say, "Should we keep it about things that fly, or change it?" If the teller says, "Change it," say, "What should make us do the gesture?"

One fifth grader chose "words with a double 'o' in them." He made a story featuring words like "woods," "foot," "look," "took," "good," and "balloon."

Other gestures. For players who may consider the flying gesture babyish, have them simply raise a hand or lift a forefinger from their desks. Or have them stand up when they hear one flying thing mentioned, and sit down when they hear the next.

Instead of the cross-handed flying gesture, have players flap their arms to the side (if space allows).

Use a gesture appropriate to the category. If the category is "something that walks," for example, use a walking gesture rather than a flying gesture.

Add additional categories and gestures. Say, for example, "This time, make the flying gesture if I mention something that flies, but pretend you are swimming if I mention something that swims in water."

Skills Reinforced

Communication:

Group: Listening for cues. Responding with a gesture.

Leader: Pronouncing cues clearly to the entire group (with immediate feedback).

Storytelling:

Leader: Creating a story that contains words of a given category. Maintaining coherence during audience participation; adjusting the rate of participation based on the group's response.

Thinking:

Leader: Using words frequently that belong to the given category, mixed with words that do not belong to the category.

On a more advanced level, including a word from the given category without drawing attention to it. Introducing other words—which are suggestive of the given category but not in it—as "red herrings" to which attention is deliberately drawn.

Group: Giving the opposite response (those who have already joined the leader give the opposite response, to try to fool the remaining players).

Curricular: Reviewing the category of things that fly (in variations, reviewing other categories).

SETS IN CONFLICT

Grade levels: Grade 4 and up.

Props needed: Blackboard or paper *(optional).*

Complexity: High.

Game type: Combining elements. Filling in a plot.

Quick summary: A player selects three unrelated objects, then chooses a set that two of the objects ordinarily belong to, but that the third does not. The player creates a story about how the third object came to become a member of that set.

Directions: Say, "I need us to think of three objects that don't have anything to do with each other. Raise your hand if you want to suggest an object."

Call on volunteers. If desired, write down their responses where all can see. One group chose:

◆ *pen*

◆ *house*

◆ *leaf*

Say, "What could the first two of these have in common, that doesn't apply to the third? What's the same about a pen and a house, but different about a leaf?" (If your group is familiar with set terminology, you can ask "What set do both a pen and a house belong to, that a leaf does not belong to?")

Call on volunteers. Answers might include "things made by humans," "things with metal parts," and "things with an opening that can be opened and closed."

If desired, repeat the question with each of the other two pairs of objects (pen and leaf; house and leaf). For example, "What's the same about a pen and a leaf, that's different about a house?" Repeating the question in this way gives more practice with sets and generates more story possibilities.

Say,

> *We're going to choose one of the answers you just gave, and make a story from it. We'll make a story about how the third object became like the other two. Which of your answers would you like to use?*

Once the group has chosen one of its earlier answers, rephrase the story idea in terms of the group's choice. For example, you might say,

> *You chose the answer that a pen and a house could be blue, but a leaf could not. Therefore, our story will be the story of how a leaf became blue so it could be like the pen and the house.*

> *Can anyone make up a story about that?*

Choose a volunteer, who will tell a story to the group.

One fifth-grader told this story, about how the leaf became blue:

> *One fall day, a brown leaf was lying on the earth. Someone walked by and dropped a beautiful blue fountain pen next to the leaf. The leaf thought, "That is the most beautiful color I ever saw!" The leaf was so excited; it looked up beyond the pen and saw a house nearby. The house was blue, too! The leaf said, "I wish I was as beautiful as the house and the pen!"*

> *The leaf wished so hard that a wind came up and blew on it. The leaf was already on the ground, so the only way it could go was up. The leaf blew up and up, to the top of the sky.*

> *The top of the sky was shiny and hard, like a mirror. The sky was even bluer than the pen and the house! The leaf threw itself at the beautiful sky. It bounced off the top of the sky, and some of the sky's color rubbed off on the leaf.*

> *The leaf floated back to the ground. But now it was as blue as the sky— even more beautiful than the pen and the house.*

If desired, call on other volunteers to make up stories based on the same answer. Or, choose another of the group's earlier answers, and have a volunteer tell a story based on it.

Hints: The question about a characteristic common to only two of the objects is abstract, but is more easily understood when a question is asked about the three particular objects (e.g., "how are a leaf and a pen. . ."). If your group is young or gets confused by abstractions, omit the abstract form of the questions.

It may be helpful to write the names of the objects three times, showing the three possible groupings:

1. pen	leaf	house
2. pen	house	leaf
3. leaf	house	pen

Variations: Choose the three objects randomly. You might draw pictures from a hat, open a dictionary randomly, or spin an object or spinner and choose the object in the room that it points to.

Choose three objects from a given environment or context that relates to an area of the curriculum. For example, choose three objects or creatures from a fresh-water pond, or from colonial North America, or from a story the group knows.

Break into pairs or small groups. Have each player tell a story to the others in her small group.

Have small groups make a story together, then share it with other groups or with everyone.

Simplifying the process. For younger players, ask them to suggest two objects that usually belong together, and a third object that does not usually belong with them. If players suggest "a knife and fork" and "a radio," help them create a story that answers the question: "How did the radio become like the knife and fork in some way?"

To create the story, ask first,

How are a knife and fork alike?

If your players answer, "They both are on the dining-room table," you can begin the story like this:

We're going to make a story about how the radio got to join the knife and fork on the dining-room table.

Every day, the knife and fork were put on the table, and the radio stayed all alone on the shelf. It thought, "How come I can't join them?"

Who can think of how the radio got on the table?

Perhaps a volunteer will suggest, "There was an earthquake, and the people wanted to hear the radio." Then you can continue the story, filling in as much detail as you wish:

*One day, the radio was sitting all alone on the shelf. The family came into the dining room, put dinner on the table—including the knife and fork, of course. The radio tried to look useful, but the knife and fork didn't even look at it. **They** were being useful!*

Suddenly, the shelf began to shake. The whole house began to shake! The knife and fork began to jump up and down on the table in a panic, and the family said, "What's going on? Let's get out of here!" They stood up and started to run outside.

With a mighty effort, the radio turned its own switch on. It began to speak, "We are now experiencing a small earthquake. There is no need to be alarmed or to leave your houses. Stay tuned for further bulletins."

The family came back and sat down! One of them said, "Let's keep the radio where we can hear it better while we eat." They carried the radio from the shelf, putting it right next to the knife and fork, who smiled at the radio. It had saved the dinner. Now they were all friends!

Skills Reinforced

Storytelling: Improvising a fantasy story explaining how an object joined a set that it did not originally belong to.

Thinking: Exploring the sets common to any two of a set of three objects. Finding an exception that would allow the third object to belong to a set common to the first two.

Curricular: Thinking about objects that are part of multiple, overlapping, and nonoverlapping sets.

Science

One of the wonders of modern science is that new developments in physics and astronomy—the most "factual" and "objective" of the sciences—have shown that even these subjects depend as much on our ability to imagine as on our ability to reason and to calculate.

Like storytelling, science involves skills of observation, in addition to skills of memory, thought, and imagination.

Story games used to teach science can help us observe, review bare facts, express relationships and concepts, and apply underlying principles. In addition, by developing our ability to think and to imagine, story games make us more prepared to enter the hard-to-imagine theoretical worlds of shrinking or expanding universes, large-scale ecological interrelationships, and subatomic wave-particles.

Games in This Section

"The Sea Is Getting Stormy" lets players review simple sets of *facts:* what creatures live in the sea, what common substances are acidic, or the names of constellations.

"Spaceship," in contrast, lets players review *relationships* among the parts of a system: the space shuttle, the nervous system, an automobile engine, or the freshwater food chain.

"Because" extends to a still higher level of abstraction, the idea of causality itself. Much scientific study seeks to understand the causes of a phenomenon or to predict the results of an action. This game gives practice in establishing fanciful sequences of causation.

Games in Other Sections

In a variation to "Proverb Guessing" (p. 60), players hide a rote scientific principle or quotation in a story.

These games deal with the subject of sound, including (in the first three games) the observation of sounds:

"Guess the Voice" (p. 17)

"Janey Jo" (p. 6)

"Knocking" (p. 16)

"You're Shaking Me Up" (p. 31)

The subject of "Squabble Body" (p. 94) is the parts of the body and their functions. A variation uses animal or insect bodies.

"Flying" (p. 106) deals with which animals fly—and can be adapted to review the contents of any category in any field of science.

"Janey Jo" (p. 6) involves the idea of causality: the leader thinks of alternative causes for a sound.

The following two games can treat the history and social implications of science and technology:

"History Mystery" (p. 76)

"Inventions" (p. 80)

THE SEA IS GETTING STORMY

Grade levels: Preschool through grade 4.

Props needed: Chairs *(optional; see variations).*

Complexity: Medium.

Game type: Audience response to story cues.

Quick summary: Players, seated, secretly choose names of sea creatures. The leader walks around, telling a story about the sea. When the leader mentions one of the secret names, that player joins behind the leader. At the phrase "The sea is getting stormy," all rush to find a vacant chair.

Directions: Make sure that all players are seated in chairs, and that any extra chairs are covered or otherwise marked as "out of bounds."

Standing up, say,

> *Your job is to choose the name of something that lives in the sea—but don't tell me what it is. Raise your hand when you have thought of your secret sea creature.*

When all have signaled that they have chosen the name of a sea creature, say,

> *I'm going to tell a story. If I say the name of your sea creature, you get up and follow me in a line. When I say, "The sea is getting stormy," we're all going to run for a chair—and all the people still sitting have to get up and find a new chair.*

Begin a story that mentions many creatures of the sea, such as:

Once, the whale [any players who have chosen "whale" now get up and join you] said, "I'm the biggest sea dweller, but I don't want to be the ruler of the sea. I'll find some other creature to rule over us all."

First, the whale went to the sharks and the giant squids. "You are giant creatures. Would you like to rule the sea?" But they refused.

Then the whale asked the sailfish, the tuna, and the dolphins. "You are large enough creatures. How about taking over as rulers of the sea?" But they didn't even answer.

Continue the story, causing the whale to ask creature after creature, all of whom refuse to rule the sea. When enough players have joined in a line behind you (half the group is probably a good number, but it depends on your group, your space, and your patience), end the story this way:

Finally, the whale went to the plankton. They were so small that the whale couldn't even see them. The whale said, "No one else will rule the sea. Will you?"

The plankton were very busy. But they knew that the sea needs someone to watch over it—and if they didn't, no one would. So they said, "Yes."

When all the plankton spoke at once, it made the sea begin to roll and roil, to trouble and to bubble. The sea got so rough that even the whale was getting sea-sick. The whale said, "Thanks! But I'd better dive now. The sea is getting stormy!"

Lead the charge for an empty seat, reminding the others to do the same, if necessary.

When all players are seated but one, ask for a volunteer to tell the next story. Let the player without a seat take the volunteer's chair.

Hints: Your group may know the names of too few sea creatures. If so, precede the game with a discussion of sea creatures. If you wish, write the names of several sea creatures in plain sight, or display photos or drawings.

On the other hand, your group may know too many sea creatures. As storyteller, you'll never name the obscure species they choose. In this case, it may help to precede the game by eliciting the names of 10 or 20 sea-dwellers and writing them on the board, and then to require players to choose from those names.

The more times a particular group plays this game, the easier it gets for the storytellers.

Variations: Have groups of three or four cooperate to choose a secret name that will apply to the group. This reduces the total number of names.

Instead of chairs, use marks on the floor, cushions—or let adults on their hands and knees act as "human chairs."

Play with the "cooperative musical chairs" ending. Reduce the number of chairs each time, but have more than one player sit in each chair. Eventually, players will need to be creative about sharing!

Use a less active ending, such as singing a song or reciting a home-made cheer about the sea.

Use a different subject from science, history, social studies, or literature, such as sub-atomic particles, the Revolutionary War, the life history of a congressional bill, or *MacBeth*. Have players choose the names of characters, places, or objects important to the subject. Choose a new final line for the story, appropriate to the new subject (e.g., "And a new nation was created," or "The nucleus divided.")

To form a line for another game, play until all are in line, then omit the ending sentence, "The sea is getting stormy." To form a circle, have the leader follow the last in line.

Skills Reinforced

Communication:

Group: Listening for cues. Responding by joining the line of players.

Leader: Pronouncing a story clue clearly to the entire group (with immediate feedback).

Storytelling:

Leader: Creating a story that contains words from a given category. Maintaining coherence during audience participation; adjusting the rate of participation based on the group's response.

Thinking:

Leader: Remembering which words from the given category have already been used in the story.

Curricular: Reviewing the creatures of the sea (or the content of another category).

SPACESHIP

Grade levels: Preschool through grade 2.

Props needed: Blackboard or butcher paper *(optional).*

Complexity: High.

Game type: Audience response to story cues.

Quick summary: A player tells a story about a spaceship. Each portion of the group represents an agreed-upon term; when their term is mentioned, they stand up, turn around, and sit back down. At the phrase "The spaceship landed," everyone in the entire group gets up, claps hands twice with another player, and finds a new seat.

Directions: Say, "What things or people might be on a spaceship?" Call on group members for their responses, writing the first four or five where all can see, if desired. A typical list might include rocket engines, booster rockets, control panel, laser guns, fuel, astronauts, and computers.

Choose four or five items from the list that you want highlighted in the story, such as:

◆ engines
◆ control panel
◆ fuel
◆ astronauts

Circle the chosen items or erase the others.

Point to part of the group (one or two rows of desks, or a quarter of the players seated on the floor), saying,

This group can be the Engines. When you hear me say, "Engines," you stand up, turn around, and sit back down. Ready for a practice? Engines!

Repeat for each of the other items, giving each group a chance to stand up, turn around, and sit back down.

Say the following, allowing players enough time to perform the required action after each cue:

When I say, "Spaceship," everyone stands up, turns around, and sits back down. Ready for a roll call? Engines! Control Panel! Fuel! Astronauts! Spaceship! Now, when you hear me say, "The spaceship landed," everyone stands up, finds someone else to clap hands with twice, and sits back down in a different chair. Ready for a test? The spaceship landed!

When all are back in their seats, tell this story, pausing after each emphasized word for the appropriate group to stand up, etc.:

*Once, there was a magnificent **Spaceship**. It had powerful **Engines,** the very finest **Control Panel,** and a year's supply of **Fuel**. Not only that, the **Astronauts** flying it were the best pilots in the world.*

*Finally, the big day came: the **Spaceship** was ready to take off. The **Engines** were ready, and there was plenty of **Fuel**. The **Astronauts** were strapped in their seats in front of the **Control Panel**. Three, two, one, liftoff! The **Spaceship** took off, and quickly flew into space.*

*Suddenly, the **Astronauts** looked at the **Control Panel,** and saw there was a problem. A big asteroid was heading right toward them. They sent more **Fuel** to the **Engines,** but the asteroid kept up with them. The asteroid was getting closer, and the **Control Panel** lights were flashing red. The **Astronauts** fired the **Engines** faster and faster, but finally they were almost out of **Fuel.***

*What could they do? Since they couldn't beat it, they had to join the asteroid. The **Astronauts** just turned the knob on the **Control Panel** that stopped sending **Fuel** to the **Engines,** and, right there on the asteroid, **the spaceship landed!***

If you wish, when all have recovered their breath and their chairs, ask for a volunteer to tell some other story about a spaceship. Guide the player through another "roll call," then let her make up another impromptu story about a spaceship.

Hints: Very young players (or players not speaking their first language) may prefer to take turns telling almost the same story. Allow the stories to be imitative while the players get comfortable with the game. Later, encourage originality by praising any players who vary the story. If no players do, model originality by telling one or more completely different stories yourself.

Variations: "Hash" the group. Once parts are assigned, have players intermingle. Since a player's neighbors will be responding to different cues, this variation makes the game more challenging.

Change the parts of the spaceship that you highlight. Another story might be built around Lunar Module, Computer, Hull, and Oxygen Supply.

Vary the number of parts of the spaceship. Older players can remember more parts, especially when they are written out in plain sight.

Vary the responses that each group makes. Instead of having every group stand up, turn around, and sit down, have each make a movement or sound that's appropriate to the function of the part it's named after. Players can even sing a song or chant a verse.

Vary the final line of the story. Let the volunteer choose it, or suggest one, such as "The spaceship returned to earth," or "The mission was successful."

Vary the action performed at the final line. Traditionally, the final line signaled a scramble for chairs; the player who failed to find one became the next storyteller.

Change the subject. Replace the idea of a spaceship with another object that has several component parts. Traditional subjects include a stagecoach, an automobile, and the objects a woman might use in the course of getting dressed. For curricular use, however, any object or system already studied will do. Examples might include a tree, Noah's ark, a family, the central nervous system, the players' home town, the Round Table, or the U.S. House of Representatives—or any other multi-part object or process from science, social studies, geography, or history.

For each new subject, establish the parts of the subject and the line that will signal the story's end.

Skills Reinforced

Communication:

Group: Listening for cues. Responding with movement.

Leader: Pronouncing the cue words clearly to the entire group (with immediate feedback).

Storytelling:

Leader: Creating a story that contains a given set of words. Maintaining coherence during audience participation; adjusting the rate of participation based on the group's response.

Thinking:

Leader: Using the given set of words frequently in an improvised story. Expressing the relationships among the parts of the spaceship (or of another multi-part object or system).

Curricular: Reviewing the parts of a spaceship (or of another multi-part object or system).

※ ※

BECAUSE

Grade levels: Grade 3 and up.

Complexity: Low.

Game type: Round-robin.

Quick summary: First player makes a statement; second player gives the cause of the statement; third player gives the result.

Directions: Say,

> *Here's a statement: "One morning, the sun did not rise." Who can make up a reason why? Say, "Because. . . ."*

Call on a volunteer, who might say something like, "Because the sun's alarm clock didn't go off."

Say,

Who can tell me what happened because of that? Say, "Therefore. . . ."

Call on another volunteer, who might say,

Therefore, ten thousand clock-makers took ten thousand flashlights and ten thousand screwdrivers, and had to fix the sun's alarm clock before it could be daylight again.

Begin again with another statement (e.g., "One day in the future, all kangaroos will know how to use computers," or "Late last night, my new pair of jeans started to dance.").

Alternatively, ask a volunteer to make a statement. Then proceed as before, with other volunteers giving a "Because . . ." and a "Therefore. . . ."

Repeat as desired.

Variations: Ask for several possible "Because's" for each statement, or ask for several possible "Therefore's" for a particular "Because." By showing alternative responses to each idea, this process can help players learn to imagine more freely.

Have the players form groups of three to work together to prepare a statement, a cause, and a consequence.

When a group feels safe enough, call on players randomly and quickly. Or go quickly around the room or around the circle, asking one player for a statement, the next for a "Because. . ." and the third for a "Therefore. . ." Ask the fourth for another statement, and so forth.

Require that the statement relate to a given subject, such as a historical period, a topic from science or social studies, or a work of literature.

Skills Reinforced

Communication: Practicing turn-taking.

Leader: Pronouncing a contribution clearly to the entire group

Storytelling: Improvising a single sentence that can be the beginning of or an addition to a brief story. Maintaining a temporal sequence that is different from the narrative sequence. (The temporal sequence is cause, statement, effect; the narrative sequence is statement, cause, effect.)

Thinking: Imagining a causal connection between events, even if the events are fantastical. Thinking of a cause. Thinking of an effect.

Thinking Skills

Thinking skills influence all learning, but are challenging to teach separately. They fall into three broad categories: consideration, generation, and evaluation. The more fundamental a thinking skill is, the more difficult it is to teach.

The most essential thinking skills fall into the category of consideration (perceptive thinking) skills. These skills involve considering all the relevant factors—making sure that everything that matters gets your attention. If you are thinking about a decision to be made, for example, there is little sense in weighing individual pros and cons until you are sure you have looked at all the relevant ones. Consideration skills help you notice what to evaluate—including causes, consequences, and the points of view of all involved. As vital as they are, these skills are not evoked directly by the games in this collection.

Generation (divergent thinking) skills, in contrast, produce multiple ways of viewing the same data. These skills build on consideration skills to help you break the bonds of your own thought structures. By their very nature, most story games promote generation of alternative ideas, and thus give practice in divergent thinking.

Evaluation (critical thinking) skills come into play only when a statement or factor has already come to your attention. If a statement is self-contradictory, evaluation skills let you see its lack of logic. If an inference is not justified by the data under consideration, evaluation skills help you question its correctness.

The games in this collection give practice with two kinds of evaluation. The first kind assesses the truth or falsehood of a statement; the second kind finds alternative interpretations of a situation, to help decide whether a statement is necessarily true.

Although easiest to present separately, critical thinking skills are often overemphasized. They depend on ideas generated by perceptive and divergent thinking skills, which are more basic. Evaluating a factor in a decision, for example, doesn't help you much if another hidden factor is more relevant, nor is it useful to spend time trying to evaluate a weak idea just because it's the only one you could come up with. Furthermore, most older children and adults try to apply evaluation skills too early in the thinking process, before they have had a chance to consider enough factors or to generate enough concepts. Playing story games may help players learn to consider many thoughts before evaluating any of them.

This section presents games for divergent thinking and for two types of critical thinking. For the thinking skills practiced by games not mentioned here, see the section "Skills Reinforced," given with each game.

Divergent Thinking

Divergent thinking skills are essential to story games. Even when a single player's story does not involve divergent thinking, hearing different stories from several players allows the entire group to experience the generation of multiple responses.

Games in This Section

"I Was Present!" takes a well-known story—presumably one that all players have already imagined in their own particular ways—and encourages players to re-imagine it in a new way. Stories familiar to a person have been imagined in the same way by the person many times; this can make the "conceptual ruts" very deep. Therefore, re-imagining such a story can be a substantial achievement in divergent thinking.

Games in Other Sections

These games help players re-imagine stories they already know:

"Grouping Stories" (p. 104)

"Occupations" (p. 97)

"Questions and Answers" (p. 87)

"They Tossed It High" (p. 22) asks players to imagine the same scene in multiple ways, while "Cross-Picture Puzzles" (p. 20) asks them to see the same picture in two or more ways.

In "Fortunately, Unfortunately" (p. 30), each triumph must be re-imagined as a defeat, and each defeat re-imagined as a triumph.

In these games, players are asked to imagine changes in or unlikely actions by familiar objects:

※ ※

I WAS PRESENT!

Grade levels: Kindergarten and up.

Props needed: Blackboard, slips of paper *(optional)*.

Complexity: Low.

Game type: Round-robin.

Quick summary: Players interrupt a well-known story by saying, "I was present," and then improvise an addition to the story.

Directions: Say, "Do you know the story of 'Little Red Riding Hood'?" (If the group's response leads you to think the story might not be familiar to the players, change to a different story or else summarize "Little Red Riding Hood" now.)

Say, "In this game, you get to change the story of 'Little Red Riding Hood.' For example, when the story gets to the part when she goes down the path to her grandmother's house, you might raise your hand and say, 'I was present! When she got to the path, she sat down and fell asleep! So the wolf just talked to her because he was worried she'd catch cold.'"

Say, "The only rule is, you can't change what someone else already said. So, the next person can't say, 'No, she didn't take a nap, she ran off to the mall instead.' Are you ready? Okay, here I go."

Begin the story, stopping when a player raises a hand to say, "I was present!"

After each turn by a player, you can choose another player to add the next new part of the story (if there are other volunteers), or you can continue the story yourself.

Continue the story as desired. If a player creates a good ending, say, "That sounds like a good place to end the story this time!" If, on the other hand, the players seem unlikely to end soon enough, you can continue the story yourself, bringing it to a conclusion without allowing further input from the group.

If you wish, play again.

Hint: This game is most exciting when players build on each others' contributions.

If a player makes an addition to the story that ignores what has been developing, you can stop and say something like, "Yes, that could be where we take this story. But wait, remember how the Seven Dwarfs had just arrived to save Red Riding Hood from the alligator? Does anyone have an 'I was present' that keeps the Seven Dwarfs in the story?"

If desired, listen to several alternative ideas before going on. Choose one idea, and say, "Let's put that idea into our story now. So, we have six of the dwarfs afraid of alligators, but one of them used to have an alligator pet and isn't afraid at all. What happens next?" Instead of making the decision yourself, however, you can also put it to the group: "Which idea should we use for now: one dwarf who isn't afraid of alligators, or the seven of them using canned sardines as bait to trap the alligator?"

All such interventions on your part require care to keep a player from feeling rejected. It may help to keep your focus on the story (Ask, "How should the story go now?") rather than on the player (Avoid asking, "Who likes Tina's idea?"). Additionally, take time to validate the suggestions you don't incorporate into the story. (If a player says, "I was present, and the alligator exploded, and they all died," say, "That's certainly a good way to end the story right now! What if we want to keep it going?") For more hints about responding to potentially inappropriate contributions, see "Dealing with Inappropriate Responses" (p. xix) and "Placing Limits on Leaders" (p. xxi).

Variations: Use a different story. Use a story familiar from home, TV, movies, computer games, folklore, or curriculum.

For an enjoyable end-of-unit review, use this game with a historical event, a novel, or even a scientific process you have just studied. For example, you might begin by saying, "The molecules of water got colder and colder, and began to crystallize." Let a player continue with, "I was present! One molecule refused to freeze! It began to dance instead! It was humming a catchy tune!"

Add another element. Require each player to use a word from a list that's on the board. For example, if one word in the list is "system," a player might say, "I was present! Red Riding Hood knew what the wolf was up to. She said to herself, 'I've been watching him; I know his system for getting free meals. I'll just play along and watch for my chance to escape.'"

Alternatively, put each word on a slip of paper and have each player draw the word that he or she must use in the story.

If desired, choose words from a curricular unit.

Instead of words, you can have players use another kind of element: the name of a character, a line from a nursery rhyme (or other piece of literature), a picture or a graphic symbol, or a tone of voice associated with a particular feeling.

Skills Reinforced

Communication: Practicing turn-taking.

Leader: Using the cue for beginning a turn: "I was present!" Pronouncing a contribution clearly to the entire group.

Storytelling:

Leader: Improvising a fantastic addition to a familiar story. Taking into account the previous additions by others.

Thinking: Imagining an alternative version of a familiar scene.

Curricular: Reviewing a familiar story.

Critical Thinking: Truth and Falsehood

We are frequently warned to discriminate truth from falsehood. In most situations, this means telling only the truth. In story games, however, both sides of the coin are open to examination. Individual players can tell stories that are purposely true or purposely false. The group can also be asked to evaluate whether a story is true or false, and why.

Games in This Section

"Old Doc Jones" approaches truth from an unusual direction—by asking for deliberate, harmless falsehood. Players tell silly lies about objects in the room.

"Apple Tree" makes greater demands on players' ability to discriminate truth from falsehood. It asks players to tell stories from their lives which may be true or false, and then it asks the group to vote whether they thought a story was true or false. This game sometimes leads to thoughtful discussions about how much deviation from literal truth constitutes a falsehood, and to consensus about an answer.

Games in Other Sections

"My Mother, Your Mother" (p. 99) uses the voting mechanism used in "Apple Tree" to encourage discrimination between true stories and false stories. The stories, however, are restricted to the theme of conflict resolution.

In "History Mystery" (p. 76), the storyteller makes a claim that the listeners know is false—but they must figure out why it is false. In a variation, players decide which of three claims is false, and why.

※ ※

OLD DOC JONES

Grade levels: Preschool through grade 2.

Props needed: Any interesting object *(optional)*.

Complexity: Low.

Game type: Alternating solo stories with group chant.

Quick summary: Players create "silly lies" about objects in the room.

Directions: Speak these lines (or chant them like a poem, or sing them to the tune of "This Is the Way We Wash Our Clothes," or sing them to the tune given on p. 151):

Old Doc Jones was a fine old man,

A fine old man, a fine old man;

Old Doc Jones was a fine old man,

He told ten thousand lies.

Say:

Did you hear what I said Old Doc Jones did?

If the answer is incorrect or uncertain, say "Listen again!" and repeat the chanted lines and the question. If the answer is "Told ten thousand lies," say,

Old Doc Jones' lies weren't mean lies. They were just silly lies, for fun. I'll tell you a silly lie about the clock on the wall over there. Ready? Here's my silly lie:

I came into this room in the middle of the night. When I got here, it was dark. I heard someone walking around. I turned on the light. It was the clock, walking on its hands!

Chant or sing:

Silliest thing I ever heard,

I ever heard, I ever heard;

Silliest thing I ever heard,

And I just heard it now.

Say,

Can anyone here make up a silly lie about something in this room?

After each silly lie, sing "Silliest thing I ever heard. . . . " Call on as many players as desired.

Hints: If no one volunteers, make up some more silly lies, such as, "The clock was dancing with the eraser," or "The clock had turned into a watermelon with two clock hands sticking out of it." After another lie or two, ask again for volunteers.

If you narrow down the possibilities for the "silly lie," it can actually become easier to think of a silly lie to tell.

The most difficult category for most groups is the broadest: "Tell a silly lie." If you narrow it down a little, it might get easier: "Tell me a silly lie about something in this room." If you narrow it down even more, it might get even easier: "Tell me a silly lie that involves that chair and the plant on the window sill."

If your group seems unable to create lies that are silly enough to be fun, tell some additional outrageous ones:

Here's another one. I went to sit down, and I heard someone saying, "Don't sit on my face!" I looked down, and there was the clock!

I said, "How did you get down from the wall? Get back up there!"

The clock said, "No way! I'm staying down here." The clock began to roll around the room.

So I began to chase it. Finally, I threw my coat over it, and trapped it. But it might get away again—so you'd better keep watching it!

If your players still have trouble, try building on their stories, saying, "I think I can make that lie even sillier! Would you like to hear how?"

Some groups have trouble telling "lies," which they have been so often warned against. Such a group may prefer to tell "fantastic tales," or just "sillies."

Variations: Say the player's name in the chanted lines:

Silliest thing I ever heard,

I ever heard, I ever heard;

Silliest thing I ever heard,

And Jenna just said it now.

For short lies, you can say the whole lie in the chanted lines:

Silliest thing I ever heard,

I ever heard, I ever heard;

Silliest thing I ever heard,

The table danced with the salt shaker.

Skills Reinforced

Communication: Saying chanted lines in unison.

Leader: Pronouncing a story clearly to the entire group.

Storytelling:

Leader: Improvising a fantasy story about an object in the room.

Thinking: Reviewing criteria for determining truth or falsehood.

Group: Imagining a single object as it appears in one or more—possibly inconsistent—fantasy stories.

Leader: Imagining the impossible.

Curriculum: Dealing playfully with objects in the immediate environment.

※ ※

APPLE TREE

Grade levels: Grade 1 and up.

Complexity: Medium.

Game type: Alternating solo stories with group chant. Guessing true or false.

Quick summary: A player tells a purportedly true personal story; after the story, the others guess whether it was true or false.

Directions: Point to individual players in turn, as though saying "Eenie meenie" or "One Potato, Two Potato," while saying this rhyme:

As I climbed up the apple tree,

All the apples fell on me.

Apple pudding, apple pie,

Did you ever tell a lie?

Point to yourself on the word "lie." Say,

It fell on me. So my job is to tell a story from my life. The trick is that the story could be true or false. Your job is to guess which it is. At the end, I'll take a vote. If you think the story is false, you will hold out two crossed fingers—as though you were crossing fingers behind your back to fool someone. If you think the story is true, hold out two straight fingers—not crossed. Let's have a practice vote. At the count of three, everyone vote false. Ready? One, two, three, vote!

Look around at the group's hands. Each player should be holding out two crossed fingers. Say, "Now let's all vote true. Ready again? One, two three, vote!" Look around again; players should be holding out two uncrossed fingers.

Next, tell a story from your life. Choose a true story that you think will interest and relax your group. For example, with junior high students, I like to break the ice by mentioning family quarrels:

When I was little, we had a big, expensive mirror over the dining room table. Sometimes my parents would argue, and every once in a while they would threaten to throw things at each other. One of them would say, "Don't you throw that, it might break the mirror!" And the other would say, "I don't care what I break." And sometimes they'd throw things at the wall. But no one ever broke that mirror.

Now say, "On the count of three, everyone vote. One, two, three, vote!" The players should all hold out two fingers, either crossed to mean "false" or uncrossed to mean "true." Look around, saying, "I'm looking around to see what people thought. Some thought 'true' and some thought 'false.' The story was . . . true!"

Give a little time for reactions ("How did they miss the mirror?" "My mother broke a window once"); then say, "Who would be willing to tell a story from your life? It could be true or false. Hold up your hands, and I'll use the rhyme to choose." Saying the rhyme, count out among those volunteering. The player you point to at the word "lie" will tell the next story.

Hints: Reluctant players. I use this frequently as a first story game with a new group. As a result, I often face players reluctant to volunteer.

To coax players to tell a story—while giving them time to think of an incident from their life—I recite the following list of possibilities:

You can tell a true story, or one that you made up. It can be something that happened this morning, or something that happened a long time ago. It could have happened just to you, or to you and a friend, or your parents, or brothers or sisters, or some other family member, or even to a pet. It could have happened at home, or on vacation, or at school, or at work.

Often enough, someone will raise a hand to volunteer by the time I finish saying all this.

If group members seem ready to tell a story but prevented by peer pressure from actually showing their readiness, I'll sometimes use the counting-out rhyme to choose among the seated players, even though none have raised their hands.

Using the counting-out rhyme. The "Apple Tree" rhyme serves as an impersonal "finger of fate" to choose a volunteer. At the same time, however, it actually allows you to choose which volunteer the last word will land on.

Why would you bother to cheat with the counting-out rhyme? First, the class will be helped if the first volunteer succeeds, rather than fails. It's your responsibility, then, to try to choose someone who can actually hold the group's attention and who won't "clutch." Second, in some groups only some players will volunteer (boys, girls, native English speakers, etc.). If someone from a different group raises a tentative hand, it may help the entire group if you give that person a chance.

To cheat, keep in mind that the rhyme has 16 beats, and that you can decide which player to start with. Therefore, if you are counting around a large circle, the 16th person will be chosen. If all the girls are on the left side of a group of 30 students (15 girls and 15 boys), starting at the left will choose a boy. Starting in the middle and continuing to the right will bring you back among the girls.

If you are choosing between just two volunteers, the rhyme will choose the one you did not start on (because 16 is an even number). If you are choosing among three volunteers, the rhyme will choose the one you started on (because you'll point to all three volunteers five times, and then point to the first one again). If you are choosing among four volunteers, the rhyme will choose the fourth one from the one you started on (because you'll point to each player four times, ending on the last one of the four).

To use these hints, decide who you want to pick, count how many volunteers you have, and then start the rhyme by pointing to the appropriate player—so that the rhyme will end on the player of your choice.

What is true? In most groups, the question will eventually be asked, "What makes a story true?" The question usually comes up when a player claims truth for a story that seems obviously false in some part—or when a player claims falsehood for a story that seems true.

I find it best to respond to the question by asking the players what they think. Their answers teach me a great deal about their thought processes. First graders, for example, tend to believe that one drop of falsehood makes a whole story false. Adults may be more apt to say, "It's a true story—but of course I simplified the part about the hospital to make it short enough."

Some people judge the truth of a story by its moral lesson or accordance with a world view: "I know that story must be true, because people pretend to be a lot meaner than they are."

Variation: If your group reserves the word "lie" for serious offenses, you can alter the rhyme to end:

Apple pudding, apple dilly,

Did you ever tell a silly?

Skills Reinforced

Communication: Saying chanted lines in unison.

Group: Using the agreed-upon gesture to "vote."

Leader: Pronouncing a story clearly to the entire group.

Storytelling:

Leader: Telling a personal experience story, free of the constraints of truthfulness.

Thinking: Reviewing criteria for and practicing the determination of truth or falsehood.

Leader: At more advanced levels, creating strategies for making a true story appear false, or a false story appear true.

Curricular: Practicing the solo-chorus form.

Experiencing a genre of folklore story, the "memorat"—the personal story told as true.

Critical Thinking: Finding Alternative Interpretations

To evaluate a statement or conclusion, it is helpful to think of alternative interpretations of known data. For example, it may seem true that Grandfather's clock must have sensed his passing, because it stopped running the day he died. That explanation will seem less likely, however, when we consider an alternative interpretation of its stopping: Grandfather might have been the only person who wound his clock!

Games in This Section

In "Such a Robbery!" players describe the loss of something that sounds valuable but is not. They must not only give a description that makes an object seem more valuable than it is, they must also think of an alternative interpretation of their description.

"Daddy Shot a Bear" makes even greater demands. In this game, players must imagine alternative explanations of the single sentence, "Daddy shot a bear"—explanations that make it clear that, contrary to our likely first interpretation, Daddy did nothing brave.

Games in Other Sections

In the game "Janey Jo" (p. 6), one player gives alternative explanations for the presence of a sound.

In "The Back Speaks" (p. 25), a single activity is performed with different attitudes. Starting with the simple activity, players must think of alternative reasons and contexts for it.

A component of finding alternative explanations is seeing possible advantages and disadvantages. In these games, players think of the pros and cons of a change:

"Inventions" (p. 80)
"Squabble Body" (p. 94)

※ ※

SUCH A ROBBERY!

Grade levels: Kindergarten through grade 5.

Complexity: Low.

Game type: Alternating solo stories with group chant.

Quick Summary: Players tell of an apparently valuable object that was stolen, then explain why it was actually worthless.

Directions: Speak the following lines (or chant them like a poem; or sing them loosely to the tune—sung twice through—of "What Will We Do with a Drunken Sailor?" or "London Bridge"; or sing them to the tune given on p. 152). As you speak, clap four times for each line (the first two times, clap hands on thighs twice; the third time, clap hands together; the fourth time, "shrug" with palms up, elbows bent, and hands out to the side at shoulder level):

At my cousin's it has happened;

It has happened at my cousin's.

At my cousin's it has happened,

Such a robbery!

Seven sweaters someone stole,

Three with patches, four with holes!

At my cousin's it has happened,

Such a robbery!

Say, "Do that with me!" Repeat the lines, with motions.

Say, "Do you know what to do when I say, 'Such a robbery!'? Do what we just did. Let's try it. Such a robbery!" Repeat the lines and motions again.

Say, "This time, I'll tell you a little story first. Do you remember what to do when I say those special words?" Tell this story:

My cousin is so poor, nothing he has is worth anything! Once, robbers broke in and stole seven sweaters. Does this sound terrible? Actually, three of the sweaters were covered all over with patches, and four of them were covered all over with holes. They were too worn out to wear. Such a robbery!

Chant the lines again with the motions, encouraging all players to join in.

Say, "Does anyone want to tell a story about something that was stolen, but wasn't really worth anything? When you want to stop your story, just say the special words, and we'll all say the verse." If no player volunteers, you may need to tell another sample story or two.

Hint: Most players tell true stories about thefts of valueless objects. Some, of course, make up preposterous stories (e.g., "Someone stole my time machine, but it had only enough fuel in it for one trip—the thief will be stranded in the past!"). I try to encourage both kinds of stories. Sometimes, it's helpful to identify each kind of story after they are told. You can do this quickly and supportively with a simple appreciation, such as "That sounds like it really happened!" or "What a great imagination!"

I'm always surprised at the number of true stories on this topic known even by kindergarten children.

Variations: The verse is from a traditional folk song of Eastern European Jews. A comic, self-deprecating song, it makes light of how poor the typical Jews were. In particular, it playfully acknowledges the poverty of the rabbis who served the small Jewish communities. If you explain this background to the players, you might say "rabbi" in place of "cousin," as in the original folk song. You can even teach the original Yiddish words:

Bay mayn rebin iz gevazn,

Iz gevazn bay mayn rebin,

Bay mayn rebin iz gevazn,

A ganayve.

Ziben hemder vi di becher

Dray mit lates fir mit lecher!

Bay mayn rebin iz gevazn,

A ganayve.

To hear these lines sung in Yiddish, listen to one of the records listed in Sources and Notes (p. 142).

Change or omit the motions, as desired. You can even add standing-up movements, or make the chanted lines into a circle dance.

Skills Reinforced

Communication: Saying chanted lines in unison.

Leader: Pronouncing a contribution clearly to the entire group.

Storytelling:

Leader: Improvising a fantasy story explaining how an apparently serious robbery was actually inconsequential.

Thinking: Exploring alternative interpretations of an event.

Curricular: Practicing the solo-chorus form. Reviewing personal experiences of material loss.

※ ※

DADDY SHOT A BEAR

Grade levels: Grade 1 and up.

Complexity: Low.

Game type: Alternating solo stories with group chant.

Quick summary: Players create brief stories that explain why "Daddy shot a bear" does not mean what it would appear to mean.

Directions: Speak these lines (or sing them loosely to the tune of "Hot Cross Buns," or sing them to the tune given on p. 150):

Daddy shot a bear,

Daddy shot a bear,

Shot it through a keyhole,

And never touched a hair.

Say, "Say that with me!" Repeat the lines.
Say,

You heard me say that Daddy shot a bear? That sounds brave, right? Well, if you know the whole story, it wasn't really brave at all.

When Daddy heard the bear coming, he ran inside the house and hid. He wanted to take a picture of the bear outside our house, but he was afraid to even stand in the window and take it. So he pointed the camera through the keyhole and shot the bear—with a camera.

Speak or sing the lines again. Say,

I'll tell you a different story about how Daddy shot a bear but wasn't being brave.

You see, Daddy is a veterinarian. One day they called him in to the zoo because they had a sick bear. They wanted Daddy to give the bear a shot of medicine, but Daddy was too scared. Finally, they had 20 people hold the bear down while Daddy sneaked up and gave the bear its shot.

Speak or sing the lines again. Then say,

Who can make up another story about how Daddy shot a bear but wasn't really brave?

Call on a volunteer. After the volunteer's story, speak or sing the lines again. Repeat as desired, or until all players who want a turn have had one.

Hints: Some young children will have trouble understanding the idea of this game. It may help to tell several sample stories. Daddy might be an animal scientist who shot the bear with a tranquilizing gun; or the bear might have been tame, already dead, or asleep; or it might have been a toy bear that was shot with a water pistol or rubber band.

Don't worry if your players give short responses in this game, or exhibit only a small range of creativity in their responses. A group that is only beginning to develop its critical thinking skills will have much to gain from repeating this game over time.

Keep sessions short: play this game for five minutes or so at a time over several sessions. If your group does not introduce new ideas on its own, you can add one new kind of response each session. If you tell the example story, "Daddy drew a picture of a bear, then shot a bullet through it," it is likely that other players will make use of the idea of shooting a picture of a bear. Another time, you can introduce the ideas of shooting an already dead bear, or of shooting with a water pistol.

If your players give very abbreviated stories, such as, "He climbed up on the roof," you can respond in several ways. First, you can ask questions, such as, "Then what happened?" or "Why did he climb on the roof?" Second, you can restate the story and then ask a question:

So, Daddy climbed up on the roof. What did he shoot the bear with?

Third, you can restate the story while elaborating it. Often, you can tell by the player's expression or other responses whether you are interpreting the story correctly. You might say,

*So, Daddy was outside, and saw a bear coming, right? And he was scared,
 but he couldn't get in the house. And there was no place to hide. But
 Daddy had a ladder, so he climbed up onto the roof.*

Variations: Use a different statement. Instead of "Daddy shot a bear," take a statement such as, "Mouthgravel is the most popular toothpaste" and make stories that show how the statement could be true, but not mean what it would appear to mean. Other possible statements:

The snow was over my head.

She caught the biggest fish anyone there had ever seen in that country.

I broke the record in the thousand meter race.

I finished my homework, but I lost it.

Of course, your players may enjoy making up their own statements, too.

When using different statements, you can use the same lines to speak or sing between stories; or you can omit them; or you can change them to fit the new subject (e.g., "The snow was awfully deep, the snow was awfully deep; At least that's what they tell me, 'cause I was fast asleep").

Skills Reinforced

Communication: Saying chanted lines in unison.

Leader: Pronouncing a story clearly to the entire group.

Storytelling:

Leader: Improvising a fantasy story explaining how Daddy could "shoot a bear" but not be brave.

Thinking: Exploring alternative explanations for a statement.

Curricular: Practicing the solo-chorus form. Reviewing multiple meanings of "shoot."

SOURCES AND NOTES

All the games have been adapted or created by the author of this book.

In the notes that follow, you'll learn the origin of the games and any verses or songs used with them. You'll also see three other types of information (where applicable):

My first source: where I first learned the game (or the song), whether in the version in this book or not.

The closest source: the source of the version closest to the one in this book, if different from the "first."

Other sources: some or all of the other sources I used.

In the case of games I created that were inspired by other games, these references apply to the games that inspired me; in the case of games I created that incorporate a song or rhyme from oral tradition, the references apply to the song or rhyme.

Full information for each source appears in the Bibliography (p. 143).

MASTERING ORAL COMMUNICATION

Wolf, Are You Ready?

This traditional game is widespread among Anglo-American and English children; forms of it are popular in other countries as well. In some forms, players ask "What time is it, Mr. Wolf?" When the Wolf answers "Supper time," or "Twelve o'clock," the Wolf chases the other players. Or the game may be a guessing game, in which the players suggest a time and the Wolf gives chase when they are correct.

Sometimes played with a Fox chasing Chickens, the game's older forms often include more extended dialogues as well as more roles. One example includes a song that ends with "What time is it?"—all of which is repeated eight times—followed by a 10-line dialogue between the Hen and the Old Woman. When the Old Woman finally chases the Chickens, the Hen tries to protect them (Williams and Frost, *Evening Amusements,* 68–69).

A version from Cairo (Opie and Opie, *Street and Playground,* 103) is quite similar to our New York version. Even a Chinese version (Hunt and Cain, *Games the World Around,* 64–65) resembles it in many ways. Other forms have been collected in Italy, Germany, Spain, and South America (Opie and Opie, *Street and Playground,* 103).

My First Source

Archive of Folk Culture, recording 3649 B2. Recorded in 1938 by Herbert Halpert from the singing of Josephine Alongi and a group of girls at the Lenox Hill Settlement House, New York, NY. (Song plus game description.)

Other Sources

Barker, *Theatre Games*, 86.

Brady, *All In! All In!* 142–43.

Gomme, *Traditional Games*, vol. 2, 396–97, 410–11.

Perrin et al., *Gymnastic Games*, 88–89.

Withers, *Treasury of Games*, 82–83, 119–20.

Janey Jo

I adapted this game from a traditional Scottish children's game—which is itself a variant of a widespread singing game of the British Isles and English-speaking North America.

"Janey Jo" seems to be a variant of "Jenny Jo," which tells a longer story. In its fullest forms, "Jenny Jo" (or "Jennie Jones") begins with suitors coming to ask for the hand of Jenny Jo. They are put off by Jenny's family with the report that she must do various chores; at last, they are told that she has hurt herself, is sick, is worse, and, finally, is dead. The suitors then ask what color to dress her in; to each color, they reply, "No, blue is for sailors," or "No, red is for soldiers." At last, they are told "white," and reply, "Yes, white is for the corpse." At this point, the game may end, but in a few versions the suitors hear a noise and ask what it is. Then the family says, "It is the ghost of Jenny Jo!" Then Jenny Jo rises from the dead and chases the other players.

My First Source

Fraser, *Langsyne*, 120–21.

Other Sources

Gomme, *Traditional Games*, vol. 1, 260–83; vol. 2, 432–35.

Newell, *Games and Songs*, 63–66, 243–45.

Opie and Opie, *Singing Game*, 254–60.

Opie and Opie, *Street and Playground*, 105–06 ("John Brown").

Aunt Dinah

I first heard this as a vigorous African-American children's game. Later, I learned that it probably had migrated from British and Anglo-American tradition.

The earliest published version available to me (Child, L.M.) describes it as a forfeit: the penalty that players pay for mistakes in another game. In that version, two players enact a small, ludicrous drama without laughing, complete with a handkerchief held at the eyes and exaggerated sobs of "Sad news!" Other variants also require players not to laugh.

Variants differ in who died: Uncle Joshua, Uncle Ned, Mr. Postman, Queen Dido, or Tom Thumb.

Some variants are cumulative, repeating all the prior postures or movements each time a new one is added. Others require the players to keep on performing a movement once it has begun, then add new movements—continue nodding the head while beginning to tap the foot, etc.

I'm not sure where I learned the exact version given here; I may have unconsciously collated several traditional versions.

My First Source

Yurchenco, *John's Island* ("Mr. Postman Died").

Other Sources

Child, L.M., *Girl's Own Book*, 100 ("The King of Morocco Is Dead!").

Newell, *Games and Songs*, 137 ("The Royal Russian Princess, Husty Fusty, Is Defunct!").

Walks of Life

This is my adaptation of a traditional game, known in continental Europe as well as in the British Isles and English-speaking North America. In versions that put two groups across from each other, the groups often recite a dialogue—although many versions of the game lack the dialogue (see Routledge).

The dialogue given here is highly adapted from Gomme, Opie and Opie, and Emrich and Korson.

My First Source

Emrich and Korson, *Child's Book of Folklore*, 125.

Other Sources

Boyd, *Handbook of Recreational Games*, 106–07.

Brewster, *American Nonsinging Games*, 4–7.

Gomme, *Traditional Games*, vol. 1, 117; vol. 2, 305–06.

Gregson, *Incredible Indoor Games Book*, 12.

Hindman, *Games and Stunts*, 59–60.

Newell, *Games and Songs*, 249–50.

Opie and Opie, *Street and Playground*, 280–84.

Perrin et al., *Gymnastic Games*, 148–49.

Routledge, *Every Boy's Book*, 29.

Spolin, *Theater Games for the Classroom*, 94.

From Me to You

I created the chant for this adaptation of an uncommon game.

My First Source

Orlick, *Second Cooperative*, 87.

Other Sources

Spolin, *Theater Games for the Classroom*, 173.

Knocking

Many traditional games involve the guessing of sounds. This game was inspired by a game in Boyd. I created the song to help set an imaginative mood as well as to structure the timing of the knocking.

My First Sources

Boyd, *Handbook of Recreational Games*, 78.

Other Sources

Spolin, *Theater Games for the Classroom*, 99.

Guess the Voice

This game is derived from "Blind Man's Wand," or "The Muffin Man," a traditional guessing game. In the traditional versions, the player in the center can demand that a player imitate three vocal sounds (which can be animal sounds), or answer any three questions, or repeat whatever the center player says. In a Czech version (Brewster), the center player calls, "Little bird, how do you sing?" The other player must make a sound. In a German game, a player can be required to say "Peep" (Rohrbough). Similar games appear in Poland and Greece (Brewster).

I added the idea of having the center player demand a story, and of using the story prompt, "Tell me how a ____ helped a ____!"

My First Source

Williams and Frost, *Evening Amusements*, 8–9.

Other Sources

Brewster, *American Nonsinging Games*, 14–15.

Child, L.M., *Girl's Own Book*, 59.

Gomme, *Traditional Games*, vol. 1, 403–04.

Home Games, 26.

Mohr, *Games Treasury*, 240.

Perrin et al., *Gymnastic Games*, 76.

Rohrbough, *All Time Games*, 16.

Cross-Picture Puzzles

Reading a description of a game in which players combine word-cards to create sentences (Schultz and Fisher, *Games for All Reasons,* 17), I suddenly thought, "What if players drew pictures instead, and put them on a board like a crossword game?" The result was this game.

They Tossed It High

For a course I teach on stories and images, I wanted a way to give students a chance to hear an evocative description of an image, then to allow the image to develop in their own minds. I decided to create a story game using the first verse of a traditional ballad.

The ballad I chose is known as "Sir Hugh; or the Jew's Daughter" in Francis James Child's famous collection. In the ballad, a child is drawn into a garden, then killed. A Nova Scotia version begins:

It rains, it rains in merry Scotland,

It rains in bower and ha',

And all the boys in merry Scotland

Are playing of the ba'.

They tossed it high, so very high,

They tossed it high and low,

They tossed it into a Jew's garden,

Where many a flower did grow.

The story is probably based on an anti-Semitic Christian belief (dating to the Middle Ages) that Jews required the blood of a Christian child for the Passover service. This belief was used as a pretext for the persecution and murder of Jews. Many Jewish households end their Passover services by opening the door "to allow Elijah to enter," a practice that stems in part from a historical desire to show their Christian neighbors that no ritual murder had been committed.

A version of the ballad—in which "Sir Hugh" has made way for "Harry Hughes"— was collected from African-American children in New York (Newell).

I adapted the words and created a new melody.

My First Source

Seeger, R.C., *American Folksongs for Children*, 68.

Closest Source

Creighton, *Songs and Ballads from Nova Scotia*, 16–17.

Other Sources

Arnold, *World Book of Children's Games*, 178–79 ("The Unfinished Story Game").

Bronson, *Traditional Tunes*, vol. 3, 72–104.

Child, F. J., *Popular Ballads*, vol. 3, 233–54 (number 155).

Newell, *Games and Songs*, 75–78.

Rakan-san

In Japan, many Buddhist temples feature an outdoor line of 31 stone statues that represent the reincarnations of the Buddha. Each statue has a distinctive costume and posture. Japanese children play a game in which they imagine that these statues come to life long enough to take on another posture. The game is accompanied by a chant that signals the players when to change their posture.

In the variants described in my sources, the game is an elimination game: those who make a mistake drop out, and may be made to perform a stunt for the others. As in musical chairs, the goal is to be the last player remaining, and the pace increases as the game continues.

My First Source

Phillips, *Far Peoples*, 126–27.

Other Sources

Rohrbough, *All Time Games*, 11 ("Temple Garden Game").

I made up the "Rakan-san" chant.

The Back Speaks

This original game was inspired by some existing traditional and educational games.

My First Source

Brandreth, *World's Best Indoor Games*, 29.

Closest Source

Spolin, *Theater Games*, 140.

Other Sources

Luvmoor and Luvmoor, *Everyone Wins!* 35.

Ó Súilleabháin, *Irish Wake Amusements*, 127–28.

Old Bloody Bones

This is adapted from a Texas play-party game. (For the history of the play-party game and some easy-to-play examples, see Lipman, *We All Go Together*.) The collector remarked that the traditional stories told during the game reminded him of the stories told by medicine-show entertainers.

My First Source

Owens, *Swing and Turn*, 104–05.

Fortunately, Unfortunately

This is a traditional joke or participation story. Mohr places it as a vaudeville routine. I have heard it as a participation story at adult parties, along these lines:

Leader: *They're tearing down the saloon.*

Group: *That's bad!*

Leader: *They're building a bigger one.*

Group: *That's good!*

Leader: *But there will only be one bar in the new saloon.*

Group: *That's bad!*

Leader: *But it will be 40 feet long.*

Group: *That's good!*

One of the joke forms was made into a children's book by Remy Charlip (*Fortunately*).

My First Source

Someone described this game to me about 1980. My informant had seen an actor use it in the classroom.

Other Sources

Mohr, *Games Treasury*, 264.

You're Shaking Me Up

A traditional game—often used as a theater warm-up—has each player in a circle create a movement; each successive player must repeat all the previous movements, then add a new one. I fashioned this game by creating a story to combine with the theater game, thereby providing a narrative purpose for the movements.

Monster Rumble

I came across a theater game in which an actor creates a monster (Barker, *Theatre Games,* 114). In creating a song and circle-game for creating monsters, I was influenced by the traditional African-American games, such as "Alabama, Mississippi" (learned in person from Bessie Jones of the Georgia Sea Islands), in which players in a line take turns stepping forward and performing a solo dance.

LEARNING ABOUT LANGUAGE

Letter Echoes

In a Victorian parlor game, each player selects a word from a list, then echoes that word whenever it is spoken by the storyteller (*Home Games,* 61–66).

As far as I can remember, I combined the parlor game with the game my cousin Roger Fox played when I was young (described in the text under "Variations"), to produce this game.

Letter Relay

I found existing games in which a word or a sentence is to start with the last letter of the previous word or sentence. I combined that idea with the idea of the "round-robin" story, to produce this game.

My First Source

Schultz and Fisher, *Games for All Reasons,* 8.

Other Sources

Mohr, *Games Treasury,* 267.

Hide the Words

Several traditional games from the nineteenth century require players to speak a sentence containing a previously assigned word, which another player must guess. Once it occurred to me that words could also be hidden in a story, I went about creating this game.

For sources of the traditional games, see:

Gomme, *Traditional Games,* vol. 2, 114–15.

Home Games, 115–17.

Sunbeam, *Child's Book of Games,* 14.

Williams and Frost, *Evening Amusements,* 64.

Story Crambo

The game "Crambo" was a popular Victorian parlor game in which players made their guesses by describing the word they guess: "Is it part of the equipment found in most playgrounds?" "No, it is not swing." I had the idea of substituting stories for descriptions.

According to Mohr, this was originally a game in which players created rhyming poems based on randomly drawn words (see the notes for "Questions and Answers," p. 138). "Crambo" apparently stems from the Greek word for "cabbage."

My First Source

Boyd, *Handbook of Recreational Games,* 98.

Other Sources

Hindman, *Games and Stunts*, 79–80.

Mohr, *Games Treasury*, 262.

Williams and Frost, *Evening Amusements*, 5–6, 193–94.

Fuddy Duddy

As a child, I learned the traditional game "Hinky Pinky" (Augarde, *Oxford Guide to Word Games,* 199–200), on which this game is based. I created "Fuddy Duddy" by adding the requirement that clues be given in story form.

Teakettle Stories

My contribution to this traditional word game is to require that the clues be given in story form.

In its traditional forms, the clues are given in a variety of ways, sometimes by two players carrying on a conversation about "teakettle," or else by the group answering questions such as "When do you teakettle?"

Most versions of this game from the United States change the English "teakettle" to "coffeepot," although it is also known as "How, When, and Where," or "How Do You Like It?"

My First Source

Mulac, *Educational Games for Fun*, 123–24.

Other Sources

Boyd, *Handbook of Recreational Games*, 93, 100.

Child, L.M., *Girl's Own Book*, 19–20.

Hindman, *Games and Stunts*, 77–78.

Home Games, 107–08.

Williams and Frost, *Evening Amusements*, 75.

Williams-Ellis and Williams-Ellis, *In and Out of Doors*, 190–91.

Withers, *Treasury of Games*, 76.

Pun Puzzles

This game was inspired by a party game given in Harbin, *Phunology*, 290–91. A specific written story ("The Romance of a Shirt-waist Girl") is passed out to players—with words omitted that relate to sewing. The players are to fill in the blanks. For example, players are expected to provide the words "cuff" and "collar" in this sentence from the story: "She often felt she would like to ____ him, but decided to ____ him instead." I had the idea of letting players create their own punning stories, on a subject of their choice.

Proverb Guessing

A traditional game involves guessing proverbs from the answers of a sequence of players. The guessing player asks random questions of each player, who must incorporate the assigned word of the proverb in an answer. My contribution was to use segments of a story instead of answers to various questions.

My First Source

Boyd, *Handbook of Recreational Games*, 96.

Other Sources

Harris, *Great Games*, 76–77.

Hindman, *Games and Stunts*, 79.

Home Games, 104–07.

Parlett, *Botticelli and Beyond*, 43–44.

Williams and Frost, *Evening Amusements*, 61–62.

Mish Mash Mush

I created this game after reading the game "Amazed American" in Shipley, *Playing with Words,* 17–18.

Would You Believe?

This game was inspired by Sutton-Smith's *Folkstories of Children,* which includes transcriptions of stories told by young children. Reading the transcriptions, I was struck by the formulaic character of some of the stories, which apparently apply a simple sentence structure to every conceivable object: "The cat went on the cakies. The cat went on the car. . . . The cookie went on the fireman's hat. The fireman's hat went on the bucket. The cookie went on the carousel. . . ." (page 6). It occurred to me that this formulaic approach could produce humorous images.

The melody I created was inspired by the traditional calypso song "Mary Ann."

Places, Persons, and Things

Esther Kaplan, Director of Arts in Progress (Jamaica Plain, MA), told me of a game she had played in which players drew three words out of hats, then created a story using them. Starting with that idea, I created a version of this game. As I used it, it evolved into its present form.

EXPLORING PLACES, PERIODS, AND PEOPLES

Towns and Counties

A traditional game of Irish children, "Towns and Counties" was collected in a housing development near Dublin. Traditionally, when it is played on the street, one team of players tries to guess the place thought of by another team, who may use "all sorts of miming actions" to give additional clues. The traditional place name used to explain the game to newcomers is "Wicklow."

My adaptations include the idea of using a team of players, each of whom tells a section of the story and incorporates a single syllable of the place name.

My First Source

Brady, *All In! All In!* 142.

Other Sources

Harbin, *Phunology,* 285, "Pictorial Geography"

History Mystery

As I was doing the research for this book, my wife, Linda Palmström, called me with an exciting discovery. She had learned that her 12-year-old niece, Susan Tussing, had read Donald Sobel's *More Two-Minute Mysteries* and was spontaneously creating her own mystery stories. Once Susan made me realize that children were capable of creating this kind of story, I tried to structure the game in a way that would cover all the steps she made unconsciously.

Inventions

This game was inspired by an example in Hennings, *Communication in Action,* chapter 6. Hennings describes a teacher's innovative presentation of a unit based on *The Human Adventure,* from the Addison-Wesley Social Studies Program.

Do It Your Way

In the traditional game "In the Manner of the Adverb," players call on someone to perform a particular action—in the manner of the adverb which they are trying to guess. My primary contribution was to require that the action be chosen from a given story.

My First Source

Gregson, *Incredible Indoor Games Book*, 25.

Other Sources

Hindman, *Games and Stunts*, 81.

Parlett, *Botticelli and Beyond*, 31–32.

Withers, *Treasury of Games*, 160.

Questions and Answers

Numerous traditional games match questions with unrelated answers. In one game, known as "Substantives," "Twisted Words," or "Crambo" (not to be confused with the word-guessing game also called "Crambo"—see the notes to "Story Crambo," p. 135), players draw a question and a noun, and must create a poem that answers the question and uses the noun. In some cases, a single sheet of paper is used by having one player write a question, fold the paper over, then pass on the paper to another who adds the noun. The third player to get each piece of paper must write a rhyme that answers the question and uses the noun.

The idea of answering the questions with a story appears in Parlett. The idea of using questions about a particular story combined with phrases from nursery rhymes comes from Vinton.

My First Source

Vinton, *Folkways Omnibus of Children's Games*, 281–82.

Other Sources

Cassell's Book of Sports and Pastimes, 761.

Deacove, *Cooperative Games Manual*, 40–41.

Hindman, *Games and Stunts*, 126.

Mott, *Home Games and Parties*, 40–41.

Parlett, *Botticelli and Beyond*, 29–30.

Williams and Frost, *Evening Amusements*, 14–15, 190–91, 195–96.

People Are Different

Like most of the storytellers in New England, I look forward to our annual "town meeting," the Sharing the Fire conference sponsored by the League for the Advancement of New England Storytelling. One year, I was asked to lead a discussion about diversity. To do so, I created this game and song.

Squabble Body

This original game was inspired, in part, by the various folk tales in which the parts of the body argue with one another, invariably with disastrous results.

For references to a few such folk stories in children's books, see MacDonald, *Storyteller's Sourcebook*, 29–30 (A1391) and 212 (J461.1).

Occupations

A game called "Trades," "The Newspaper," or "The President of the Board of Trade" appears in several nineteenth-century game books. In it, each player chooses a trade. Then the Reader reads aloud a story, poem, or other written passage, pausing at each noun. When the Reader points to a player, the player responds with a noun appropriate to the player's selected trade. In some versions, the nouns are assembled before the reading begins; in others, they are contributed on the fly, during the reading of the story.

I adapted "Trades" to create the present game.

My First Source

Routledge, *Every Boy's Book*, 40.

Other Sources

Graeffe and Kearney, *255 Party Games to Play*, 85–86.

Williams and Frost, *Evening Amusements*, 56–57, 100–01.

My Mother, Your Mother

I created this game for use with children at the Edison School, Boston, MA, as part of a program sponsored by Arts in Progress (Jamaica Plain, MA).

I borrowed a traditional counting-out and jump-rope rhyme to use as a chorus.

My First Source

Withers, *Counting Out*, n.p.

Other Sources

Abrahams, *Jump-Rope Rhymes*, 135–36.

Abrahams and Rankin, *Counting-Out Rhymes*, 154–55.

Emrich and Korson, *Child's Book of Folklore*, 117.

PRACTICING MATH, SCIENCE, AND THINKING SKILLS

Grouping Stories

Mbundu children from Angola play a game in which a leader calls out a number. The players then divide into groups of the size called out. Their game inspired this one.

My First Source

U.S. Committee for UNICEF, *Games Around the World*, n.p.

Other Sources

A game similar to the Angolan game is described as "Bump" in Harrison, *For the Fun of It*, G-10.

The variation in which players must apply an arithmetic operation to the number in the story was inspired by "Arithmetical Catch-the-Cane" (Hindman, *Games and Stunts,* 163).

I added the storytelling element to the game.

Flying

This game is based on a common parlor game of the nineteenth century, often known as "Ducks Fly," "Fly Away, Pigeon," or "Horns." It was collected as a children's game by Newell in New York and by Gomme in England. It also functioned as a traditional wake amusement among adults in Ireland (Ó Súilleabháin).

Brewster mentions versions from several Scandinavian countries, as well as versions from Latvian, Greek, and Hispanic lore. He quotes a Greek proverb based on the game, applied to a credulous person, "If you tell him that the donkey flies, he will say, 'Yes, it flies.'"

In most versions, the leader speaks a series of short sentences, such as "Cats fly!" or "Cows have horns!" In one variant (*Cassell's Book of Sports and Pastimes*, 765), however, the leader relates a story, mentioning various animals, some of which fly. The example given begins:

> *One lovely morning in June I sallied forth to take the air. The honeysuckle and roses were shedding a delicious perfume, the **butterflies** and **bees** were flitting from flower to flower, the **cuckoo's** note resounded through the groves, and the **lark's** sweet trill was heard overhead.*

The responsive movements range from the "flying motion" described in this work, to arm flapping, to raising a single finger off the table or off a knee. In some cases, players don't move at all, but repeat correct sentences in unison and remain silent after incorrect ones—or else they make the sound of the animal that was correctly described.

In the traditional forms, players who make a mistake are eliminated or required to pay a forfeit—which they must redeem by performing some amusing or humiliating task.

The idea of having players who make a mistake become hecklers was inspired by the "Satori Heckler" in Fluegelman, *More New Games,* 79.

My First Source

Newell, *Games and Songs,* 119.

Other Sources

Brewster, *American Nonsinging Games,* 24-25.

Gomme, *Traditional Games,* vol. 1, 228.

Ó Súilleabháin, *Irish Wake Amusements,* 105.

Sets in Conflict

I created this game to capitalize on the emotional correlates to elementary set theory.

The sample story is adapted from one created in November 1993 by Emily, grade 5, Matthew Thornton School, Derry, New Hampshire.

The Sea Is Getting Stormy

This traditional game, a variant of "Musical Chairs," is known in many countries. It is closely related to the game "Huntsman," which lacks the storytelling element. Other relatives include "Thunder"—a Czech game that also lacks a story—and "Blowout," an Arkansas variant that includes storytelling.

My First Source

Phillips, *Far Peoples,* 257.

Other Sources

Brewster, *American Nonsinging Games,* 98–101 ("Thunder," "Blowout").

Harris, *Great Games,* 40.

Hindman, *Games and Stunts,* 89–90, 108 ("Huntsman").

Hunt and Cain, *Games the World Around,* 89.

Williams and Frost, *Evening Amusements,* 25, 73–74 ("Huntsman").

Spaceship

Several nineteenth-century parlor games (among them "The Bird Catcher," "The Picnic," "The Sportsman," and "The Stage Coach") use the same basic idea: one player tells or reads a story, while others take the names of various characters or objects in the story. When a character or object is mentioned, the assigned player responds with a movement or sound. Usually, there is one word or phrase to which all must respond. Frequently the game ends with a mad dash for empty chairs, the player failing to find a chair becoming the next storyteller.

I modernized "Stage Coach," to "Spaceship," adapting the game in small ways over the years. More recently, young players I work with have adapted it further to become "Space Shuttle."

My First Source

Emrich and Korson, *Child's Book of Folklore,* 149.

Other Sources

Bancroft, *Games for the Playground*, 185–86.

Boyd, *Handbook of Recreational Games*, 102.

Cassell's Book of Sports and Pastimes, 786–87.

Harbin, *Phunology*, 196–97, 295.

Hindman, *Games and Stunts*, 98.

Home Games, 29–35, 35–39, 40–42.

Maclagan, *Argyleshire*, 87–88.

Sunbeam, *Child's Book of Games*, 5–9.

Williams and Frost, *Evening Amusements*, 15–20, 21–23, 77–80, 80–81, 102–03.

Because

My First Source

Arnold, *World Book of Children's Games*, 162–63.

Other Source

Gregson, *Incredible Indoor Games Book*, 44.

Lovinger, *Learning Disabilities and Games*, 107.

I Was Present!

I learned this game from a quick reading of Weinstein and Goodman, *Playfair*, 142–43. Only when I began to write this book did I notice that their source was my late friend and colleague, Mara Capy.

Old Doc Jones

The song was collected in 1917 by Cecil Sharp, who heard it sung by children at the Pine Mountain Settlement School in Harlan County, Kentucky. A similar version was collected by Angela Melville in Wooton, Kentucky (see Rohrbough).

A game in which players make up a lie about an object is given in Gregson.

My First Source

Sharp, *Southern Appalachians*, 368, 416.

Other Sources

Gregson, *Incredible Indoor Games Book*, 18.

Rohrbough, *Handy Play Party Book*, 120.

Apple Tree

In a class for adults about teaching music to children, I assigned my students to create a game based on a traditional rhyme. One student came in with a version of this game. I loved it and began teaching it in my storytelling classes.

A few months later, when I wanted to credit the student who had created the game, I had forgotten which student it was. Even though I asked every student who had been in the class, no one admitted to having taught it to me. I was puzzled!

Years later, I came across someone who remembered learning this game before I had ever taught my classes. I still don't know the ultimate origin of the game, but I suspect I've solved the puzzle of the reticent student: the student may **not** have made the game up and was therefore reluctant to claim public credit for creating the game, for fear of being exposed as having "cheated" on the assignment.

The variation was contributed by Rosemary Glenn.

My First Source

The rhyme has many versions in oral tradition. I first learned this Irish variant from Hamilton, *So Early in the Morning*.

Other Sources

A game about guessing whether a story is true or false appears in Gregson, *Incredible Indoor Games Book*, 19.

Such a Robbery!

I created this game, basing it on my translation of the traditional Yiddish folk song "A Ganayve."

My First Source

Rubin, *Jewish Folk Songs*, 10–11.

Other Sources

Rubin, *Treasury of Jewish Folksongs*, 130–31.

Silverman, *Yiddish Song Book*, 130–31.

To hear the original Yiddish, listen to these recordings:

Rubin, *Jewish Children Songs and Games*.

Olf, *Mark Olf Sings Jewish Folksongs*.

Daddy Shot a Bear

I created this game by combining an idea from a game book—based, the author claimed, on a tradition of the Tatar (also "Tartar") peoples of Poland and Eastern Europe—with a folk song from the southern United States. The song—a "patting song" used with children—was collected by John Lomax from Annie Brewer of Montgomery, Alabama, in 1937.

I have listed the song as Anglo-American, but I do not actually know whether the singer or the song is from Anglo- or African-American tradition.

My First Source, Game

Vinton, *Folkways Omnibus of Children's Games*, 190–91.

My First Source, Song

Seeger, R.C., *Animal Folksongs for Children*, 78.

Other Sources, Game:

Deacove, *Cooperative Games Manual*, 29–30.

Other Sources, Song:

Archive of Folk Culture, recording 942 A2.

Lomax and Lomax, *Our Singing Country*, 95–96.

Seeger, P., *Folk Songs of Peggy Seeger*, 88.

BIBLIOGRAPHY

Almost every item in this bibliography can be put into one of five rough categories, indicated by these abbreviations:

Pop. Popular game books. These were written primarily for families or leaders of informal recreation—with children or with adults. Those books with copyrights before the 1940s are, in general, available only in specialty collections.

Educ. Educational game books. These were written primarily for teachers, church educators, or leaders of formal recreation programs.

Coop. Cooperative game books. This subset of popular or educational game books focuses on cooperative games or else "new" games.

Folk. Collections by folklorists of authentic texts—of games, songs, or rhymes—from oral tradition.

Rec. Recordings of folk songs.

When a source falls into more than one category, it is marked with multiple abbreviations.

Abrahams, Roger D., ed. *Jump-Rope Rhymes: A Dictionary.* Austin: University of Texas Press, 1969. *Folk*

Abrahams, Roger D., and Lois Rankin, eds. *Counting-Out Rhymes: A Dictionary.* Austin: University of Texas Press, 1980. *Folk*

Archive of Folk Culture. Library of Congress, Washington, DC. *Folk, Rec*

Arnold, Arnold. *The World Book of Children's Games.* Greenwich, CT: Fawcett, 1972. *Pop*

Augarde, Tony. *The Oxford Guide to Word Games.* Oxford: Oxford University Press, 1986. *Pop*

Bancroft, Jessie. *Games for the Playground, Home, School and Gymnasium.* New York: Macmillan, 1934. *Educ, Pop*

Barker, Clive. *Theatre Games.* London: Methuen, 1977. *Educ*

Boyd, Neva L., comp. *Handbook of Recreational Games.* 1945. Reprint. New York: Dover, 1975. *Educ, Pop*

Brady, Eilís. *All In! All In!* Dublin: Comhairle Bhéaloideas Éireann, 1975. *Folk*

Brandreth, Gyles. *The World's Best Indoor Games.* New York: Pantheon, 1981. *Pop*

Brewster, Paul. *American Nonsinging Games.* Norman: University of Oklahoma Press, 1953. *Folk*

Bronson, Bertrand Harris. *The Traditional Tunes of the Child Ballads.* 4 vols. Princeton, NJ: Princeton University Press, 1966. *Folk*

Brotchie, Alastair, comp. *Surrealist Games.* Boston: Shambhala, 1993. *Pop*

Cassell's Book of Sports and Pastimes. Rev. ed. London: Cassell and Company, 1903. *Pop*

Charlip, Remy. *Fortunately.* New York: Macmillan, 1993.

Child, Francis James. *The English and Scottish Popular Ballads.* 5 vols. 1884–98. Reprint. New York: Dover, 1965. *Folk*

Child, L. Maria. *The Girl's Own Book.* 1833. Reprint. Chester, CT: Applewood Books, n.d. *Pop*

Creighton, Helen. *Songs and Ballads from Nova Scotia.* 1932. Reprint. New York: Dover, 1966. *Folk*

Deacove, Jim. *Cooperative Games Manual.* Perth, Ontario: Family Pastimes, 1974. (R.R. 4, Perth, Ontario, Canada K7H 3C6). *Coop*

Emrich, Marion Vallat, and George Korson. *The Child's Book of Folklore.* New York: Dial, 1947. *Folk, Pop*

Fluegelman, Andrew. *More New Games.* Garden City, NY: Doubleday, 1981. *Coop*

Fraser, Amy Stewart. *Dae Ye Min' Langsyne?* London: Routledge and Kegan Paul, 1975. *Folk*

Gomme, Alice Bertha. *The Traditional Games of England, Scotland, and Ireland.* 2 vols. 1888. Reprint. New York: Dover, 1964. *Folk*

Graeffe, Clare A., and Paul W. Kearney. *255 Party Games to Play.* Pioneer Publications, 1938. *Pop*

Gregson, Bob. *The Incredible Indoor Games Book.* Carthage, IL: Fearon, 1982. *Educ*

Hamilton, Diane. *So Early in the Morning.* Tradition TLP 1034. *Folk, Rec*

Harbin, E. O. *Phunology.* Rev. ed. Nashville: Cokesbury, 1923. *Educ*

Harris, Frank W. *Great Games to Play with Groups.* Belmont, CA: Fearon Teacher Aids, 1990. *Educ*

Harrison, Marta. *For the Fun of It.* In *A Manual on Nonviolence and Children,* edited by Stephanie Judson. Philadelphia: Friends Peace Committee, 1977. *Coop*

Hennings, Dorothy Grant. *Communication in Action: Teaching the Language Arts.* 4th ed. Boston: Houghton Mifflin, 1990.

Hindman, Darwin A. *Complete Book of Games and Stunts.* 1950. Reprint. New York: Bonanza, 1956. *Educ, Pop*

Home Games for the People. New York: Philip J. Cozans, 1855. *Pop*

Hunt, Sarah Ethridge, and Ethel Cain. *Games the World Around.* New York: A.S. Barnes, 1941. *Pop*

Lipman, Doug. *We All Go Together: Creative Activities for Children to Use with Multicultural Folksongs.* Phoenix: Oryx, 1994.

Lomax, John, and Alan Lomax. *Our Singing Country.* New York: Macmillan, 1941. *Folk*

Lovinger, Sophie. *Learning Disabilities and Games.* Chicago: Nelson Hall, 1979. *Educ*

Luvmoor, Sambhava, and Josette Luvmoor. *Everyone Wins!* Philadelphia: New Society Publishers, 1990. *Coop*

MacDonald, Margaret Read. *The Storyteller's Sourcebook.* Detroit, MI: Gale Research, 1982.

Maclagan, Robert Craig. *The Games and Diversions of Argyleshire.* 1901. Reprint. New York: Arno, 1976. *Folk*

Mauk, Carolyn. *Storytelling: A Game.* Jonesborough, TN: Mauk's of Jonesborough, 1991. (Main St., Jonesborough, TN 37659, 615-753-4648). *Pop*

Mohr, Merilyn Simonds. *The Games Treasury*. Shelburne, VT: Chapters, 1993. *Pop*

Mott, Mrs. Hamilton. *Home Games and Parties*. New York: Doubleday and McClure, 1898. *Pop*

Mulac, Margaret. *Educational Games for Fun*. New York: Harper and Row, 1971. *Educ*

Newell, William Wells. *Games and Songs of American Children*. 1883. Reprint. New York: Dover, 1963. *Folk*

Ó Súilleabháin, Sean. *Irish Wake Amusements*. Cork, Ireland: Mercier, 1967. *Folk*

Olf, Mark. *Mark Olf Sings Jewish Folksongs*. Folkways Records FW 6826. *Rec*

Opie, Iona, and Peter Opie. *Children's Games in Street and Playground*. Oxford: Clarendon, 1969. *Folk*

Opie, Iona, and Peter Opie. *The Singing Game*. Oxford: Oxford University Press, 1985. *Folk*

Orlick, Terry. *The Second Cooperative Sports and Games Book*. New York: Pantheon Books, 1982. *Coop*

Owens, William A. *Swing and Turn*. Dallas: Tardy Publishing Co., 1936. *Folk*

Parlett, David. *Botticelli and Beyond*. New York: Pantheon, 1981. *Pop*

Perrin, Ethel, et al. *One Hundred and Fifty Gymnastic Games*. Boston: Geo. H. Ellis, 1904. *Educ*

Phillips, Grace Darling. *Far Peoples*. Chicago: University of Chicago Press, 1929. *Pop*

Rohrbough, Lynn. *All Time Games*. Delaware, OH: Cooperative Recreation Service, 1955. *Educ*

Rohrbough, Lynn. *Handy Play Party Book*. Delaware, OH: Cooperative Recreation Service, 1940. *Educ, Folk*

Routledge, Edmund, ed. *Every Boy's Book: A Complete Encyclopedia*. London: George Routledge and Sons, 1868. *Pop*

Rubin, Ruth. *Jewish Children Songs and Games*. Folkways Records FC 7224. *Rec*

Rubin, Ruth. *Jewish Folk Songs*. New York: Oak Publications, 1965. *Folk*

Rubin, Ruth. *A Treasury of Jewish Folksongs*. New York: Schocken Books, 1964. *Folk*

Schultz, Matthew, and Alan Fisher. *Games for All Reasons*. Reading, MA: Addison-Wesley, 1988. *Educ*

Seeger, Peggy. *Folk Songs of Peggy Seeger*. New York: Oak, 1964.

Seeger, Ruth Crawford. *American Folksongs for Children*. Garden City, NY: Doubleday, 1948.

Seeger, Ruth Crawford. *Animal Folksongs for Children*. Garden City, NY: Doubleday, 1950.

Sharp, Cecil. *English Folk Songs from the Southern Appalachians*. London: Oxford University Press, 1932. *Folk*

Shipley, Joseph T. *Playing with Words*. Englewood Cliffs, NJ: Prentice-Hall, 1960. *Pop*

Silverman, Jerry. *The Yiddish Song Book*. Briarcliff Manor, NY: Stein and Day, 1983. *Folk*

Sobel, Donald J. *More Two-Minute Mysteries*. New York: Scholastic, 1971.

Spolin, Viola. *Theater Games for the Classroom*. Evanston, IL: Northwestern University Press, 1986. *Educ*

Star+Gate. P.O. Box 1006, Orinda, CA 94563, 1984. (Fortune-telling game with card deck and cloth playing board.) *Pop*

Sunbeam, Susie. *The Child's Book of Games*. Boston: G.W. Cottrell, 1856. *Pop*

Sutton-Smith, Brian. *The Folkstories of Children*. Philadelphia: University of Pennsylvania Press, 1981. *Folk*

U.S. Committee for UNICEF. *Games Around the World*. New York: U.S. Committee for UNICEF, 1981. (Package of unbound game sheets.) *Pop*

Vinton, Iris. *The Folkways Omnibus of Children's Games*. Harrisburg, PA: Stackpole, 1970. *Pop*

Weinstein, Matt, and Joel Goodman. *Playfair*. San Luis Obispo, CA: Impact, 1980. *Coop*

Williams, Henry T., and S. Annie Frost. *Evening Amusements*. New York: Henry T. Williams, 1878. *Pop*

Williams-Ellis, Susan, and Charlotte Williams-Ellis, et al. *In and Out of Doors*. New York: Coward-McCann, 1938. *Pop*

Withers, Carl. *Counting Out*. 1946. Reprint. New York: Dover, 1970. *Folk, Pop*

Withers, Carl. *A Treasury of Games*. 1947. Reprint. New York: Grosset and Dunlap, 1974. *Folk, Pop*

Yurchenco, Henrietta, recorded by. *John's Island, South Carolina: Its People and Songs*. Folkways Records FS 3840. *Folk, Rec*

MELODIES OF THE SONGS

■ ■ ■

These melodies are optional. All the games can be played without them by chanting the words like poems or by singing the words to the well-known tunes given with each game.

In the case of the folk songs, these tunes are traditional variants, arranged and adapted by Doug Lipman.

In the case of the composed songs, the tunes are composed by Doug Lipman.

The keys have been chosen to allow easy guitar chords while keeping the tunes in the range of most children's voices. Please transpose for other instruments or to match the singing range of your group.

Guitar chords in parentheses may be omitted for ease of playing, or included for variety.

Knocking

Monster Rumble

Daddy Shot a Bear

Traditional (Alabama)

Dad-dy shot a bear, Dad-dy shot a bear,
Shot it through the key-hole, and nev-er touched a hair.

Old Bloody Bones

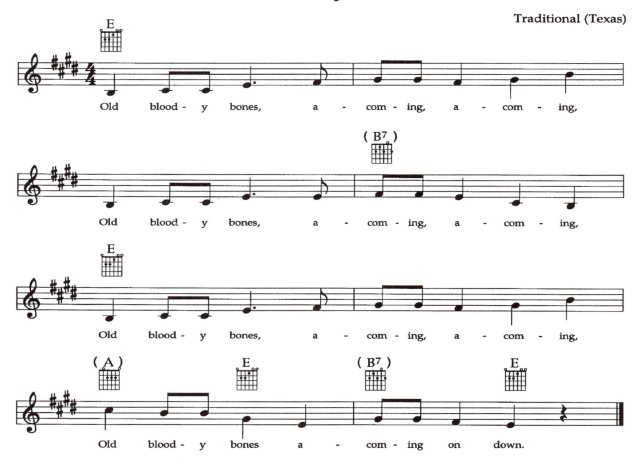

Traditional (Texas)

Old blood-y bones, a-com-ing, a-com-ing,
Old blood-y bones, a-com-ing, a-com-ing,
Old blood-y bones, a-com-ing, a-com-ing,
Old blood-y bones a-com-ing on down.

Old Doc Jones

Traditional (Kentucky)

Old Doc Jones is a fine old man,

A fine old man, a fine old man;

Old Doc Jones is a fine old man,

He told ten thou sand lies.

People Are Different

Doug Lipman

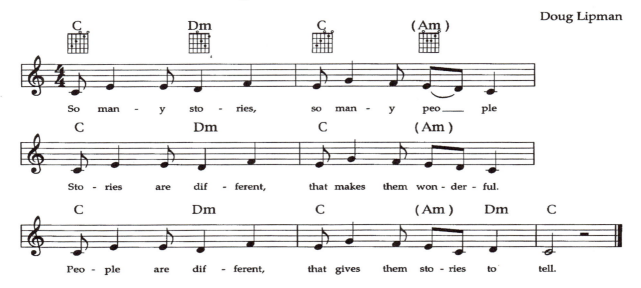

So man - y sto - ries, so man - y peo___ ple

Sto - ries are dif - ferent, that makes them won - der - ful.

Peo - ple are dif - ferent, that gives them sto - ries to tell.

Such a Robbery!

They Tossed It High

Wolf, Are You Ready?

Would You Believe?

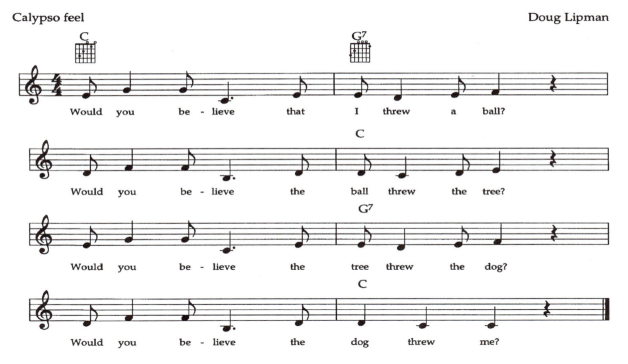

CULTURAL BACKGROUND INDEX

■ ■ ■

The following games (or the rhymes or songs accompanying them) are derived from the folklore of particular cultures. For details, see Sources and Notes, starting on page 130.

GAME FINDER INDEX

■ ■ ■

This index will help you find games to meet your needs. It is divided in sections by age group; games appropriate for more than one age group are listed more than once. "Pre." stands for "preschool"; "K" stands for "kindergarten."

Games especially suited for a given age group are listed in **bold face**.

1st. Games marked with a "✔" in the "1st" column are especially appropriate for a first introduction to story games for the indicated age group.

Size. All games are suitable for groups from 5 to 30 players. Games especially suitable for smaller groups are marked with a number showing the smallest practical group size (e.g., "2" or "4"). Games especially suitable for playing with larger groups are marked "large." Some games fit both categories. "Aunt Dinah," for instance, is suitable for a 2-person group and a large group.

The columns *space* (physical space needed in which to play the game) and *props* (objects needed to play the game) do not refer to requirements that are optional or needed only for a variation of the game. Such requirements are listed at the start of each game.

Space. The abbreviations for *space* are:

circle ...... A clear area for a circle of players (with or without room for one player to walk around the outside).

line .... Enough space to form a line of all players, with the Leader in front.

run .... An area for chasing (which may include a "safe place"—such as an empty expanse of wall) large enough for the entire group.

stage .... An area that the whole group can see, and that's large enough for 1-5 players at a time to walk across (or for 1–10 to stand).

stand .... Enough space for all players to make movements while standing in place.

Props. The abbreviations for *props* are:

P&P .... Paper and pencil or other writing materials.

BB .... Blackboard or other large writing surface.

GAMES FOR PRESCHOOLERS

title	page	grade level	1st	complexity	game type	size	space	props
Aunt Dinah	8	Pre. to grade 5		Low	Imitating posture, with dialogue	2 large	stand	
Janey Jo	6	Pre. to grade 2		Low	Stationary tag, with improvised dialogue		circle	
Occupations	97	Pre. and up		Med.	Filling in a plot			

title	page	grade level	1st	complexity	game type	size	space	props
Old Doc Jones	121	Pre. to grade 2	✔	Low	Alternating solo stories with group chant	3 large		
Rakan-san	23	Pre. to grade 5		Low	Imitating posture, with rhyme	large	stand	
Sea Is Getting Stormy, The	112	Pre. to grade 4		Med.	Audience response to story cues			
Spaceship	114	Pre. to grade 2		Med.	Audience response to story cues	large		
Wolf, Are You Ready?	4	Pre. to grade 2	✔	Low	Chase, with improvised dialogue		run	
Would You Believe?	66	Pre. to grade 2	✔	Low	Filling in a plot	2 large		
You're Shaking Me Up	31	Pre. to grade 4		High	Filling in a plot	large		

GAMES FOR PRIMARY GRADES

title	page	grade level	1st	complexity	game type	size	space	props
Apple Tree	123	Grade 1 and up		Med.	Alternating solo stories with group chant	4		
Aunt Dinah	8	Pre. to grade 5	✔	Low	Imitating posture, with dialogue	2 large	stand	
Back Speaks, The	25	Grade 2 and up		Med.	Guessing a quality of movement	large		chair
Because	116	Grade 3 and up		Low	Round robin	2		
Cross-Picture Puzzles	20	Grade 1 and up		High	Combining elements	2		pictures
Daddy Shot a Bear	128	Grade 1 and up	✔	Low	Alternating solo stories with group chant	large		
Do It Your Way	84	K. to grade 4		Med.	Guessing a quality of movement	2 large	stage	
Flying	106	K. to grade 4	✔	Low	Audience response to story cues		stage	
Fortunately, Unfortunately	30	K. and up		Med.	Round robin	3		
From Me to You	13	K. and up		Low	Choosing the next player		circle or line	
Fuddy Duddy	49	Grade 3 and up		Med.	Guessing a word used in a story/Guessing a phrase	2		
Grouping Stories	104	K. to grade 3		Med.	Audience response to story cues	large	stand	
Guess the Voice	17	K. to grade 4		Med.	Guessing a sound/ Combining elements			stick
Hide the Words	43	Grade 3 and up		High	Guessing a word used in a story/Combining elements			P&P
I Was Present!	119	K. and up	✔	Med.	Round robin	3		

title	page	grade level	1st	complexity	game type	size	space	props
Inventions	80	K. and up		High	Filling in a plot	2		
Janey Jo	6	Pre. to grade 2	✔	Low	Stationary tag, with improvised dialogue		circle	
Knocking	16	K. to grade 3	✔	Low	Guessing a sound	2		hard objects
Letter Echoes	39	Grades 1-3	✔	Low	Audience response to story cues	2 large		
Letter Relay	41	Grade 3 and up		Med.	Round robin	2		
Monster Rumble	35	K. to grade 3		Low	Alternating solo movements with group chant		circle	
My Mother, Your Mother	99	Grade 1 and up		Med.	Alternating solo stories with group chant	large		
					Guessing true or false			
Occupations	97	Pre. and up		Med.	Filling in a plot			
Old Bloody Bones	28	K. to grade 5	✔	Med.	Alternating solo stories with group chant		circle	
Old Doc Jones	121	Pre. to grade 2	✔	Low	Alternating solo stories with group chant	3 large		
People Are Different	90	K. and up		Low	Alternating solo stories with group chant	large		
Places, Persons & Things	67	K. to grade 5		High	Combining elements			P&P
Rakan-san	23	Pre. to grade 5	✔	Low	Imitating posture, with rhyme	large	stand	
Sea Is Getting Stormy, The	112	Pre. to grade 4		Med.	Audience response to story cues			
Spaceship	114	Pre. to grade 2	✔	Med.	Audience response to story cues	large		
Squabble Body	94	K. to grade 3		Med.	Filling in a plot			
Story Crambo	47	Grade 2 and up		High	Guessing a word used in a story	2		
Such a Robbery!	126	K. to grade 5		Low	Alternating solo stories with group chant	large		
They Tossed It High	22	Grade 3 and up		Low	Alternating solo stories with group chant	large		
Walks of Life	10	Grades 3-7		Med.	Guessing a movement	large	stage	
Wolf, Are You Ready?	4	Pre. to grade 2		Low	Chase, with improvised dialogue		run	
Would You Believe?	66	Pre. to grade 2		Low	Filling in a plot	2 large		
You're Shaking Me Up	31	Pre. to grade 4		High	Filling in a plot	large		

GAMES FOR UPPER ELEMENTARY GRADES

title	page	grade level	1st	complexity	game type	size	space	props
Apple Tree	123	Grade 1 and up		Med.	Alternating solo stories with group chant/ Guessing true or false	4		
Aunt Dinah	8	Pre. to grade 5		Low	Imitating posture, with dialogue	2 large	stand	
Back Speaks, The	25	Grade 2 and up		Med.	Guessing a quality of movement	large		chair
Because	116	Grade 3 and up	✔	Low	Round robin	2		
Cross-Picture Puzzles	20	Grade 1 and up		High	Combining elements	2		pictures
Daddy Shot a Bear	128	Grade 1 and up		Low	Alternating solo stories with group chant	large		
Do It Your Way	84	K. to grade 4		Med.	Guessing a quality of movement	2 large	stage	
Flying	106	K. to grade 4		Low	Audience response to story cues		stage	
Fortunately, Unfortunately	30	K. and up	✔	Med.	Round robin	3		
From Me to You	13	K. and up		Low	Choosing the next player		circle or line	
Fuddy Duddy	49	Grade 3 and up		Med.	Guessing a word used in a story/Guessing a phrase	2		
Guess the Voice	17	K. to grade 4		Med.	Guessing a sound/ Combining elements			stick
Hide the Words	43	Grade 3 and up		High	Guessing a word used in a story/Combining elements		P&P	
History Mystery	76	Grade 5 and up		High	Filling in a plot/ Guessing a fact	2		
I Was Present!	119	K. and up	✔	Med.	Round robin	3		
Inventions	80	K. and up		High	Filling in a plot	2		
Letter Relay	41	Grade 3 and up		Med.	Round robin	2		
Mish Mash Mush	63	Grade 6 and up		Med.	Guessing a word used in a story/Guessing a phrase	2		
My Mother, Your Mother	99	Grade 1 and up		Med.	Alternating solo stories with group chant/ Guessing true or false	large		
Occupations	97	Pre. and up		Med.	Filling in a plot			
Old Bloody Bones	28	K. to grade 5		Med.	Alternating solo stories with group chant		circle	
People Are Different	90	K. and up		Low	Alternating solo stories with group chant	large		
Places, Persons, & Things	67	K. to grade 5		High	Combining elements			P&P
Proverb Guessing	60	Grade 5 and up		High	Guessing a word used in a story/Combining elements	2		

title	page	grade level	1st	complexity	game type	size	space	props
Pun Puzzles	56	Grade 5 and up		High	Guessing a word used in a story/Guessing a topic Combining elements	2		
Questions and Answers	87	Grade 4 and up		High	Combining elements			
Rakan-san	23	Pre. to grade 5		Low	Imitating posture, with rhyme	large	stand	
Sea Is Getting Stormy, The	112	Pre. to grade 4		Med.	Audience response to story cues			
Sets in Conflict	108	Grade 4 and up		Med.	Combining elements/ Filling in a plot	2		
Story Crambo	47	Grade 2 and up		High	Guessing a word used in a story	2		
Such a Robbery!	126	K. to grade 5		Low	Alternating solo stories with group chant	large		
Teakettle Stories	53	Grade 4 and up		Med.	Guessing a word used in a story	2		
They Tossed It High	22	Grade 3 and up		Low	Alternating solo stories with group chant/	large		
Towns and Counties	73	Grades 4-9		Med.	Guessing a word used in a story	2		
Walks of Life	10	Grades 3-7	✔	Med.	Guessing a movement	large	stage	
You're Shaking Me Up	31	Pre. to grade 4		High	Filling in a plot	large		

GAMES FOR JUNIOR HIGH

title	page	grade level	1st	complexity	game type	size	space	props
Apple Tree	123	Grade 1 and up	✔	Med.	Alternating solo stories with group chant/ Guessing true or false	4		
Back Speaks, The	25	Grade 2 and up		Med.	Guessing a quality of movement	large		chair
Because	116	Grade 3 and up		Low	Round robin	2		
Cross-Picture Puzzles	20	Grade 1 and up		High	Combining elements	2		pictures
Daddy Shot a Bear	128	Grade 1 and up		Low	Alternating solo stories with group chant	large		
Fortunately, Unfortunately	30	K. and up		Med.	Round robin	3		
From Me to You	13	K. and up		Low	Choosing the next player		circle or line	
Fuddy Duddy	49	Grade 3 and up		Med.	Guessing a word used in a story/Guessing a phrase	2		
Hide the Words	43	Grade 3 and up		High	Guessing a word used in a story/Combining elements			P&P

title	page	grade level	1st	complexity	game type	size	space	props
History Mystery	76	Grade 5 and up		High	Filling in a plot/Guessing a fact	2		
I Was Present!	119	K. and up		Med.	Round robin	3		
Inventions	80	K. and up		High	Filling in a plot	2		
Letter Relay	41	Grade 3 and up		Med.	Round robin	2		
Mish Mash Mush	63	Grade 6 and up		Med.	Guessing a word used in a story/Guessing a phrase	2		
My Mother, Your Mother	99	Grade 1 and up		Med.	Alternating solo stories with group chant/ Guessing true or false	large		
Occupations	97	Pre. and up		Med.	Filling in a plot			
People Are Different	90	K. and up		Low	Alternating solo stories with group chant	large		
Proverb Guessing	60	Grade 5 and up		High	Guessing a word used in a story/Combining elements	2		
Pun Puzzles	56	Grade 5 and up		High	Guessing a word used in a story/Guessing a topic/ Combining elements	2		
Questions and Answers	87	Grade 4 and up		High	Combining elements			
Sets in Conflict	108	Grade 4 and up		Med.	Combining elements/ Filling in a plot	2		
Story Crambo	47	Grade 2 and up	✔	High	Guessing a word used in a story	2		
Teakettle Stories	53	Grade 4 and up		Med.	Guessing a word used in a story	2		
They Tossed It High	22	Grade 3 and up		Low	Alternating solo stories with group chant/	large		
Towns and Counties	73	Grades 4-9	✔	Med.	Guessing a word used in a story	2		
Walks of Life	10	Grades 3-7		Med.	Guessing a movement	large	stage	

GAMES FOR SECONDARY GRADES

title	page	grade level	1st	complexity	game type	size	space	props
Apple Tree	123	Grade 1 and up	✔	Med.	Alternating solo stories with group chant Guessing true or false	4		
Back Speaks, The	25	Grade 2 and up		Med.	Guessing a quality of movement	large		chair
Because	116	Grade 3 and up		Low	Round robin	2		
Cross-Picture Puzzles	20	Grade 1 and up		High	Combining elements	2		pictures
Daddy Shot a Bear	128	Grade 1 and up		Low	Alternating solo stories with group chant	large		

title	page	grade level	1st	complexity	game type	size	space	props
Fortunately, Unfortunately	30	K. and up		Med.	Round robin	3		
From Me to You	13	K. and up		Low	Choosing the next player		circle or line	
Fuddy Duddy	49	Grade 3 and up		Med.	Guessing a word used in a story/Guessing a phrase	2		
Hide the Words	43	Grade 3 and up		High	Guessing a word used in a story/Combining elements			P&P
History Mystery	76	Grade 5 and up		High	Filling in a plot/Guessing a fact	2		
I Was Present!	119	K. and up		Med.	Round robin	3		
Inventions	80	K. and up		High	Filling in a plot	2		
Letter Relay	41	Grade 3 and up	✔	Med.	Round robin	2		
Mish Mash Mush	63	Grade 6 and up	✔	Med.	Guessing a word used in a story/Guessing a phrase	2		
My Mother, Your Mother	99	Grade 1 and up		Med.	Alternating solo stories with group chant/ Guessing true or false	large		
Occupations	97	Pre. and up		Med.	Filling in a plot			
People Are Different	90	K. and up		Low	Alternating solo stories with group chant/	large		
Proverb Guessing	60	Grade 5 and up		High	Guessing a word used in a story/Combining elements	2		
Pun Puzzles	53	Grade 5 and up		High	Guessing a word used in a story/Guessing a topic/ Combining elements/	2		
Questions and Answers	87	Grade 4 and up		High	Combining elements			
Sets in Conflict	108	Grade 4 and up		Med.	Combining elements Filling in a plot	2		
Story Crambo	47	Grade 2 and up	✔	High	Guessing a word used in a story	2		
Teakettle Stories	53	Grade 4 and up		Med.	Guessing a word used in a story	2		
They Tossed It High	22	Grade 3 and up	✔	Low	Alternating solo stories with group chant	large		

GAMES FOR ADULTS

The same games that will work with secondary grades will work with adults. The games that are especially suited for adults are:

title	page	grade level	1st	complexity	game type	size	space	props
Apple Tree	123	Grade 1 and up	✔	Med.	Alternating solo stories with group chant/ Guessing true or false	4		
Cross-Picture Puzzles	20	Grade 1 and up	✔	High	Combining elements	2		pictures
Letter Relay	41	Grade 3 and up	✔	Med.	Round robin	2		
Pun Puzzles	56	Grade 5 and up		High	Guessing a word used in a story/Guessing a topic/ Combining elements	2		
Questions and Answers	87	Grade 4 and up		High	Combining elements			
Story Crambo	47	Grade 2 and up	✔	High	Guessing a word used in a story	2		

SUBJECT INDEX

Please see also the Game Finder Index (p. 156) and Cultural Background Index (p. 155). Game titles and the page numbers of their descriptions are in **boldface**.

Coffeepot (game), 136
Colors, xviii, 52, 131
    papers of different, 26, 68, 87
Community helpers, 12
Complexity ratings, explained, xii
Computer game, 120
Concealing words, 47, 59, 62, 75, 108
Concepts, 12, 72, 76. *See also* Categories
Conflict resolution, 76, 96, 101
Contributions from players, xv–xvi, xix–xx, xxi–xxii
Coordinating story with team members, 47, 59, 62, 75, 83
Counting, 5, 37, 51, 81. *See also* Mathematics
    number of questions, 7
    number of turns, 30
    people, 81, 106
    syllables, 49, 51, 52, 75
    words, 62
Counting-out rhymes, 101, 124
Country, rural, 9
Courage, 129
Crambo. *See* Story Crambo
Creating. *See also* Improvising; Sentences; Story
    characters, 34-37
    a monster character, 37
Creativity, 27, 65
Crimes, 79
Critical thinking, 102, 118, 120-129
Cross-Picture Puzzles, 19, **20-21**, 76, 104, 118, 133
Cues, 4–5, 6–7, 90–93, 112–14, 114–16
Cultural diversity, xv, xviii, 46, 89-96, 155
    and eye contact, 13, 14
Cumulative stories, 31
Curriculum, xi, xvi, 72
Czech games, 132, 140

Daddy Shot a Bear, 4, 53, 126, **128-29**, 142
Danish game, 155
Death, 7, 9
Decoding
    marker words, 49, 52, 65
    movements, 12, 27, 86
Detective, 79
Dialogue, 4, 6, 8, 64
Dice, 21
Dictionary, 41, 43
Differences and similarities, 89, 93, 96, 103, 111
Differences, human, 89-96
Disruptive behavior, 34
Divergent thinking, 102, 118-20
Do It Your Way, 8, 23, 35, 76, **84-86**, 137
Drawings, stories made about, 21, 76, 113. *See also* Photographs
Drunken Sailor (melody), 126

Echoing, 40
Embroidering a story, 29, 75
Emotions. *See* Feelings
Ending a story, 27
England, 130, 136, 139
Environment, 17, 46, 110

Europe, Eastern, 127
Expressions, 60-65. *See also* Phrases
Eye contact, 12-15

Falsehood vs. truth, 79, 101, 118, 120-25
Fantasy stories, 19, 27, 52, 71, 83, 89, 90, 94, 96, 111, 117, 120, 122, 123, 127, 129
Father (Daddy), 128
Fear, ix, 5, 16, 27, 37
Feelings, 7, 9, 23, 24, 25, 26, 27
    about historical period, 76
    belonging, of, 111
    communicating through movement, 27, 86
    discomfort, 14
    expressed, 17, 23
    fear, ix, 5, 16, 27, 37
    impatience, 34
    places, feelings associated with, 73
    rejection, when choosing teams, xvii
    safety, xiv, 14
Fingers, snapping, 29
Fish, 129
Flow, maintaining, 47, 62, 75, 83
Flying, 8, 28, 103, **106-08**, 112, 139
Form, solo-chorus, 37, 93, 101, 125, 128, 129
Formulas, mathematical, 106
Fortunately, Unfortunately, 4, 27, **30**, 84, 118, 134
Friends, 32
From Me to You, **13-15**, 90, 132
Fuddy Duddy, 43, 47, **49-52**, 73, 104, 136
Future, imagining the, 21, 23

Game Finder Index, xi, 156
Games, vii, xi, xiii, 38
    chasing, 4
    choosing, 13
    circle, 6, 13, 17, 24, 28, 29, 35, 89, 93, 127
    computer, 120
    dandling, 40
    guessing, xviii, 10, 16, 17, 25, 43, 47, 49, 53, 56, 60, 63, 73, 76, 85, 93
    parlor, 98, 135, 138, 139, 140
    round robin, 30, 41, 56, 116, 119
    tag, 7
Geography, 73-75
Germany, 132
Gestures, 9, 25, 108. *See also* Movements
    for voting, 101, 125
    imitating and initiating, 10, 25
Ghost, 6
Gibberish, 15
God Rest Ye Merry, Gentlemen (melody), 22
Grammar, 65-71, 75. *See also* Parts, of speech; Sentences, structure
Greece, 132, 139
Grid, 21
Grouping Stories, 28, 84, 103, **104-06**, 118, 139
Guess the Voice, 4, 15, **17-19**, 20, 28, 66, 76, 84, 97, 112, 132

Mother, 7
Movements, 7-12, 31, 40, 92, 115, 116, 126, 127
    as response to story cues, 40, 104, 106, 112, 114
    decoding, 12, 27, 86
    expressive, 27, 86
    guessing, 10, 25, 84
    improvising, 37
    to match an activity, 34
Muffin Man (game), 132
Multiculturalism, xv, xviii, 46, 89-96, 155
    eye contact in various cultures, 13, 14
My Mother, Your Mother, 76, 90, 96, **99-101**, 121,
    139
Myths, 64, 75, 89

Names, xviii, 19, 120
    Bible characters, 75
    feelings, 27
    Greek gods, 75
    numbers, 106
    objects, 19
    places, 52, 73, 75
New York, 131, 155
Night, 16
Nova Scotia, song from, 133, 155
Nouns, 47, 48, 52, 65, 66, 67-71, 74, 97-98, 138
Numbers, xviii, 21, 106. *See also* Counting; Mathematics
Nursery rhymes, 89

Object, direct (grammar), 67
Objects, 19, 52, 67, 78, 123
    sounds made by, 16
    stories about, 18, 111, 119, 123
Observation, 111
Occupations, 10, 11, 56
    detective, 79
Occupations (game), 43, 66, 73, 76, 84, 96, **97-99**, 118,
    138
Ocean creatures, 114
Oh, Susannah (song), 22
Old Bloody Bones, xxi, 27, **28-29**, 134
Old Doc Jones, 4, 20, 27, 119, **121-23**, 141
Old Mother Hubbard (rhyme), 22
One Little Indian (melody), 28
Opposites, 108

Parent, 7, 128
Parlor games, 98, 135, 138, 139, 140
Participation
    adjusting rate of, 41, 106, 108, 114, 116
    maintaining coherence during, 41, 99, 106, 108, 114,
    116
    stories, 39, 104, 106, 112, 114
Parts
    of the body, 25, 94-96, 112
    of an object or system, 116
    of speech, 65, 66, 70-71, 86. *See also* Adjectives;
        Adverbs; Nouns; Verbs
    of a "statue", 25
Passover, 133

Past, imagining the, 21, 23
People Are Different, 90-93, 139
Personal experience, stories from, 72, 90, 93, 101, 125,
    128
Persons. *See* Characters; Places, Persons, and Things
Photographs, 19, 20-21, 73, 76, 89, 113, 120
Phrases, 60-65, 67, 70, 89, 138
    cue, 5, 27, 29, 112, 114, 120, 140
    to end story, 29, 112, 114
    guessing, 49, 63
Piano, 25
Places, 52, 67, 75
Places, Persons, and Things, 43, 66, **67-71**, 73, 84, 97,
    137
Playfulness. *See also* Silliness
    speaking and listening, ix–x
Plot
    combining elements to create, 17, 20, 43, 56, 60, 67,
        87, 108
    filling in a, 31, 66, 76, 80, 94, 97, 108
    improvising, 27-30
    players' contributions to, 9-10, 12
    positive vs. negative developments in, 30
Poetry, 15, 22, 65. *See also* Rhyming
    counting-out rhymes, 101, 124
    nursery rhymes, 89
Poland, 132, 142
Posture, 8, 9, 10, 25, 37. *See also* Imagery, kinesthetic
Poverty, 127
Professions, 10, 11, 56, 97-99
    detective, 79
Pronouncing, 34, 40
    contribution to entire group, 30, 42, 46, 49, 52, 86,
        96, 117, 120, 127
    cue phrase to entire group, 5, 29
    story clue to entire group, 56, 59, 62, 114
    story to entire group, 79, 83, 89, 93, 99, 101, 123,
        125, 129
    words to the entire group, 40, 67, 75, 99, 106, 108,
        116
Proverb Guessing, 43, 53, **60-62**, 76, 84, 136
Proverbs, 60-62, 139
Public speaking, 3-4
Pun Puzzles, 43, 53, **56-60**, 97, 136
Puns, 56-60, 88, 129. *See also* Homonyms

Questions, 6, 18, 19, 82, 87-89
    about history, 76
Questions and Answers, 53, 76, 84, **87-89**, 118, 138
Quotations, 62, 89

Rabbi, 127
Rakan-san, 8, **23-25**, 134
Recognizing letter sounds, 41
"Red herring" strategy, 47, 59, 62, 75, 108
Red River Valley (melody), 66
Relationships, 31, 103, 111, 116
Remembering, 25, 31, 34
    sequences, 21, 31-34, 60, 79, 99, 117
    words, 114

Translating. *See also* Language, second
  between concepts and movements, 12
  between feelings and movements, 27, 86
Truth vs. falsehood, 79, 101, 118, 121-25
Turn-taking, xvii, 5, 7, 10, 19, 25, 30, 37, 42, 52, 99,
  117, 120
  managing, xvii
Twelve Days of Christmas, The (melody), 90
Twinkle, Twinkle, Little Star (melody), 16

Umbrella (as prop), 17
Understanding. *See also* Meanings
  relationships, 31
  story with omitted words, 56
Unison, say chanted lines in, 5, 7, 17, 25, 34, 37, 67,
  93, 101, 123, 125, 127, 129

Vaudeville, 134
Verbs, 7, 19, 46, 48, 52, 66, 67, 70-71, 98
Violence in players' stories, xxii, 101
Visual imagery, 19-23
Voice, 19
  tone of, 7, 35, 120
Volunteers, xv, xix. *See also* Contributions from players
Voting true or false, 99, 101, 125

Walking, 10-12, 37
Walks of Life, 7, **10-12**, 97, 132
What Will We Do with a Drunken Sailor? (melody), 126
Wolf, Are You Ready?, **4-5**, 66, 103, 130

Words, 42-47, 62, 71. *See also* Adjectives; Adverbs;
  Nouns; Phrases; Sentences; Verbs
  choosing, from a category, 49, 52, 120
  concealing, 47, 59, 62, 75, 108
  counting, 62
  creating story with given category of, 108, 114
  creating story with given set of, 47, 59, 75, 89, 116,
    120
  cues, 24, 28, 39-40, 93, 99, 114-16, 135
  declined forms, 42, 75
  guessing, 43, 47-48, 49-52, 53-56, 56-59, 60-2, 63-
    64, 73-75
  homonyms, xi–xii, 52-60, 129
  infer meanings from context, 49, 52
  isolating from story, 47, 60, 62, 75, 106
  marker, 47, 49, 56, 65
  omitted, 49, 52, 56, 65, 99
  sentence beginning with given, 42
  substitution, 67, 71, 99
  with given initial letters, 41, 42
  with two syllables, 46
  writing, 47, 62, 71, 88, 96, 120
Work, 10
Would You Believe?, 4, 43, 65, **66-67**, 137
Writing a word, 47, 62, 71, 96, 120

Yiddish, 127
You're Shaking Me Up, xvi, 4, 8, 15, 28, **31-34**, 66,
  112, 135

DATE DUE

SEP 0 5 2008			
SEP 1 6 2009			
OCT 0 5 2009			
			Printed in USA

HIGHSMITH #45230